REMEMBERING THE ALAMO

HISTORY, CULTURE, AND SOCIETY SERIES
CENTER FOR MEXICAN AMERICAN STUDIES
UNIVERSITY OF TEXAS AT AUSTIN

# Remembering
## the Alamo
### MEMORY, MODERNITY,
### AND THE MASTER SYMBOL

BY RICHARD R. FLORES

UNIVERSITY OF TEXAS PRESS

*Austin*

The publication of this book was assisted by a University Cooperative Society Subvention Grant awarded by the University of Texas at Austin.

A version of chapter 1 previously appeared as "Mexicans, Modernity, and *Martyrs of the Alamo*" in *Reflexiones* 98 (1999).

An earlier version of chapter 2 previously appeared as "Memory-Place, Meaning, and the Alamo" in *American Literary History* 10, no. 3 (1998), and is reproduced with the permission of Oxford University Press.

A portion of chapter 4 previously appeared as "Private Visions, Public Culture: The Making of the Alamo" in *Cultural Anthropology* 10, no. 1 (1995).

Another portion of chapter 4 previously appeared as the introduction to *History and Legends of the Alamo and Other Missions in and around San Antonio,* by Adina De Zavala, and is reproduced here with permission from Arte Público Press, University of Houston, 1996.

LIBRARY OF CONGRESS CATALOGING-IN-PUBLICATION DATA

Flores, Richard R.
    Remembering the Alamo : memory, modernity, and the master symbol /
by Richard R. Flores. — 1st ed.
        p.    cm. — (History, culture, and society series)
    Includes bibliographical references and index.
    ISBN 0-292-72539-6 (cloth : alk. paper) — ISBN 0-292-72540-x
(pbk. : alk. paper)
    1. Alamo (San Antonio, Tex.)—Siege, 1836.    2. Alamo (San Antonio,
Tex.)—Siege, 1836—Influence.    3. Memory—Social aspects—United
States.    4. Symbolism—Social aspects—United States.    5. Popular
culture—Texas.    6. Texas—Ethnic relations.    7. Whites—Texas—
Social conditions.    8. Mexican Americans—Texas—Social conditions.
9. Texas—History—1846–1950.    I. Title.    II. Series.
F390 .F58    2002
976.4'03—dc21

                                                          2001052230

TO MY FATHER AND MY MOTHER

*With wisdom and love*
*they teach;*
*By example and heart*
*they live.*

# CONTENTS

# PREFACE AND
# ACKNOWLEDGMENTS

This book had its inception when, after my last research project, I returned to San Antonio, Texas, to begin working on questions of tourism, culture, and the public sphere. After several days of talking to people, it quickly became apparent that the Alamo was not only the most visited site in the city, much less the state of Texas, but also a place that figured large in the local and national imagination. But this public understanding was not always productive or agreed on. Having grown up, literally, in the Alamo's shadow, I was quite aware of the visceral reaction of many who wander through this old mission's stone walls. I knew the reasons for my own ambivalence to the Alamo, but what of others? Were the stories and legends, films and folklore, that shaped the public cultural memory of this place so potent that they prescribed all understanding of the past? Had any notion of a nonfictitious past been lost to the various genres of public culture that construed the cultural memory of the Alamo? But what *was* a nonfictitious past? A true past? My intellectual training told me that "the past" was a messy assemblage of dates, events, chronologies, and stories and any effort to know it definitively spoke more to the politics of knowing than to knowledge itself.

And yet I knew the stories I heard and grew up with were "wrong." It is here that I began to rethink my project, not under the rubric of historical "truth" and "facts" of the past, but through the "effects" these stories had as they circulated through multiple locations and sites of public culture. Narratives of the past, known as history, memory, legend, or myth, circulate and swirl, as my friend and colleague Katie Stewart describes, through a wide array of sites, locations, and tellings. They are present in traditional genres and multimedia forms; we experience them as historical tales at sites of public history, from Hollywood productions, stories told late at night around a table of dominoes, or the podiums of lecture halls across college campuses. Stories of the past envelop us: they inscribe our present and shape our future; stories of the past are linked to the formation of selves and others in a complex tapestry of textured narratives. Are they real? Perhaps. Are they true? Who can know. But it is their *real* effects that concern me. Myth or history, cultural memory or public history, stories of the past track through us and over us as they provide narrative representations and public imaginaries that help us to make our way through the world.

For this reason, and perhaps others, I could not let go of the stories, memories, legends, and histories of the Alamo. These were the most influential stories told about "Texans" and "Mexicans," stories whose tellings had effectively shaped daily life and public interactions between these two groups for years. And yet little was known about "how" or "why" such tellings traced the way they did. The pages that follow are my attempt to track these traces.

Most questions, from the simple to the more complex, are never investigated in a vacuum but through the give-and-take of research, inquiry, presentations, lectures, debate, and writing. This could not be more true for this book. It started on the shores of Lake Mendota at the University of Wisconsin and comes to completion in the shadows of the tower at the University of Texas. In between, friends, colleagues, students, family members, and others who have heard various parts of what is written here have all contributed in some measure.

At the University of Wisconsin, Kevin Bohrer, Geoff Bradshaw, Kirstin Erickson, Jim Escalante, Ben Márquez, Ruben Medina, María Moreno, Peter Nabokov, Kirin Narayan, Emiko Ohnuki-Tierney, Francisco Scarano, Karen Strier, Harry West, and Neil Whitehead heard and responded to earlier versions of this book. While at Wisconsin I also had the pleasure of spending a semester at the Institute for Research in the Humanities. There I want to thank Paul Boyer, Susan Stanford Friedman, Gordon Hutner, Rudy Koshar, Thongchai Winichakul, and my other institute colleagues for creating a supportive and stimulating research environment.

Midway through this book, I returned to the University of Texas, where I found a cohort of new friends and colleagues who have been invaluable to this project. First, at the Center for Mexican American Studies, Neil Foley, José Limón, David Montejano, Lisa Montoya, Alba Ortiz,

Yolanda Padilla, Bárbara Robles, Angela Valenzuela, and Emilio Zamora have made my return to Austin an exciting and stimulating one. José Limón and David Montejano, mentors and colleagues both, merit special recognition for their critical perspectives, encouragement, and commitment to this project. In the department of anthropology, James Brow, Maria Franklin, Ted Gordon, Charlie Hale, Ward Keeler, Martha Menchaca, Henry Selby, Katie Stewart, Polly Strong, Kamala Visweswaren, Sam Wilson, and others have made this a dynamic and productive place to think through many of the questions of this book. Also of note are the graduate students in my seminars, "History, Power, Symbol" and "Marxism and Expressive Culture," where much of this material was used to exemplify almost every point of discussion for the past two years. The questions and comments, critiques and clarifications, from all of these students have made this material all the more interesting.

Outside of Austin there are a number of individuals whose work and critiques have been invaluable. Jim Crisp, Brian Huberman, and, especially during the early parts of this project, Tim Matovina are three friends who introduced me to the world of Alamo "culture" and whose questions and suggestions have been instructive and insightful. I thank Jim Fernandez for graciously commenting on my discussion of the master symbol; Peter Nabokov, again, for his deep commitment and passionate concern for many of the issues presented here; Harry West, also again, who has heard most of the arguments put forward in these pages as we sipped brandy and reflected on the African-Mexican diaspora; and my debate partner from the shores of Lake St. Catherine, John Mecchella, who makes a living as a business executive but is a philosopher through and through.

Over the years, portions of this material have been presented at various universities and conferences. In particular, I am grateful to faculty at Cornell University, Steve Ferzaca and his colleagues at Bryn Mawr College, Mario Montaño and Victor Nelson Cisneros at Colorado College, John Donahue and Char Miller at Trinity University, the University of Houston, Texas A&M University–Corpus Christi, Andres Tijerina and the history faculty at Austin Community College, and various groups at the University of Texas at Austin. I am grateful to Jim Crisp who brokered a number of presentations, in particular those at the Western Historical Association, the Texas State Historical Society, and the Texas Association of Museums. Material was also presented at the annual meetings of the American Anthropological Association, the National Association for Chicana and Chicano Studies, the American Ethnological Society, and the Dallas Historical Society. I thank them all for the opportunities they afforded.

Research for this book was conducted in a number of archives and libraries. In particular, I want to thank the staff at the Center for American History at the University of Texas at Austin; Linda Edwards, although she is no longer there, and other personnel at the Daughters of the Republic of Texas Library; Tom Shelton and Chris Floerke at the Institute of Texan Cultures at the University of Texas at San Antonio; Gilberto Hinojosa and Basil Aivaliotis at the University of the Incarnate Word for allowing me access to the then uncataloged Adina De Zavala Collection; the library staff at Trinity University; the San Antonio Public Library; the Wisconsin Center for Film and Theatre Research and the State Historical Society located at the University of Wisconsin–Madison; Charles Silber at the Film Study Center of the Museum of Modern Art; and the staff of the Library of Congress. Finally, at the University of Texas Press, I want to thank Theresa May and Rachel Chance; their support and belief in this project did not go unnoticed. And *mil gracias* to Kathy Vargas for permission to use her wonderful photography for the cover.

This book would not have been completed without the understanding and support of my family. First, there are Katherine, Rebecca, and Rachel. They have grown up with this project, listening patiently, at least most of the time, to my dinner table musings and early morning ramblings about every aspect of it. Finally, there is Christine. Over and above all those mentioned here, she listened and queried, probed and prodded, and through it all taught me more than I would have known otherwise.

# INTRODUCTION

I no longer recall the month or the week, only the place. Wrapped in our winter coats, gloves, scarves, and hats, my third-grade class was on its first field trip of the year. The thrill of leaving behind workbooks filled with three-place addition and subtraction problems was electrifying. The trip, like many of those that would follow in my elementary school years, was to the Alamo: bastion of Texas liberty and memorial to brave men. I had passed by it numerous times before, on my way to see my father, who worked at the pharmacy across the street. I remember wondering if he ever ventured there during his lunch break and felt what I would surely feel walking amid the Alamo's ancient stone walls where, I had learned, heroes died.

My every expectation was met. The stones cried out to me with their sense of history. I looked closely at the wall, searching for pockmarks, imagining muskets displacing rock with each shot. The silence of the main room, the mission church, filled me with awe and heightened my senses. There, beneath the floor that I and my classmates trod, was where legends fell in martyrdom for my freedom. Bowie. Travis. Crockett. Texan heroes all of them.

Once outside, the air fresher and the light brilliant, I lost my equilibrium. I recall it vividly. Robert, my best friend, nudged my elbow and whispered, "You killed them! You and the other 'mes'kins'!"

It is not that I didn't know I was Mexican, I couldn't escape it. I just hadn't realized the liability it was in the eyes of my best friend. My initial response was to argue. "I never killed anyone. And my *papá* [my maternal grandfather, whose age I must have thought made him more a contemporary to the Alamo battle than anyone else in my family] never did either." Although I recalled overhearing his laments, on several late-night occasions when the men were playing dominoes and I should have been sleeping, about working for "esos caranchos gringos." But he didn't kill them.

I do not know what I lost that day. Innocence? Certitude? Identity? Or some other existentially derived nine-year-old sense of self? Whatever it was, it was gone. And, like many other losses in my life, this one could not be replaced. Somehow, deep inside, I knew that moment would last forever, etched into my youthful memory. Unfortunately, this experience is not mine alone. Over the last few years as I have retold this story at various places throughout the United States — some as distant from Texas as Ithaca, New York — someone would invariably approach me with his or her own Alamo story.[1]

Soon after starting this research project, I began to ask close associates and friends their thoughts on the Alamo. While all had their particular understanding of the subject, many of my Mexican American and Latino/a friends and colleagues were ambivalent, if not hostile, to the place. It became very clear to me that the Alamo, and its various representations, did not reference the battle that took place more than one hundred fifty years ago. The Alamo resonated with something deeper, more powerful, and less obvious.

Why was it that the stories, legends, and myths spawned by the Alamo created both pride and ambivalence, patriotism and disregard, heroes and tyrants? Was it because it told a story of winner and losers? Perhaps but rather unlikely. Was it related to the taken for granted axiom that victors tell history from their own vantage point? This was not it either. Did it concern the relationship among the past, its representation, and identity? Perhaps, but it was much more than this. Such were the questions that shaped my early interest in the Alamo and that have led to the writing of this book.

It is my contention that both the breadth of the Alamo story — its reproduction in film, literature, and folklore, and more generally its presence in the repertoire of American cultural memory — and the divergent understandings of it — the competing, even at times silent interpretations — are the result of its transformation from a site of defeat in 1836 into a powerfully rendered and racially produced icon of American cultural memory. While similar sites — Gettysburg, Little Big Horn, and Pearl Harbor — easily come to mind, their transformation into major sites of public history and culture do not match the Alamo for their continued effect on racial identities.

But why the Alamo of all places? While the full weight of my argument can only be assessed at the completion of this book, I want to suggest, and begin my own telling, by taking seriously the two features of meaning making that were influential in the Alamo's rise to its place in American popular culture: memory and modernity.

The Alamo did not emerge full blown as a site of public history but is the cumulative effect of multiple representations that have etched its compelling story into the reservoir of American cultural memory. In many ways, the response of my third-grade accuser was mediated by the narrative he had learned from teachers, picture books, movies, and our visit that day. In a work much like this one, Marita Sturken (1997) persuasively argues for the examination of cultural memory as it has shaped the cognitive contours of sites like the Vietnam War Memorial and events related to the AIDS epidemic. For Sturken (1997:5), cultural memory refers to those aspects of memory that exist outside of official historical discourse, yet are "entangled" with them. Like Sturken's work, this book is not a "history" in the traditional sense of the word, nor is it principally concerned with the events of 1836. Instead, what follows is an exploration of how the Alamo is *remembered* through various genres of public and popular culture and how these rememberings are entangled with official historical discourses on the events of 1836. But this book moves in different directions from Sturken's as well. The process of "remembering" requires, as Sturken suggests, a certain level of "forgetting." But forgetting is not a passive experience; like remembering, it is an active process that involves erasure. Memory, in being selective, actively forgets or "silences the past," as Michel-Rolph Trouillot (1995) writes.

While I do not want to engage the various popular or academic distinctions between historiography and memory, distinctions forged from various forms of discursive practice, I must state that this work moves away from the concerns one might find in a traditional historiography. I am dealing with what some might call "historical" materials, but I do so from a position that asks questions about identity, power, and their relationship to the construction of meaning. David J. Weber (1988:135–136), the preeminent historian of the Spanish borderlands, writes that "a number of the cherished stories about the Alamo have no basis in historical fact, but have moved out of the earthly realm of reality into the stratosphere of myth." I agree with Weber's statement, with one exception. Myths, and cultural memories more generally, are not stratospheric tales but deeply grounded narratives through which communities express their heartfelt convictions. Understanding the place of the Alamo in memory and historiography is not a task of picking through the rubble of fact and fiction, discarding the invented and upholding the real. Any interpretation and critique of the Alamo must examine the contents of the story (the battle of 1836) and come to terms with the raw materials of fact and fiction as genuine elements in a larger tale. This tale, now recovered, reveals how and why "the story of the Alamo" came to hold such a place in the cultural reservoir of the United States (see Linenthal 1988). This recovery recast the materials of cultural memory as inflections of a society coming to terms with itself in real historical time. My general thesis is that this inflection — the symbolic work accomplished through "remembering the Alamo" — consists of signifying a radical difference between "Anglos" and "Mexicans" so as to cognize and codify the social relations circulating at the beginning of the twentieth century.[2]

The Alamo, as a major feature of American cultural memory, references not only the events of 1836 but the social and historical moment of its remembering as well. I would even suggest that its primary importance lies not with remembering 1836 but with inscribing, in the moment of its retelling, a more contemporary lesson. Recall that the men of Sam Houston, as they attacked the forces of Santa Anna at the Battle of San Jacinto, did so, we are told, shouting, "Remember the Alamo." Thus what may be the first public act of remembering the Alamo serves as a call to arms and action. Remembering is a deeply embedded social practice that informs the present. The act of remembering and the acts such rememberings inform are the subject of this work.

The ubiquity of the Alamo narrative stems, in part, from the multiple forms through which the Alamo is remembered: historiography, film, literature, and other genres of memorialization. These rememberings constitute what Trouillot (1995:22) calls the "historical production" of history, those deeply experienced and highly entangled narratives of remembering that form for us the workings of historical discourse. Unlike Trouillot, however, who speaks of the "silences" of history, this book examines the significance of remembering. Silencing and remembering, I offer, serve as Janus-faced articulations of power embedded in the production of the past. Recovering the silenced voices of historical production restores the voices of the subaltern; uncovering why and how the past is remembered reveals the strategies and ideologies that silence social actors in the present.

My focus on memory and remembering is coupled with a second, equally important aspect of this work: modernity. My argument throughout this book is that we cannot understand the importance, preservation, and fundamentally central role of the Alamo in American cultural memory without understanding its profound relationship to the project of modernity. I do not mean that the Alamo is invented, whole cloth, in the modern period: the events of 1836 did occur. What I do suggest is that the cultural memory of the Alamo is both produced and invoked as a means of sustaining the deep social changes associated with the transition to modernity in Texas. As such, the cultural memory of the Alamo provides semantic justification for slotting Mexicans and Anglos into an emerging social order brought forth by the material and ideological forces that gripped Texas between 1880 and 1920.

I discuss my understanding of modernity in chapter 1. Let me briefly state here that—particularly through its local inflection, what I call the Texas Modern—it references a series of economic changes, social processes, discursive articulations, and cultural forms that result in the transformation of Texas from a largely Mexican, cattle-based society into an industrial and agricultural social complex between 1880 and 1920. This transformation is at once creative and destructive, promising and debilitating, a "unity of disunity" (Berman 1982:15) that sets in motion forces of nationalism, post–Civil War politics, wage labor, bureaucratic rationalism, and the restructuring of racial and ethnic difference. It is here, in the cleavages and fissures of this transformation, that the Alamo is born. Modernity, while uneven and disparate as a social force, nonetheless serves as a periodizing frame to organize the material of this book. My focus on modernity and the Texas Modern more specifically is not undertaken in a causal manner. My thesis that the Alamo is part of the project of modernity does not in itself provide the specific ideological and practical articulations of the modern that serve as the unique or general developments from which the cultural memory of the Alamo arises. It is, in fact, the task of the pages ahead to do just that.

The Texas Modern, therefore, is both the social ground on which the Alamo enters into American cultural memory as well as the key analytic frame through which I interpret its various articulations. My decision on which expressive forms to investigate—memory, historiography, film, literature—has not been haphazard but has been influenced, in part, by the relative dearth of discussion on some forms and the vast material on others. In both cases, however, decisions on what to "include" and "exclude" emerged from the material itself. For example, that little has been written on the Alamo as a place in the built environment of San Antonio indicates how such a process seems a "natural" occurrence of everyday life. And yet, as I demonstrate in chapter 3, this process requires both the dissolution of one way of organizing space and its replacement by another. On the contrary, the vast historiographic writings on the Alamo, like the prepon-

derance of films, indicate the continuing role the Alamo plays in the reproduction of a Texas and, more specifically, U.S. social imagination. I do
not claim to have captured all facets of the Alamo; this was never my intent.
Instead, my plan has been to rethink the Alamo, not as a place in history,
but as a historical place made meaningful through the practices and ideologies of the Texas Modern. My objective has been to uncover the social
conditions—those material and ideological practices and values—that
serve as the fodder from which the very possibility of a place like the
Alamo emerges in the social imagination of a people. Such a task requires
that I first search the past for the various seedbeds that serve as the social
"matter" for the formation of the Alamo; and second, once present, chart
the various effects the Alamo, as a symbolic form, has had on the social
landscape. Understanding the conditions that gave rise to the Alamo cannot ignore the equally necessary pursuit of analyzing how the emergence
of this "master symbol" affected the lives of Mexicans and Mexican Americans. I conclude, therefore, that those who remember the Alamo in the
early twentieth century do so not primarily to remember the events of 1836
but to re-member a social body through a specific hierarchical and class
rubric endemic to the arrival of modernity in Texas. In effect, re-member-
ing the Alamo as a site of cultural memory, as a sacred site in the pantheon
of American public history, serves to hide the material social relations and
conditions that require such sites in the first place. This process of remembering has already stamped the Alamo as a naturally given icon of
American cultural memory, leaving us to understand not its historical
character but its "meaning." My reflections on the Alamo, as a symbolic
form, follow a route directly opposite to that of its actual historical development, although I present events and actors from the past. The task of
this book is to move backward from the "Alamo as given" to the historical
and social conditions that serve as the necessary elements of its making
and the work these elements achieve in the everyday world of social life.

Contemporary anthropological practice favors, rightly so, I believe, the
portrayal of "cultural" groups as complex, historically specific entities
that can no longer be discussed through reductive binaries such as those
used here: "Anglo" or "Texan" and "Mexican." Such dichotomies, James
Clifford (1988:23) warns, lead to the depiction of "abstract, ahistorical
'others.'" I agree. My usage of "Anglo" and "Mexican" is a necessary one,
however, since what I am undertaking is a historical ethnography of the
formation of "Angloness" and "Mexicanness" as categories of difference
and power constructed through the making of the Alamo itself. I realize
that historically specific social actors may or may not have subscribed to

these terms and their particular ideologies even as the effects of their practical activity constituted the formation of historical modes of dominance and representation. Unlike contemporary ethnographic works that move from the binaries of cultural differences to the complexities of subject positions, *Remembering the Alamo* underscores the production of difference and the reification of identity achieved through the "making of the Alamo." My task, then, is, in the words of Akhil Gupta and James Ferguson (1992:16), a study of how the Alamo affected notions of cultural otherness through the "production of difference."

This book begins with a discussion of the Texas Modern, crucial to my overall argument about the Alamo as it is tied directly to this social formation. I see the "birth" of the Alamo as coterminous with the events of the Texas Modern, a begetting that provides representational and ideological fodder to this period.

In part 1 I am principally concerned with the Alamo as a *place* of cultural memory. Chapter 2, therefore, assesses the public history presented at the Alamo today. This "official" Alamo story, provided by the Daughters of the Republic of Texas (DRT), the custodians of the Alamo for the state of Texas, is juxtaposed to historical material that has been "left out" of the official version as well as to the subjective impact this story has on those who experience it. My interest is not to merely contrast "my" story with "theirs," although this is done, but to underscore how the power and weight of the Alamo story—a combination of popular culture, memory, and public history—affects and shapes social identities in the contemporary period.

Chapter 3 considers how the original urban geography of San Antonio shifted from the Mexican plazas to the square surrounding the Alamo. In this shift, one that began long before the physical structures were themselves fully recognized as monuments to the past, we see how the Alamo comes to signify, nondiscursively, an emerging and distinctively American social order. Chapter 4 examines the efforts to "preserve" the physical structures of the Alamo through the work and writings of Adina De Zavala and Clara Driscoll. It not only provides a reading of how the Alamo is codified into a place of public history and culture but also uses this event as a way to understand the larger cultural and social processes of the early twentieth century.

Part 2 takes seriously the social and cultural *project* of modernity and explores how the cultural memory of the Alamo advances deeply racialized, ambiguous, even invented understandings of the past. Chapter 5 looks at the role of cinema. In particular, I am concerned with how two films, *Martyrs of the Alamo,* released in 1915, and *The Alamo* by John Wayne, released in 1960, provide visual representations and ideological substance to the changing social conditions of their time. While telling the story of the Alamo, these films also reveal the complex social and racial underpinnings of their historical moments.

The story of the Alamo cannot be told without reference to its "heroes." While much has already been written about the Alamo defenders, chapter 6 deals specifically with the production of Davy Crockett as an American hero. Since at least 1975 "how" Crockett died has been a topic of debate. It is clear, I believe, that most historical evidence points to Crockett's execution *after* the battle; I am less concerned here with how he died than with why he continues to "live" as a heroic figure.

Finally, in the conclusion, I bring the full weight of my argument to bear on the role of symbols, here the Alamo, in shaping the identities and social locations of those signified by them. I consider the role of the Alamo as a master symbol, how as a myth of origin it construes social actors in the present through a story that assures clear divisions between winners and losers, Anglos and Mexicans, Self and Other. I suggest that the Alamo is also a particular token of a more general type of symbolic form coterminous with modernity.

The research for and writing of this book introduced me to a world of scholars and everyday citizens for whom the Alamo is more than a subject of history. For many of them, it is a passion. Perhaps for me as well. But my interest has never been in discovering the "real" events of 1836 but in exploring the how and why of the reproduction of 1836 in other social and historical moments. There are some who believe that questioning and interrogating the relics and shrines of our national past handicaps the present. I disagree. It is only in "examining" the past, not in accepting it as the workings of mythology or cultural memory, that we truly learn from it. There are also those who believe that questioning the Alamo in any way disvalues the decisions and valor of those who died in 1836. I disagree here as well. But again this is not my focus. I will let historians debate the merits of the social actors of 1836 as actors of their own time. My concern is how the cultural memory of the events of 1836 shapes, influences, and represents the changing relationship between Anglos and Mexicans during the Texas Modern. Thus this is a book about the Alamo as symbol: how the Alamo speaks to the politics of its remembering and references the social conditions of that moment. Unpacking the various rememberings and meanings surrounding the Alamo is critical if we are to understand how historical meanings shape contemporary social actors and realize the deep implications of power, meaning making, and the past. When such unpacking brushes up against the production of national or regional myths, icons, memories, and ideologies that have contributed to the racialization, stereotyping, and social displacement of others, it behooves us to probe deeply and honestly into regions some would rather leave unexplored. This is a book of cultural and historical criticism that should be read as an effort to understand how and why the Alamo continues to be both celebrated and disparaged. My hope is that those whose lives have been shadowed by the walls of this old mission may find in these pages a glimmer of light that allows them to see the past more critically and the present more clearly.

REMEMBERING THE ALAMO

And had the Alamo, Goliad, and Mier not existed,
they would have been invented, as indeed they seem
to have been in part.
— AMÉRICO PAREDES,
*With His Pistol in His Hand*

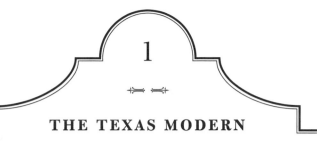

# THE TEXAS MODERN

The nineteenth century was a time of war, of maneuver, position, and outright violence. The seeds of war were scattered alongside the ashes of those killed in the 1836 Battle of the Alamo, and local and regional conflicts emerged soon after, but it was not until the early twentieth century that the seeds of conflict would fully germinate. The story of how the Alamo emerged as a major site of American cultural memory does not begin in 1836 but in the latter part of the nineteenth century as Texas was undergoing a vast social transformation. It is then that efforts were initiated to preserve the remaining physical structures of the old mission of the Alamo and to claim Davy Crockett as an American hero. But why some sixty years after the battle? There is no single answer; we can only look to the numerous events and forces that began to shape the social face of Texas at this time.

Several critical changes affected the Texas economy between 1880 and 1900: the closing of the range, the introduction of the railroad, and the beginning of commercial farming. Between 1900 and 1920 the rate of these changes accelerated, leading to increased social pressure and conflict. Overall, the period between 1880 and 1920 was marked by the working out of new relationships, habits, and practices, resulting in the establishment of a social order segmented into various ethnic and class divisions.

By 1915, however, these struggles for position—struggles Antonio Gramsci (1971:108) identifies as passive or nonviolent forms of negotiation—had erupted into violent conflict. The various social and class contradictions of this period could no longer be restrained by earlier social and ideological arrangements, like those between elite ranchers and their workers, revealing the depth and magnitude of social change. These eruptions are markers of a "cultural revolution"—that unsettling and transitional period in which new practices and customs, forged from new relations of material and ideological production, ascend to a position of dominance (Jameson 1981:85). I refer to the emerging and newly established social forms and the numerous responses they engendered, both for and against, as the Texas Modern.

While modernity had its beginning far from the Texas-Mexican border, events there provide an important perspective on how global processes and forces are both constitutive of and repositioned by local practices and concerns. The project of modernity resulted from the attempts of writers, philosophers, intellectuals, and others to free the world from the confines of "tradition," to establish scientific rationalism in place of "magic" and "superstition," to understand and control "nature," and to organize society through rationalized bureaucratic institutions. While it is clear that these achievements developed in uneven stages and, by some accounts, are still in process, it is also clear that they brought both promise and tragedy. Modernity, therefore, references a complex, uneven, and multi-faceted process of transformation through which earlier social and cultural complexes are dislodged from the habitats of their making and reconstituted, under the weight of rationalized, technocratic forces, into distinct and qualitatively new forms.[1] One of the effects of this process is the redefinition and reinvention of society and self as earlier social rubrics are stretched beyond their capacity to recognize, organize, and map emerging relations. A primary engine of modernity is capitalism, with its incessant drive to create new markets and its incorporation of earlier productive practices and relations into its guiding principles of wage labor, surplus value, and commodity fetishism. While pointing to capitalism as an "essential" ingredient of the modern, I want also to clarify that modernity refuses linear or causal explanation and is better understood as a "complex structure" of multiple and uneven events, forces, practices, and ideologies that emerge in their own time and place and through the rhythm of their own development (Althusser and Balibar 1979:312).[2]

Modernity can be seen directly through changes in the various articulations of its complex structure. Such changes grow out of historically specific conditions that, while interacting with larger social networks, are rooted in the concrete conditions of the local. It is this conjuncture of material relations and their articulation though a meaning-making system of signs that constitutes my discussion of the Texas Modern and the Alamo. To speak of the Texas Modern and its various inflections serves, not to define all social relations of this period, but to rethink its social and expressive features in terms of a conceptual unity, or as Louis Althusser (Althusser and Balibar 1970:186) suggests, "a structural causality." Periodizing concepts allow us to place in relation events and practices that all too often are disjointed by the rationalizing forces of Western, modern thought.

The changes associated with the Texas Modern are evident in the rapid transition to commercial farming and the erosion of local agricultural and cattle-related practices. In deep South Texas farmers from Kansas and Illinois played a principal role in this transformation, influenced by developers promising cheap land worked by even cheaper Mexican labor (Zamora 1993). Between 1910 and 1920 these midwestern transplants were responsible for doubling the number of farms in Cameron County and increasing the number sevenfold in neighboring Hidalgo County. The influx into South Texas of outsiders — or *fuereños* — resulted in a population boom: from 79,974 inhabitants in 1900 to more than 159,000 in 1920 (Montejano 1987:109). Although these events affected all sectors of the population, the displacement of Mexican skilled workers, landowners, and vaqueros was disproportionate to their overall numbers.

Urban areas were equally affected. San Antonio's West Side developed as an enclave of Mexican social and cultural life whose population mushroomed by the early 1900s. Although they were founders of the city and early civic and business leaders, by 1915 Mexicans were primarily poor, and stayed poor because of their "forced social and economic segregation" (R. García 1991:27–28). William Knox, remembering his boyhood in the 1870s, speaks of

> [a] proud class of Mexicans who owned the center of town, living in the best houses, and also owning the hundreds of irrigated acres lying in this well-watered valley. . . . That was old San Antonio, where the educated Mexican gentlemen of Spanish blood lived in ease and splendor. (1927:3–4)

Such a site, he claims, rapidly changed with the arrival of the Southern Pacific in 1875. "Old San Antonio," he continues, "of brilliant court and docile peasant was no more" (Knox 1927:4).

The forces of capital and economic change, responsible for the demise of the Mexican worker in Texas, were augmented by political bossism and racism. Granted, these were not new experiences in Texas, but racism worked in tandem with capitalism to accelerate the transition to industrialization and commercialism that started several decades earlier. David Montejano states,

> By 1920 the Texas Mexican people had generally been reduced, except in a few border counties, to the status of landless and dependent wage laborers. . . . The result everywhere was the same: where commercial agriculture made significant headway, the previous understanding [peace structure] between Mexican and Anglo was undermined. Mexicans now found themselves treated as an inferior race, segregated into their own town quarter and refused admittance at restaurants, picture shows, bathing beaches, and so on. (1987:114)

In an influential, although now heavily criticized work, Mario Barrera (1979:103) describes the emerging class divisions of the Southwest as an "internal colony." While Tomás Almaguer (1987), among others, has taken issue with this model—primarily because of the ways in which the Southwest differs from many international colonialisms at this time but also because of Barrera's inherently essentializing discussion—several features of this model are salient here. Without buying, whole cloth, the notion of the internal colony and in terms specifically of the Texas Modern, I am persuaded by Barrera's (1979:212) discussion of an "ascriptive class segment." Building on labor market segmentation theory—the notion that labor markets are structured into primary, well-paying jobs with good benefits and secondary, low-paying jobs with few benefits—Barrera develops further divisions based on race, ethnicity, and gender. Accordingly, an ascriptive class segment is one divided not only by the structural occupation of the workers but also by their ascribed racial, ethnic, and gender identities. For Barrera, elements of race, ethnicity, and gender play a key role in understanding the participation and displacement of Mexican workers. This dynamic was not unique to Texas but was reproduced throughout the American side of Greater Mexico as Mexican workers were structured into the U.S. capitalist economy through dual labor market practices or as reserve, unskilled workers in spite of their craft and labor specialties (Vélez-Ibáñez 1996). The imprints of these labor practices continue into the present. As recently as 1993, Gilberto Cardenas, Jorge Chapa, and Susan Burek could write:

Although the relative importance of agriculture in South Texas has diminished in the past 30 years, it continues to exert a strong influence in the southern part of the region along the Texas-Mexico border. Historically, a complex system of racial discrimination governed the insertion and devaluation of Mexican labor in San Antonio and throughout the Southwest. This system has had an extraordinarily harsh impact throughout the area. (P. 162)

My intent is not to explore the various economic models that help to explain the displacement of Mexican workers but to indicate that at the turn of the twentieth century in Texas, as in Greater Mexico and the American South, a complex system of labor segregation existed that was circumscribed by class, race, and gender.[3] In short, the social and economic transition I am calling the Texas Modern is made possible by the economic and social displacement of the Mexican worker. As Emilio Zamora (1993:53) claims, "Mexican workers played a central role in this transformation by shouldering a major portion of the unwelcome cost of economic change as laborers." The effects of the Texas Modern on the lives of the local Mexican population were severe: most experienced underemployment that ensured poverty; little access to public institutions, enforced by practices and policies of segregation; and loss of political power, guaranteed through gerrymandering and the institutionalization of poll taxes. These practices, reproduced through the political and social apparatuses of the state, served to assure a differential social body (Kearney 1991:55).

### OF WAR . . .

In all social upheavals there are nodes of resistance—both cultural and political. The same is true in Texas. A key example is the *corrido,* the well-known tradition of Mexican balladry of border conflict. Américo Paredes (1958), the preeminent scholar of this aesthetic form, has documented this rich corpus and demonstrated its critical stance toward the dominant Anglo-Texan community. That the Texas-Mexican *corrido* articulates, in aesthetically inflected forms, a deep suspicion of and critical perspective on the forces of the Texas Modern is not coincidence. Indeed, it is through direct engagement with the upheavals of the moment that we can describe the *corrido* as a counternarrative of the Texas Modern, one whose aesthetic shape and narrative content descends directly from the historical conditions being discussed.

In terms of social and political mediation, I want to briefly discuss two critical events from this period. The first is the 1911 *primer congreso mexicanista* (First Mexican Congress) and the second is a violent uprising occasioned by the *Plan de San Diego* and its subsequent narrativization in the *corrido* "Los Sediciosos."

The *primer congreso mexicanista* took place in Laredo, Texas, and was organized by Nicasio Idar, editor and publisher of *La Crónica,* a local Spanish-language newspaper. Concerned by the rise of violence against Mexicans, *La Crónica,* staffed by several of Idar's children, ran a series of articles in 1910 concerning the harsh treatment and disturbing socioeconomic conditions experienced by Texas Mexicans. One example was the lynching of Antonio Rodríguez on November 2, 1910. Within hours of being arrested near Rocksprings, Texas, for allegedly killing an Anglo woman, a mob formed and Rodríguez was tied to a tree and burned. Other issues that concerned Idar were the already perceptible loss of Mexican culture and the Spanish language and discrimination in education (Limón 1974:87–88).

In an effort to bring these issues into the public realm, Idar and his family organized a statewide congress through the Orden Caballeros de Honor, a Texas-Mexican and Mexican lodge, as well as Masonic organizations, mutual aid societies, and other associations. Two delegates from each order were to attend the congress along with invited guests. The congress opened on September 14, 1911, and drew a large, but unknown, number of representatives. The activities of the congress were widely reported in Spanish-language newspapers throughout South Texas, including San Antonio, while English-language papers generally ignored it or downplayed its significance.

One outcome of the meetings was the founding of a statewide organization, La Gran Liga Mexicanista de Beneficencia y Protección. Although the association did not survive, its agenda was unprecedented in terms of the objectives it set and the issues it raised. Noted as an important "precursor" to later Chicano and Chicana political activism (Limón 1974), the congress debated the importance of Mexican culture and history, Mexican unity against oppressors, the cohesion of the working classes, the role of language and culture, including bilingual education, the lack of criminal justice, the education of women, and social and educational discrimination (Limón 1974).

The efforts of the *primer congreso* remind us that the displacing and brutal facts of the Texas Modern, the local practices of lynching, land stealing, discrimination, and racism, did not go uncontested. I would even argue that it serves as an example of the strategic wars of position enacted by the local Mexican population that developed in tandem with more confrontational political maneuvers.

In 1915 a group of Mexicans and Texas Mexicans known as Los Sediciosos (the Seditionists) instigated a series of skirmishes and raids against elements of the new dominant class. These men were associated with the *Plan de San Diego* and were led by Aniceto Pizaña and Luis de la Rosa, who waged open warfare in South Texas. In their effort to wreak havoc on the emerging modern economic infrastructure, Los Sediciosos sabotaged bridges, attacked post offices and trains, and raided several large ranches, only to spur the wrath of the Texas Rangers and the U.S. military.

Although the circumstances surrounding the writing of the *Plan* are debated by historians, it is believed to have been partially written by six or seven Mexicans imprisoned in Monterrey, Mexico, in January 1915 and finalized in San Diego, Texas, from which it receives its name (Cumberland 1954; Gómez-Quiñones 1970; Richmond 1980). Texas authorities found a copy of the *Plan* on one of its authors, Basilio Ramos, when he was arrested in McAllen, Texas, later that month. Ramos was charged with treason for possession of the revolutionary document, but when the revolt, as outlined in the *Plan*, failed to materialize, the charges were dismissed. Ramos was released on May 13, 1915 (Longoria 1982:214).

The *Plan* called for a general uprising of all Texas Mexicans living on the border at 2:00 P.M. on February 20, 1915. The objective was to retake the territories lost to the United States in the wars of 1836 and 1848. This territory, consisting of the states of Texas, New Mexico, Arizona, Colorado, and California, was to become a new independent Mexican republic from which land would be granted to blacks, Indians, and Asians to form their own autonomous states (Gómez-Quiñones 1970; Hager 1963).

With the incarceration of Ramos, February 20 passed uneventfully. However, in late May and continuing until late fall of that year, border raids led by Pizaña and de la Rosa were carried out almost weekly against the Anglo-Texan community. Special aggression was directed at the Texas Rangers, who served as the strongmen for many of the new elite power brokers in the area. Pizaña and de la Rosa carried out these attacks with no more than a hundred men, often fewer, and they raided as far north as the King Ranch in Kleberg County. The U.S. government responded by increasing its military force on the border with troops from the U.S. Army and the Texas Rangers (Cumberland 1954; Hager 1963). On October 21, 1915, the last raid by the Seditionists took place at Ojo de Agua, putting an end to the revolutionary effort connected with the *Plan de San Diego*.

While the actual warfare engaged in by Los Sediciosos ended by fall

1915, their exploits were remembered for years to come through the *corrido* "Los Sediciosos." As in the ballads that preceded it and those that followed, "Los Sediciosos" reproduced aesthetically and semantically a crucial countermodernist Texas-Mexican position. As I have described elsewhere (1992), this text serves as a key example of the possibilities for collective ideological resistance while it simultaneously exhibits fractures in its formal narrative features. The irony of both song and event cannot be lost: while the Seditionists are involved in violent and intense maneuvers of border resistance, "Los Sediciosos," as a text, already represents a growing division in the Mexican community between "los puros mexicanos" (pure-blooded Mexicans) and "los mexico-tejanos" (Texas Mexicans). What could be read as a high point of communal and political solidarity fragments beneath the weight of modern nationalist and regional forces.

Before continuing, I want to make clear that the discussion above does not suggest that these are the only, or even the most important, forms of mediation and resistance during this period. For example, in the realm of economics, labor unrest and collective organizing were continuous throughout the same time. The mechanisms of segregation, Zamora (1993) shows, even at the level of labor unions, forced Mexican workers to devise "informal" organizational structures through which to oppose their continued labor exploitation. By admitting informal worker networks into his analysis, Zamora (1993:84) discovers "an impressive level of organizing that manifested a unifying set of working-class and minority concerns."

### . . . AND STRUCTURES OF PEACE

Los Sediciosos, the Mexican irredentists waging war against the emerging economic reorganization, remind us that in Texas, as elsewhere, the forces of modernity generated not only change but also, and more important, attempts at social and cultural erasure through assimilation, labor displacement, and land acquisition. It is here that the peace structure outlined by Montejano (1987) and articulated in chapter 3 merits reconsideration. Montejano states that postannexation Texas was marked by a period of accommodation between Anglo and Mexican elites that helped to keep conflict in abeyance by maintaining a semblance of the Mexican ranching social structure. While I believe Montejano's point is well placed, it merits serious reconsideration when viewed in terms of the Texas Modern.[4]

One must consider that the reorganization of nineteenth-century relations between Anglos and Mexicans was itself a social displacement of Mexican elites. While some semblance of a "Mexican" social order persisted in the ranching communities of South Texas, it was now adjudicated through the power of Anglo interests. This relationship of accommodation served to introduce a hierarchical relationship between these two groups. And while "peace" may have prevailed, at least at the more general level of elite social relations, it constituted the historical condition for the development of a class hierarchy structured along the same ethnic and racial divide. My argument, therefore, is that the peace structure serves as the condition that facilitates the formation of a racially fractured capitalist labor market. The indiscriminate lynchings, practices of racial exclusion, and labor devaluation formalized during the Texas Modern were made possible by earlier, "peaceful" social displacements and their concomitant social and cultural changes. At this level, then, Barrera's (1979) early work merits reconsideration, since the structure of peace sets in place a set of social relations typical of conquest and colonial situations wherein both class struggle and racial hierarchies coalesce into a new system of relations. While in theory Anglo-Mexican relations were structured along an axis of classic capital–labor relations within a representative democracy, the de facto practices of racial segregation and ascriptive labor segmentation, as well as formal and informal institutional barriers to political participation, served to reproduce a situation much like colonialism.

While my main focus of discussion is South Texas, it must be noted that changes experienced locally were also occurring at other levels of society. The effort to "reinvent" the United States resulted in various preservation movements across the country as cultural historians and various organizations became involved in the looming task of redefining American history, culture, and society (Kammen 1991). These projects were not random occurrences but events influenced by xenophobia as increased immigration and expanding national economies brought U.S. citizens into contact with other racial and ethnic groups. Foreigners were viewed as a major obstacle to American nationalism by the ruling bodies of the nation-state. These concerns were based, as Michael Kammen (1991:238) demonstrates, on bringing "under the flag of the United States millions of men, women, and children who had 'neither language nor traditions nor habits nor political institutions nor morals in common with us.'"

Concern over national identity, both here and abroad, was prompted by the movement of world capital as new markets and resources were "discovered" and created. It was the "Age of Empire" (Hobsbawm 1987). Just as the industrial revolution changed the face of Texas in 1880, its expansion worldwide created an increasingly complex web of relations among labor, resources, producers, markets, and the fledgling nation-states from which it emerged. The formation of an American empire moved in two directions: one within its national boundaries — as those on the western frontier, southern plantations, and southwestern borderlands were encompassed into a national project — and the other outside its territories. While the U.S. move to empire began before the 1900s — mostly through incorporating local economies, practices, and native or enslaved communities — turn-of-the-century technologies and ideologies reconfigured local communities through capitalist penetration. According to José E. Limón (1998:16), "The subaltern sectors of both Greater Mexico and the American South experienced the worst effects of Northern capitalist domination, a domination always deeply inflected with racism." While a nation-state like the United States must produce a certain level of accommodation, it also must, by capitalist necessity, reproduce itself through a process of differential access and control. Nation-state ideologies and bureaucratic practices thus worked in tandem with the class-differentiating forces of capitalism to assure a society crosscut, but not in open warfare, by various sectors.[5]

## THE ALAMO AS MASTER SYMBOL

It is here, at the conjuncture of the local and the global, that the Alamo as sign is wedded to the modern project and reproduced to underscore the social needs of the Texas Modern. The growing significance and signification of the cultural memory of the Alamo at the turn of the century makes interpretive sense only when read as both emerging from and constitutive of the changing material conditions of this period and its formalization into segregated, prejudicial, and devalued social relations between Anglos and Mexicans.

This is not to suggest that the Alamo was without meaning or significance before this era. It is clear that immediately after 1836 the death of the Alamo defenders fueled anti-Mexican sentiment throughout the Southwest for a great many years. What I am suggesting is twofold. First, the production and representation of the Battle of the Alamo during the Texas Modern serves as a master symbol that is itself constitutive, not merely reflective, of the material and social changes outlined above. I would even suggest that without the reproduction of the Alamo during this period, Texas modern life would not be as we know it. This is not to say that modernity would not have erupted in Texas, for it surely would have; it is to suggest that the historical specificity through which Anglo-Mexican social, economic, and political relations conjoined the forces of the Texas Modern would exhibit a different configuration and structure. While Anglo-Mexican relations would, I am sure, still be constituted along an axis of domination, the ideological specificity of this arrangement would be distinct.

My second point, and one that anticipates the chapters that follow, is that the significance of the Alamo is itself reconstituted in this process. The "making" of the Alamo during the Texas Modern uncouples its significance from the narrow confines of the past so that historical lessons and figures from the events of 1836 are recast to serve the ideological and social needs of the twentieth century. The forces of modernity reconfigured both material practices and symbolic forms, since the latter could no longer contain the changing social relations of the modern world; the "cognitive maps," as Fredric Jameson (1988 : 347) calls them, of this earlier period could no longer represent the radical (root) changes of modernity, resulting in the need to reimagine, through new technical rubrics, society, culture, and, in this case, the Alamo. It is for this reason that we must consider the different attitudes Anglos and Mexicans have toward the Alamo. For Anglos, the Alamo serves as a sign of rebirth, the coming-of-age for a state and, eventually, a nation in the modern period. It is not quite the same for Mexicans. For them, the Alamo reverberates with ambivalence. It serves as a reminder, a memorial to a stigmatized identity. Such an identity emerges not from the events of 1836 but as a result of the place of the Alamo developed through the Texas Modern.

The ensuing chapters underscore how the Alamo as sign constructed historical and social differences between Anglos and Mexicans, leading one group to interpret its significance as one of patriotism and the other as one of domination.[6] That is, this newly imagined history plays a constitutive role in the formation of Anglo-Mexican relations during the early part of the twentieth century. The events of the Texas Modern, therefore, give birth to the Alamo while the Alamo as sign shapes Anglo-Mexican relations. But the Alamo as sign cannot signify without referencing its foundational object: the Mexican subject. It is in the transition to modernity, 1880 to 1920, that the construction of Mexican subjectivity as "subjugated Otherness" is codified. The Alamo, and its reproduction through various forms of cultural memory, thus serves as a key example of what Michel Foucault (1980 : 65) refers to as a "procedure" of othering. The rupture of previous social alignments between Anglos and Mexicans required a reimaging of Mexican subjectivity and a remapping of Anglo-Mexican relations so as to underwrite the social and cultural forces of the Texas Modern. In this process, the cultural memory of the Alamo represented Mexican subjects, regardless of citizenship or country of origin, as "subjugated Others."

At every stage of its preservation and reproduction, the Alamo served a semantic purpose, not always unified in historical or social content but nearly always as a means of influencing, selecting, and containing various semantic postures of the dominant. While it has long been understood that symbolic forms provide such shape and value to social life, I want to extend this understanding by thinking more critically about the relationship between symbolic processes and the historical conjuncture of the Texas Modern. I want to foster a particular, if not unique, understanding of the Alamo as a major token of what I am calling a master symbol of modernity.[7]

The cultural memory of the Alamo emerged in conjunction with and in the service of the rapid social transformations of the Texas Modern. Nineteenth-century encounters between Mexicans and Anglos constituted a vast array of positions as competition for land, resources, wealth, labor, and various ideological understandings of civil society were being negotiated. By the beginning of the twentieth century, however, these struggles coalesced into an uneven yet pervasive struggle heralded by the forces of rationality, bureaucracy, industrialization, and technology. Understanding these events as individual, even isolated attempts by settlers, newcomers, and cattle and railroad barons to flex their liberal democratic and capitalistic muscles yields some interpretive understanding. When read, however, as individual acts in a vaster process of social and economic transformation, propelled by the forces of material gain and ideological dominance, the changes occurring in South Texas merit critical rethinking. One aspect of this rethinking is the role of the symbolic and its use in the production of meaning. This is the continuing story of the Alamo.

# *Part One*

⇥ ⇤

## THE ALAMO AS PLACE,
## 1836 – 1905

But collective memory is not only a conquest, it is also
an instrument and an objective of power.
— JACQUES LE GOFF,
*History and Memory*

Being obliged to forget becomes the basis for
remembering the nation, peopling it anew, imagining
the possibility of other contending and liberating forms
of cultural identification.
— HOMI BHABHA,
*Nation and Narration*

# 2

## HISTORY,

## MEMORY-PLACE, AND SILENCE

### THE PUBLIC CONSTRUCTION

### OF THE PAST

Twenty-seven years after my initial visit I return to the Alamo, sitting in a small, low-ceilinged room, facing a large monitor, waiting for the film to begin. The renovated stone room, what is known as the *convento*, or long barracks, grows dark as the "officially authorized" story of this place begins.

"In 1691 an exploratory expedition chanced on the precise spot where the modern city of San Antonio now stands," claims the narrator. The film is provided free of charge to all tourists and visitors, by the Daughters of the Republic of Texas.[1] After a few more chronological notes about Spanish and French explorers, the early history of the Alamo, initially the mission of San Antonio de Valero, begins. The role of the early Franciscan missionaries in Christianizing and civilizing the native population and the subsequent abandonment of the mission, in 1793, when Mexico's secularization laws took effect, is recalled.

The year is now 1835, and the Mexican general Martín Perfecto de Cós, charged with protecting the province of Tejas from Anglo-American unrest, is defeated at the siege of Béxar, now San Antonio. After being captured, he and his soldiers are sent south of the Rio Grande.

Sam Houston takes charge of the Texas forces and after Cós's defeat orders Col. Jim Bowie to destroy the Alamo lest it become occupied and fortified by Mexican forces. But Bowie, according to the narrative, becomes "fascinated" with the old mission and declares that he "would rather die in these ditches than to give them up to the enemy." He refuses to destroy the fortress.[2]

Soon, Lt. Col. William Barrett Travis and Bowie assume joint command of the Alamo and are joined by David Crockett and his dozen or so volunteers from Tennessee. There are about one hundred fifty men in the Alamo, few of whom are trained soldiers. The majority are from outside Texas, a number from Europe. "They had come to aid the revolution." The only outside help the defenders receive are thirty-two men from Gonzalez, Texas, who believed that "[t]his was the place and this was the hour to stand opposed to tyranny."

On February 22, "governed by the ruthless will of the dictator, Santa Anna's cavalry arrived" in Béxar. On arrival, Santa Anna orders the men in the Alamo to surrender. Unwilling to do so, Travis answers with a cannon shot aimed at the Mexican forces. "One hundred fifty valiant volunteers against the dictator's trained brigades. The siege had begun."

The men at the Alamo begin the battle alone. The help they request is not delivered, as the battle continues. Bowie, sick and bedridden, passes the full command of the Alamo forces to Travis. After twelve days of fighting, on the morning of March 6, Santa Anna sounds the *deguello*, the Mexican bugle melody that announces "no prisoners will be taken, no quarter will be given."

As the Mexicans begin their attack, Travis gives the order, "The Mexicans are upon us. Give them hell!" The Texans fight bravely, pushing back two assaults on the Alamo. The third assault breaks the Texans' forces and the Mexicans soon reach the inner fortress of the old mission. Travis falls holding his sword, Crockett dies fighting in the plaza, and Bowie, still bedridden, fights with his pistol and knife in his hand. All the defenders are killed.

The battle of the Alamo was not in vain, for Santa Anna's army is tattered and needs weeks to recuperate from its victory. Less than six weeks later, Sam Houston's army defeats Santa Anna's forces at San Jacinto, screaming, "Remember the Alamo! The Alamo! The Alamo! The Alamo!"

⊷ ⊶

This film provides visitors with the most extensive portrayal of the 1836 battle available at the Alamo.[3] The DRT provides a pamphlet titled "The Story of the Alamo: Thirteen Fateful Days in 1836," but it is less than two pages long and offers only a summary. The presentation of the past at the Alamo merits special attention since "the powerful grip of collective cultural memory," as Michael Frisch (1989:1155) writes, must be differentiated from "real people and the processes of history." Or, as Trouillot (1995:2) suggests, we must distinguish between the past as process, or "what happened," and the past as narrative, or "that which is said to have happened."

Like Frisch, Sturken (1997:3) suggests that we pay close attention to the working of cultural memory, those narratives involved with "cultural products and imbued with cultural meaning." But we must also distinguish between cultural memory and "official historical discourse" (Sturken 1997:3). For Sturken and Frisch, cultural memory and history are not oppositional but entangled: memory plays a critical role in the formation of history. Pulling at the entangled strings of history and memory, especially as they work together at sites of public history and culture like the Alamo, is a daunting but necessary task. Such an effort serves not to highlight, with any finality, the parameters of memory and history but to underscore how the Alamo has emerged in American cultural consciousness as a cultural product.

Because cultural memory imbues narratives with meaning, they are also involved in the formation of identities. As narrative resources, cultural memory emerges as objects of memory are shared, further enhancing their utility as identity markers and makers. The ability to create and control cultural memory, therefore, is an act invested with power (Le Goff 1992:98).[4] On the other hand, history, or more specifically, official historical discourse, is quite distinct. First, "historical discourse" refers to specific norms and values concerning evidence and interpretation (Ruffins 1992; Sturken 1997).[5] However, as discourse, history is available to us primarily through narrative and therefore shares many of the characteristics of other discourses such as literature, myth, and cultural memory. This is to say that historical discourse participates in a process of meaning production in a fashion similar to other forms of narrative.[6]

How then do we evaluate narratives of the past — cultural memory from history in this case — when the narratives are entangled from the start? Or how do we examine the engagement of cultural memory with history at sites like the Alamo that tend to erase this distinction?[7] It is here that memory-place, as a means of scrutinizing the semantic dimensions of the site of public history and culture, serves a critical interpretive purpose.

My understanding of memory-place builds on Pierre Nora's (1989) discussion of *lieux de mémoire,* or sites of memory, as well as the recent interest in the relationships among memory, history, and semiotics (Frisch 1989; Le Goff 1992; MacCannell 1992; Nora 1989). For Nora, *lieux de mémoire* are constructed from the interplay between memory and history, with memory attaching itself to "sites" and history to "events." But the relationships among memory, place, history, and event are not so clearly delineated in sites of public history and culture such as the Alamo. Walking through the stone-fortified Alamo church, listening to historical renditions of the battle, recalling last week's history lesson or the previous night's Disney episode of "Davy Crockett" collapses the distinctions between the events of 1836, its historical emplotment, the aura of the place, and one's memory of it.[8] It is this conjuncture of the learned and the experiential that emerges with the presence of place. The result is a past made real because one stands — quite literally — in its wake; the cultural memory of the Alamo bursts into truth by walking through its silent chambers.

Cultural memories, disguised and "entangled" with the workings of historical discourse, are spatially and physically embedded in geographically fixed sites of public history and culture. Memory-place is critically linked to practice, emerging from and within the concrete relations of social power that inform the social construction of meaning. Unraveling the relationship between cultural memory and history at the Alamo requires that we cast a glance in two directions at once: toward the past and the narrative entwinement of memory and history and toward the present, so as to examine the construction of place in terms of discursive formation and physical representation.

In the Alamo film, the cinematic narrative of the battle is based on a binary division between Texans and Mexicans structured in the following way:

|  | *Texans* | *Mexicans* |
| --- | --- | --- |
| Leaders: | Travis; Bowie; Crockett | Santa Anna |
| Character: | brave, valiant men | ruthless dictator |
| Purpose: | independence; liberty; freedom | tyranny |
| Soldiers: | volunteers | trained brigade |
| Outcome: | victorious even in death | defeated (6 weeks later) and tattered in victory |

Binary structures such as these are useful not because they provide a "map of the real," states Ramón Saldívar (1990:123), but for the kind of foundational principles that give credence to them in the first place. This symmetry is not the foundation of historical discourse, where the murky waters of the past are defined by their sheer multiplicity and ambiguity, but the structural features of memory.

In spite of its pretense to accuracy, the film does not represent the historical evidence of the "Battle of the Alamo." The film begins by citing 1691 as the year when the first explorers in the area "chanced on the precise spot" where the city of San Antonio now stands. Like all chronotopic devices, this opening sentence collapses time and space, historical distance and geographic location, into a unified frame (Bakhtin 1981). It bridges the gap between the presence of those first explorers and our own, uniting the historical fates of the observer and the historical actors through the physical place of the Alamo. A series of other dates and historical characters are presented, recalling the chronology of the founding of the mission, the names of those who established it, and its depopulation before becoming a military outpost in the early 1800s. These devices are part of the strong voice of the narrative, mixing dates and places and offering anecdotal vignettes as proof of its historical authority. The film organizes everything into a single, unified frame that leaves no confusion as to the social and geographic borders that separate Texans from Mexicans.[9]

Midway through the film, the narrator recounts Travis's action before the final siege:

> According to legend, Travis drew a line on the ground with his sword,
> offering every man a choice to remain or save his life.
> According to the legend, only one man fled.
> History records that 187 remained to die.

This segment is instructive for the way it constructs its own historical authority. By announcing this segment as "legend," the narrator readily admits that fabrications have filtered into the collective story of the Alamo. But in marking it in this way, all other aspects of the narrative, that which is unmarked, are framed as "fact." The narrative thus produces its own authority by claiming to distinguish "legend" from "fact," reinforced through the parallel repetition of the phrase "According to legend . . ."

The binary logic of the Alamo narrative is further implicated in the last phrase of this segment: "187 remained to die." But this figure only takes into account those on the Texas side, clearly qualifying them as the only historical actors who matter. The phrase provides another example of how the film constructs its own authoritative stance. The narrator, in a slow, methodical cadence, claims, "History records . . ." Through these words, the narrator represents history as a transcendental subject that keeps track of minute events and details, making them available to the investigative eye of the historian. While the phrase derives from a certain poetic and dramatic license indicative of the intended audience, its message is that the past is objectively knowable and readable.

+⇛  ⇚+

Once the credits are complete, I again explore the mission complex, scrutinizing the physical features of the place. Walking through the mission church, what most people recognize as the Alamo, I take careful note of the displayed artifacts and their descriptions. Before exiting from the back side door that leads to the Alamo museum and store, I recall the sign on the front entrance that reads:

> Be Silent Friend
> Here Heroes Died
> To Blaze a Trail
> for Other Men

The Alamo is silent.

+⇛  ⇚+

Because of the interreferentiality between the cultural memory of the Alamo and the place itself, the full force of this site can only be experienced ethnographically, which is to say, by one's presence. In keeping with the protocol of public shrines and memorials, patrons are asked to "be silent," and this request is readily observed.

Silence is not only an aspect of public protocol—observers moving quietly and reflectively as they slip by artifacts, paintings, and other objects housed in the mission church—but also underlies the ambiguous relationship between memory and history that anchors meaning in place. As a semantic component of memory, silence is crucial for understanding how places like the Alamo are validated. Andrew Lass (1988:467) argues that the "nation-state's concern for remembrance, or encoding, is paralleled only by its obsession with forgetting, or erasure." Memory is not only forgetful; in attempting to preserve the past, it selectively silences those elements that attempt to rupture the quiet. One example, of the many to follow, concerns the debate over whether Crockett died in combat during the battle or was executed after being captured at the end.[10] According to José Enrique de la Peña (1975), one of Santa Anna's men, and Dan Kilgore, in *How Did Davy Die?* (1978), Crockett was executed, on

Santa Anna's orders, after the battle. However, according to Susan Prendergast Schoelwer (1985:16), the DRT, intent on keeping Crockett's memory intact, stated in 1985 that his death in battle, as portrayed in John Wayne's cinematic version of the event, is more in accord with the official narrative of the Alamo.

While I agree with Trouillot's (1995:27) claim that "any historical narrative is a particular bundle of silences," I want to suggest that the silences of memory and history serve different purposes and move in different directions. Here I return to Nora once again. Crucial to his understanding of memory and history is the relationship between space and time. For Nora, memory is attached to sites that are concrete and physical while history is concerned with the fleeting, the fluid, and the processual. As such, memory-place, and its physical and concrete evidence, validates and authenticates a specter of the past, whereas official history—intent on unraveling the temporal movement of the past with sources and archives—is only as solid as the narrative it produces.[11] While the silences of history, as Trouillot rightly demonstrates, are linked to the differential exercises of power whose effects reinforce regimes of truth that control the past, the silences of memory serve to anchor the past concretely, naturalizing both the social order and its social actors' identities. The silence of history leads to power; the silence of memory creates cultural meaning.

The call to silence on the Alamo door resonates with the silences of memory that serve to write the past in a way that leaves no room for ambiguity. The Alamo film functions in the same way. It produces winners, losers, tyrants, heroes, Mexicans and Texans. Any evidence that would complicate the picture is silenced by the weight of its structure. While the film makes a slight attempt to portray an unbiased view ("The Mexicans charged with discipline and courage"), its binary configuration is closed to such a reading. The silent walls of the Alamo serve to remind us of those who died and shield us from the multiple histories of the past.

The narrative presented to the public at the Alamo erases a number of critical aspects of the Battle of the Alamo so as to render it misleading. Clearly, public historical accounts suffer from their need to condense and simplify, but such efforts bear a certain responsibility to understand and portray the various complex forces that shaped the past. Public history should open the door to curiosity about the past, not render it conclusive and known. The historical portrayal of the Alamo is no different, and numerous aspects effaced from the official narrative merit reinscription. To this end I offer other texts and other readings.

╬═ ═╬

In February 1836 Gen. Antonio López de Santa Anna, dictator and president of Mexico, approached the town of San Antonio de Béxar in the province of Coahuila y Tejas for the purpose of enforcing a centralist regime against those who sought to follow the federalist constitution of 1824. The events leading to Santa Anna's northward campaign are critical for understanding the march of 1836. While these events do not change the outcome of the battle, they serve to underscore the erasures of the public accounts and point to an interpretation of why such silences have existed.

Mexico gained its independence from Spain in 1821, and, like many postcolonial governments, its search for a political and national identity was forged through factionalized parties. One main source of strife was political organization and ideology: should Mexico develop as a strong centralist state or as a cohesively structured federalist nation that allows more autonomy to its member states? Centralists supported special rights for clergy and military personnel long practiced by the Spanish Crown. Furthermore, they argued persuasively for an elite form of control, relegating power to the *hacenderos* (wealthy landowners) and other select groups over the populace. Federalists were influenced by the recent success of the United States, with its separation of power into three branches, as well as the political philosophy of Montesquieu.[12] The balance of power teetered in one direction, then the other for several years, until 1824 when the issue was seemingly settled with the writing of a constitution forming the United States of Mexico as a federalist republic.

It was during the struggle for independence from Spain that Moses Austin petitioned the Spanish Crown for permission to settle in Coahuila y Tejas. He died before achieving his goal, but his son, Stephen F. Austin, received colonization rights from the newly established Mexican government in 1821. Austin was allowed to emigrate with three hundred families from the United States, provided that they were "of good moral character, would profess Roman Catholic religion, and agreed to abide by Mexican law" (Meyer and Sherman 1995:335). Arriving in Coahuila y Tejas, Austin and his fellow settlers soon learned what it meant to live under Mexican rule. While many of Austin's early frontiersmen, and others who soon followed, came seeking opportunity in this new land, many found the unwanted presence of Mexicans. As Arnoldo De León aptly states:

> The immigrants, then, did not arrive in Texas with open minds concerning the native Tejanos: their two-hundred-year experience with

"different" peoples had so shaped their psyche that their immediate reaction was negative rather than positive. . . . They had retained im-
pressions acquired before their arrival in the state then reapplied and
transposed those racial attitudes upon the native casta. (1982:11)

By 1827, 12,000 Anglo-Americans had entered Mexico and were living in
the province of Coahuila y Tejas, outnumbering the Mexicans by 5,000.
Foreigners continued moving into the province in large numbers, and by
1835 Mexican citizens in Tejas numbered 7,800 to 30,000 Anglo-Americans. Mexican officials became alarmed. In an effort to curb the growing
immigration from the United States, in 1829 the Mexican government
passed an emancipation proclamation outlawing slavery. Slavery was not
practiced in Mexico, but the law was aimed at curbing the number of U.S.
citizens moving into the Mexican provinces.

Another factor causing concern among the citizens of Tejas—both
Mexican and Anglo-American—was the cumbersome distance between
Tejas and Saltillo, where government offices and appellate courts for the
province were housed. In 1833 Austin traveled to Mexico City to try to
persuade President Santa Anna to allow Tejas to become an independent
Mexican state with control over its own affairs. Although Santa Anna refused, he agreed to allow citizens of the province more latitude in conducting their legal matters, including a revision of the tariff laws, repeal of
the anti-immigration law, and trial by jury (Hardin 1994).

But tension and fear were not the only sentiments between Anglo-
Americans and the local Mexican population. Mexicans in Tejas were
pleased to find assistance in warding off the raids of Comanches, Apaches,
and Kiowas, who often attacked settlements in search of horses and other
goods. And Anglo-Americans, unaccustomed to the harsh conditions of
the Texas prairies, learned the skills of cattle ranching from the Mexican
vaqueros. It was not uncommon for Mexican women to find husbands
among the incoming settlers, especially those of the elite classes.

Tensions between the Mexican citizenry in Tejas and the Mexican government came to a head when Santa Anna discarded the Constitution of
1824, causing great consternation among both Mexicans and Anglo-
Americans. Perhaps the biggest misconception in Texas history concerns
the immediate effects of Santa Anna's annulment. Historians agree that his
actions led to the military engagements that resulted in the independence
of Texas, but it is also quite clear that the move to independence was not
the immediate stance taken by all. Many settlers had come to Tejas to seek
new ways of life and were slow in responding to the calls for military ser-

vice, and even fewer fought at the Alamo. As Hardin (1994:156) demonstrates, "Few of the real Texians were there, for few of the old settlers had originally sought independence or war."

There are numerous factors that must be considered in attributing a motive to those who bore arms against the Mexican state. The most common, at least in the initial stages of the revolt, was the intent of local citizens to return Mexico to a federalist republic. In fact, as settlers in Texas organized during the early months of conflict, their effort to form a provisional independent government led to open feuding on the issue of independence. These initial efforts led in November 1835 to the formation of a provisional government "as a state within the Mexican federation" (Hardin 1994:57), not a separate independent Texas republic, although this was only a few months away. The rationale for this position was that local citizens of Tejas believed that many of their troubles with the Mexican government would be endurable if decisions were left in their own hands. *Federalistas* and *centralistas,* then, bear the primary responsibility for the open hostility that erupted in 1835. Among these two camps, neither ethnicity nor national origin served as the primary factor in choosing sides. One could find Mexican citizens siding with the *federalistas,* opposing the dictatorial regime of Santa Anna, and Anglo-Americans backing the centralist forces of the dictator.

Even after blood was spilled in battle, there was a lack of broad general support by the long-term Anglo-American residents. James Walker Fannin, a colonel in the Texas forces and commander at the Battle of Goliad who was executed along with his men soon after the Alamo battle, complained to Acting Governor James Robinson about this lack of support on February 7, 1836:

> Out of more than four hundred men at or near this post, I doubt if twenty-five citizens of Texas can be mustered in ranks—nay, I am informed, whilst writing the above, that there is not half that number;— does this fact bespeak an indifference, and criminal apathy, [which is] alarming? (Quoted in Hardin 1994:158)

The disputes, events, and initial steps that precipitated the Battle of the Alamo and the formation of the Republic of Texas are important for understanding how the story unfolds.

In October 1835, after his return from Mexico and his unsuccessful bid to convince Santa Anna to allow Texas more latitude in conducting its internal affairs, and where he was imprisoned for several months, Austin was called by federalist supporters to govern the rebel forces. Austin, a man with no military training, accepted this new responsibility reluctantly. The federalists in Texas were enthusiastic at this point, for in two skirmishes with Mexican forces they came out victorious, although they remained wholly untried in large-scale battle.

In late September 1835 citizens of De Witt's Colony—longtime supporters of the Mexican government—grew more concerned about the consolidation of centralists in Santa Anna's regime. When their rumblings were heard by Mexican officials, Col. Domingo Ugartechea, commander of the Mexican forces in San Antonio de Béxar, requested the return of a Mexican cannon on loan to members of the colony at Gonzales. Ugartechea, rightly concerned about equipping rebel forces with Mexican artillery, feared that members of the colony might use the cannon against his own men.

But the citizenry of Gonzales balked at returning the cannon, especially in light of increasing tensions with the Mexican government. Ugartechea sent Lt. Francisco Castañeda and one hundred men to request the cannon, giving them strict orders not to entice the colonists into a military skirmish. The forces at Gonzales, alerted to the Mexican government's intent, organized and fortified Gonzales and were prepared to fight. With both forces in full sight, Castañeda met with the leader of the Gonzales militia, Col. Henry Moore. Castañeda's request for the cannon was met with rebuke by Moore, and when it was clear that the military piece could not be taken without incident, Castañeda returned to his men without it. The Texan forces, encouraged by his withdrawal, fired the cannon at Castañeda's men, who were already in retreat.

The second skirmish took place at the presidio of La Bahía outside Goliad. General Cós arrived in Texas in mid-September at Copano Bay with five hundred men. Cós, Santa Anna's brother-in-law, was sent on a mission to disarm the rebels in Tejas and was rumored to be carrying a supply chest with $50,000. Hearing of this, rebels in Matagordo conspired to "seize the money or else capture General Cós and hold him for ransom" (Hardin 1994:14). Led by George Morse Collinsworth, the volunteers plotted to make their move on Cós while he stayed at La Bahía. As they made their way to the presidio, however, they learned that Cós had already left the garrison and was en route to Béxar. Intent on continuing their mission, the federalists in the town of Victoria drafted a document dated October 9, 1835, stating:

> The volunteers . . . declare in a clear and unequivocal manner, their
> united and unalterable resolution to give ample and complete protec-

tion to the citizens of this town, and to those also of every other which may enter—requiring only, that, the citizens of said towns stand firm to the Republican institutions of the Constitution of 1824. (Hardin 1994:15)

Collinsworth and his men were intent on demonstrating their allegiance to the Mexican Constitution and avoiding suspicion and fear among the local citizens who might see them as an itinerant band of brigands seeking their own rewards.

For his part, Cós left La Bahía without reinforcing it with more men or weaponry. When Collinsworth and his forces attacked on October 10, it was overtaken within thirty minutes. Not only did this move encourage other rebel forces in Texas, but the capture of La Bahía effectively cut off Cós's supply line to the coast, leaving him little chance of receiving reinforcements or supplies.

By mid-October, encouraged by news of these two minor victories, Austin decided to move his troops to San Antonio de Béxar, where Cós had arrived to join the forces of Ugartechea. Together, the Mexican forces in Béxar numbered 647 (Barr 1990:13), divided between the central section of town around the plazas and the garrison at the Alamo on the east side of the river. Cós received word in early October of the skirmish at La Bahía and, realizing his supply route was taken and the importance of Béxar, kept his forces on alert.

The Battle of the Alamo has dominated the history of Texas-Mexican military events, but the Battle of Béxar remains an important event that informs the 1836 fight. En route to Béxar, Austin's forces were joined by Juan Seguín, a leading Mexican citizen of Béxar, and other *bexareños*. Hardin (1994:28) describes the assistance of Seguín and his men in this way: "Tejanos thus brought much needed range skills to the rebel army, rendering it a blend of two frontier traditions. For Anglo-Celtic Americans out of their element, such assistance was critical."

Arriving outside Béxar at the end of October, Austin's forces encountered Mexican troops near Mission Concepción, southeast of town, and summarily sent them retreating back into town. The long rifles of the rebel forces, coupled with the vantage point of higher ground during the skirmish, left the Mexican army ill equipped for military operations in that terrain. The event created a false sense of superiority among Austin's men, since open field fighting could not compare to a military engagement undertaken from fortified positions.

November proved to be a difficult time for the federalist movement in Texas, one marked by "confusion, disorder, and indecision" (Hardin 1994:53). Tensions ripped at the fragile federalist ideals. Most longtime settlers disdained Santa Anna's leadership, but many newcomers, inspired by the victories of the rebel forces, were calling for independence from Mexico (Hardin 1994:53). The lack of clear goals or a plan of action affected Austin's decision making as well. Camped outside Béxar, he waited until early December before moving against Cós's forces. In the interim, his men and lieutenants, tired of waiting, despaired, fled, and nearly mutinied against his leadership. As Hardin (1994:55) describes it, "The independent and ill-disciplined frontiersmen were often more of a problem for Austin than the Mexicans were. They had volunteered to fight, not to sit around and watch their enemy starve and their officers bicker." Disheartened by the rising internal conflicts and suffering from ill health, Austin pressed forward in planning an attack on Béxar, set for November 22 at 3:00 A.M. However, at 1:00 A.M. Austin was awakened and told that several of his officers opposed the assault. At a meeting with all his staff, Austin found the same sentiment among most of the officers. With only two hundred men supporting the attack, Austin ordered his troops back to camp (Barr 1990:36).

It was later learned that Sam Houston, whom the provisional government had named commander in chief of the regular army, had leaked word to several officers that he was against the attack. Disturbed by the situation, Austin announced on November 24 what he had learned on November 18, that he had been relieved of his command by the provisional government and requested to serve as a commissioner to the United States. Col. Edward Burleson and Francis Johnson were elected to replace Austin as commander and adjutant, respectively. On November 25 Austin left the forces at Béxar, ending his brief military efforts during this campaign.

But disorganization and desertion continued to plague Burleson, and on December 4 he decided to end the siege and retreat with his forces to Goliad where they would spend the winter. "For the first time since the fighting began at Gonzalez, Texians had to admit they were beaten, not by the enemy, but by their own disorganization and discord" (Hardin 1994:68). As the rebel forces were beginning to break down camp, Ben Milam returned from a scouting trip on the south side of Béxar and was outraged to learn that the siege had been called off. He met with Johnson, then Burleson, and within hours a plan of attack was in place. The next morning Milam and a group of volunteers began their assault on Béxar in what proved to be a decisive but difficult battle. The fighting lasted four days and was waged house by house, block by block. The Mexican forces were in short supply of food and munitions, while the rebels had access to outside lines of support.

At one critical juncture, Milam was killed by a sharpshooter's bullet, enraging and spurring on the federalist forces. On December 9, pushed to the limits of his resources, Cós sent word to Burleson through his lieutenant, José Juan Sánchez-Navarro, that he wished to surrender and negotiate a ceasefire. Sánchez-Navarro negotiated very favorable terms, resulting in Cós and his men leaving Texas with ammunition, a cannon, and provisions, along with a promise from Cós that neither he nor his men would oppose "the re-establishment of the Federal Constitution of 1824" (Hardin 1994:91). The rebel forces celebrated their victory, as did the federalist leaders in Texas, believing they had met their goals. But Santa Anna had other ideas.

The Battle of the Alamo is, in effect, Santa Anna's response to the siege of Béxar and the disgrace and embarrassment brought on him by his brother-in-law, General Cós. If Tejas had to be reclaimed and ushered back into his centralist regime, the project had to begin in Béxar. In late December 1835 Santa Anna's army set out for South Texas, a trek through the harsh and difficult terrain of the northern Mexican desert.

In late January 1836 Santa Anna and the Mexican army arrived in Monclova and reunited with Cós and his men. In Béxar the rebel forces were busy fortifying Mission San Antonio de Valero, the Alamo, against attackers. With the assistance of engineer Green Jameson and under J. C. Neill's command, the Alamo had been outfitted with nineteen of Cós's cannons. But Neill departed the Alamo for personal reasons, and the leadership of the Alamo was passed to Travis. The men, a compilation of volunteers and "veterans" from earlier skirmishes, were not pleased to have Travis as their commander. And the presence of the well-liked Jim Bowie and the gregarious David Crockett did not help. Travis agreed to lead the members of the regular army and Bowie, the volunteers.

When Travis learned that Santa Anna had crossed the Rio Grande on February 16, he figured Santa Anna would not arrive in Béxar until mid-March. This was not the case. Santa Anna avoided the Laredo road into Béxar and instead took the Camino Real, which brought him in from the west. Travis and his men were taken aback when a sentry posted in the bell tower of San Fernando Cathedral spotted the Mexican forces marching up the Presidio Road on February 23, 1836.

Between the siege of Béxar and the Battle of the Alamo, rebel forces and political leaders grew more confident of their ability to squash the Mexican army led by Santa Anna. Concomitantly, these victories precipitated a stronger independence movement among the citizens of Tejas. Officially, however, when the Mexican general arrived in Béxar, there still was no declaration of independence, a matter that was not resolved until March 2 by members of the Constitutional Convention meeting at Washington-on-the-Brazos. It is clear that Travis and the defenders of the Alamo died for an independent Texas, but at their death they had not received word from their compatriots if indeed independence had been gained.

On arriving in Béxar, Santa Anna's men hoisted a red flag atop San Fernando Cathedral, a protocol of siege warfare announcing that no quarter would be given to prisoners taken during the battle. The Mexican general also offered the rebel forces an opportunity to surrender before the fighting had begun, an offer responded to by Travis with a cannon shot. The battle had commenced.

Travis immediately sent word to Fannin in Goliad to join his forces at the Alamo, but Fannin, not particularly intent on this military move, remained in Goliad after a one-day feeble attempt at transporting his men west. Travis's request to the convention leaders for more troops also went unheeded; however, a cohort of thirty-three men from Gonzalez responded to his call.

The attacks on the Alamo lasted thirteen days, the first twelve of which consisted mainly of cannonade fire and sniper shooting. During this time, munitions and food in the mission compound were slowly being depleted while Travis awaited reinforcements. But on March 3 Travis received word through a courier that Fannin's forces would not be arriving. By this time, the constant barrage of the Mexican artillery had weakened the Alamo's outer walls and Santa Anna needed to make a decision. On March 5 he met with his officers, who generally favored a strategy of waiting until the provisions of the rebel forces were exhausted and they would have no choice but to surrender. Santa Anna, however, had other plans.

Santa Anna took pride in his military acumen and in maintaining his self-proclaimed title, Napoleon of the West. He also believed he needed to inspire his young and inexperienced forces with a decisive victory. To his officers' surprise—and dismay—he ordered a full-scale attack on the Alamo for the next day.

Early on March 6 the Mexican forces made their way to the mission. The final siege had begun. The 187 men inside the Alamo were no match for the thousands of Mexican forces. But Travis's men fought bravely, and from their vantage point, even with limited artillery, they were able to inflict great damage on Santa Anna's marching columns of soldiers. By the end of the battle, Travis and Bowie were dead, as were all but a few. A handful of prisoners were captured, including David Crockett, and taken to Santa Anna, who, in keeping with his mandate of no quarter, ordered them executed.

The entire scene was one of death and destruction. As de la Peña described Santa Anna's arrival:

> He could see for himself the desolation among his battalions and that devastated area littered with corpses, with scattered limbs and bullets, with weapons and torn uniforms. . . . The bodies, with their blackened and bloody faces disfigured by a desperate death, their hair and uniforms burning at once, presented a dreadful and truly hellish sight. (De la Peña 1975:52)

It is estimated that Santa Anna lost six hundred men in his victory, a loss that would cost him in a few short weeks.

Those who died defending the Alamo did so for a "borrowed cause," Hardin (1994:156) claims: "[T]he majority had only recently come from the United States to fight for Texas independence. Among them were Scots, Welsh, Danes and English, as well as U.S. citizens. Few of the real Texians were there." But there is no doubt that news of the defeat, and the death of all the Alamo defenders, gave impetus to an already growing but not wholly embraced independence movement.

Houston — now commander in chief of all forces in Texas — dismissed the loss until he encountered Suzanna Dickenson, the wife of an Alamo defender and in the mission herself at the time of the battle. She, her young daughter, and Travis's slave, Joe, had been released by the Mexican forces and were heading north for safety.

Soon after the Alamo battle, Fannin's forces were defeated at Goliad and he and his men executed by order of Santa Anna. This left the soldiers under Houston's command the only obstacle between the Mexican general and his goal of reincorporating Tejas into the Mexican union. But Houston was not decisive. Hardin demonstrates that until the day of the battle between his forces and Santa Anna's, Houston had no clear plan of where or how to encounter the Mexican army. By either chance or design, but certainly through the influence of those serving in his ranks, Houston's forces met Santa Anna's at the Battle of San Jacinto on April 21. Mostly through the element of surprise, itself the result of indecisiveness on Houston's part, the rebel forces overtook the Mexican army swiftly and captured Santa Anna as he retreated south the next day.

Several factors are critical to this historical portrait. First, the initial dispute in Texas stemmed from both Mexicans and Anglo-Americans seeking to restore a federalist government in Mexico. Mexicans in the province also tired of Santa Anna's exploits and of the political difficulties associated with their distance from the provincial and national capitals in Coahuila and Mexico City. Second, in spite of his unilateral control of Mexican affairs and politics and his personal ambitions, Santa Anna's actions can be viewed as an effort to quash an internal uprising in his own country.

The third factor, which seems quite overlooked, is the men who died. The public version of this event provided by the custodians of the Alamo claims that this was a battle between Texans and Mexicans, a categorization that merits special scrutiny since it collapses ethnic and political categories into an ambiguous binary. Ethnically, those who fought on the "Texan" side were anything but a homogeneous lot. There were thirteen native-born Texans in the group, eleven of whom were of Mexican descent. Of those remaining, forty-one were born in Europe, two were Jews, two were blacks, and the remainder were Americans from other states in the United States. Intermarriage between Anglo-Americans and Mexicans was common, with that of Jim Bowie and Ursula Veramendi, the daughter of the Mexican governor, serving as the closest case at the Alamo. On the Mexican side, Santa Anna's forces as well as the local population in Béxar were an amalgamation of former Spanish citizens now Mexican, Spanish-Mexican *criollos* and mestizos, and indigenous young men whom Santa Anna had conscripted from the interior of Mexico. Politically, one has only to recognize that this was Mexican territory and that "foreigners" were not citizens of Texas but residents of the Mexican state. Coupled with this are the presence of European immigrants and the loosely understood notion of U.S. citizenship as well as the fact that many immigrants to Tejas were seeking relief from social and economic problems in their countries of origin. Finally, prominent Mexican citizens fought on both sides, dividing their allegiance along political and ideological lines rather than ethnically or nationally circumscribed identities popularized by the memory of this battle.

## SILENCE, HISTORY, POWER

The film presented at the Alamo is silent on many of the issues and perspectives that render the Battle of the Alamo an event of the past and results in a presentation that inherently limits the range of meanings, fixing memory (not history) to place. But what is the history of memory-fixed-to-place? Why must memory—and the specter of these hallowed walls—take precedence over history at the place of the Alamo?

The public presentation of history at the Alamo is quite specific about the 1836 battle, but it is silent about its own making within the sociocultural matrix of South Texas society. For example, why is it that the Alamo structures were not recognized as important until the late 1800s? Why is it that the years soon after 1836 saw these buildings fall into disrepair and physical neglect? Unlike the site where the Battle of Gettysburg was fought, the Alamo was not confirmed as a memorial immediately after its occurrence (Patterson 1989). This history, of memory-fixed-to-place, is one of power.

Without presenting a full summary of Texas history, let me briefly state that the years between 1836 and 1880 were filled with ambivalence, not only for Texas, but for the United States as well. Between 1836 and 1846 Texas existed as an independent republic but one not recognized by the Mexican state until the signing of the Treaty of Guadalupe Hidalgo in 1848. This treaty was followed by the Civil War, an event that destroyed the illusion of unity and propagated an economic and social agenda that functioned to catapult the United States into an emerging capitalist economy. By 1880 the United States was ready to tangle with the emerging world nations, a process that required a certain level of national introspection and identity construction.[13]

The place of the Alamo is silent about this history for several reasons. First, the "remembering" of the Alamo serves as a local narrative of displacement against the local *mexicano* population. Consider the significance of the Alamo in Texas legend and oral tradition that impelled a discourse of fear and recompense against Mexicans. As A. M. Gibson notes critically in his introduction to Will Hale's *Twenty-four Years a Cowboy*, "'Killing a Mexican was like killing an enemy in the war.' Since this was a conflict 'with historic scores [the Alamo] to settle the killing carried a sort of immunity with it'" (Hale 1959:xxii–xxiii). One does not have to wait long after the Battle of the Alamo to witness the social incrimination directed at Mexicans, even those who supported the federalist and independence movement. Juan Seguín, who played a critical role in the Battle of San Jacinto and who also was an Alamo defender who escaped death because he was sent by Travis on a courier mission, was driven out of Béxar in 1842 for being Mexican. This experience was not unique to *bexareños*. A. B. J. Hammert describes how "Mexican families were driven from their homes, their treasures, their cattle and horses and their lands, by an army of reckless, war-crazy people, who overran the town of Victoria. These new people distrusted and hated Mexicans, simply because they were

Mexican, regardless of the fact they were both on the same side of the fighting during the war" (quoted in Montejano 1987:27).

The Alamo backlash against Mexicans not only serves a social purpose but an economic one as well. To this end, the Alamo fixes a narrative against Mexicans that "naturalizes" the class identities that erupted at this time. Understanding Mexicans through the story of the Alamo is a strategy that normalizes what otherwise could not be stated—that the economic reorganization of South Texas was based on a system of social dominance. Remembering the Alamo kept present the collective memory of "Texan heroes" and "Mexican tyrants" and served as a public reminder "to keep Mexicans 'in line'" (Montejano 1987:229).

## SILENCE, MEMORY, CULTURE

The emergence of the Alamo as a place of public history and culture is generated from the memory of fixing a social discourse to a public place. The Alamo film is read as a "true" account because it points to the very "spot" that explorers found, to the "real" walls on which Texans stood, to the "real" church where heroes fell, to the "ditches" that Travis chose to defend. The historical narrative at the Alamo is conjoined to the place of the Alamo so as to provide a cohesive, coherent, and closed reading of the events of 1836. In this way, the film maps the contours of the physical structure, forming a sign-vehicle relationship that emerges from and is grounded in its presence.

That the Alamo is considered a shrine admits to its two-dimensional construction of the past. But this is also its very contradiction: maintained as a shrine and memorial, it is presented through multiple layers of historical texts that apotheosize the past. It is a shrine committed to memorializing a past event by authenticating a singular version of it. The preservation of stone walls, cannons, and other artifacts, the presence of exhibits and the film that portrays the battle are presented as historical evidence. Such aspects "overcode" this place so as to read it as a historical site. This overcoding is further recognized in the juxtaposition of colonial mission architecture and the modern edifices of San Antonio. The historical markings of the Alamo, however, are not about historical evidence. They are artifacts, displaced from the movement of history, that reinforce a collective memory of Texan superiority. And like most discourses of this kind, the reproduction of this cultural memory serves to inform the present rather than to enlighten the past (Le Goff 1992).

The silences found at the Alamo—the way selective discourses of Texans and Mexicans is wedded to the physical place where this historical

33

event occurred—are the making of cultural meaning. This cultural representation provides a socializing narrative that discloses the identities of "Texans" and "Mexicans." Such representations mark the contours and bring into relief appropriate moral and ideational values that constitute both the social terrain and one's location in it. Such representations construct the cultural and social map through which social agents find their way to themselves and their place in the world. These cultural representations, as social maps, shape the practices and views of those circumscribed by them. Only by disembedding the multiple layers of aggregate signs can we begin to understand the power they wield. As my young classmate demonstrated, the chord of collective memory and identity reproduced at the Alamo is a highly effective form of meaning construction. This forging of memory to place, constructed through the interaction of recollections of the past and physical places, reveals how knowledge of the past is constituted and spatialized in public structures.

For me, the inscription of my "mes'kin" social place was amended years later through a politically invoked "Chicano" sense of self. But what of my "best friend" and the millions of others who visit this Shrine of Texas Liberty each year? Does the image of "treacherous Mexicans" constructed from the emergent memory-place of the Alamo continue to fashion their perceptions, closing their American minds? I suggest it does, for the ability of the Alamo to wield social identities is a powerful and evocative form of meaning construction. I do not intend to point a finger at those duped by ideology but to demonstrate that the prescriptive influences of memory-place are but one aspect of the lived experience of hegemony that not only affects those whose identities are so thickly fixed, but also those whose views are so thinly drawn. That one particular memory of the Alamo was fixed to this public place is not an accident of history but an example of how cultural memories construct meaning and, in this case, shape the future of the dominant.

## 3

### FROM SAN FERNANDO
### DE BÉXAR TO THE ALAMO CITY
### THE POLITICAL UNCONSCIOUS
### OF PLAZA SPACE

In 1854 Frederick Law Olmsted arrived in what is now the city of San Antonio and described what he saw:

> From these [the German houses in the center of town] we enter the square of the Alamo. This is all Mexican. Windowless cabins of stakes, plastered with mud and roofed with river-grass, or "tula," or low, windowless, but better thatched, houses of adobes (gray, unburnt bricks), with groups of brown idlers lounging at their doors.
>
> The principal part of the town lies within a sweep of the river upon the other side. (1857:149)

By the 1890s Olmsted's portrayal was no longer accurate. The "square of the Alamo" was becoming a major city of the American West. Bernice Rhoades Strong (1987:84), writing of this later period, claims that "[the Alamo] plaza went from a dusty, often muddy area oriented to the military and transportation facilities to a parklike setting surrounded by beautiful buildings that attracted people from banking, entertainment, and mercantile professions."

Before 1850 San Antonio experienced little spatial differentiation in its built environment, with its Mexican plazas serving as the center of town. But after 1875, with the introduction of the railroad and the economic incentives and changes associated with modernity, the spatial organization of San Antonio changed dramatically, with the Alamo and its plaza becoming the new heart of the city. The development of Alamo Plaza, as a plaza, reproduced familiar features of such sites but in this period reflects a different set of organizational principles.

Henri Lefebvre (1991), David Harvey (1973, 1985), and others have demonstrated that a critical feature of social transformation is the reorganization of space as it is increasingly occupied and shaped by a new set of social actors and cultural practices.[1] It is here that San Antonio's particular history of change merits scrutiny, for as Strong testifies, the effects of modernity on San Antonio were precipitated by the emergence of the mercantile and entertainment industries and their attendant reorganization of social and spatial relations.

Equally important is the articulation of a spatially embedded ideology that advances a growing social disjuncture between Anglos and Mexicans. Abundant evidence documents the emergence of San Antonio as a modern city, but what remains hidden between the storefronts, alleyways, and public projects that result from this process is an ideology of dominance imprinted in the changing spatial relations between Mexican San Fernando de Béxar and its American descendant. What I am suggesting is that a nondiscursive ideology is embedded in the changing contours of San Antonio's urban topography that features the Alamo as its focal point. Even before formal efforts at purchasing the Alamo property and structures were initiated, the material presence of these ruins and their underlying significance were effecting change in San Antonio. As such, the dissolution of a Mexican spatial rubric and its reorganization through the practices associated with capitalist modernity mark a growing class division between Anglos and Mexicans in Texas.

### EUROPEAN AND INDIGENOUS PLAZAS

When Hernán Cortés landed on the coast of what is now Mexico, at a site near present-day Veracruz, he heard stories of what was long rumored: marvelous cities filled with gold and other treasures. A few weeks later, as he marched into Tenochtitlán, he saw an impressive and expansive city surrounded by bodies of water connected by aqueducts. Tenochtitlán, like other cities in Mesoamerica, was built with a *templo mayor,* or main temple, as its centerpiece, surrounded by large plazas where religious events took place and the elites resided, and which also served as a locus for the conduct of trade. The sheer magnitude, utility, and importance of indigenous plaza architecture represented the strictly organized social and religious structure of Aztec society. These plazas did not go unappreciated by the Spanish. As Setha M. Low (1995:749) comments, "The cere-monial and commercial uses of these plazas, as well as their sacred and civil meanings and regular form, also inform the subsequent colonial plazas built after the conquest." The impression these built environments left with the Spanish, Low suggests, led to their codification in the Laws of the Indies in 1573.

There were European antecedents to New World plaza forms that were influenced by the architectural advancements of the Italian Renaissance (Low 1993). Spanish cities exhibited three distinct styles of plazas: market, organic, and monumental. Market plazas were sites of commercial activity, mostly trading and small-scale bartering; organic plazas were open areas designed to work with street grids that allowed for social gatherings; and monumental plazas were locations of public festivities such as bullfights and religious ceremonies (Arreola 1992:57). Unlike the indigenous urban tradition, these plazas were located some distance from the center of town and not the "hub of the community" (Arreola 1992:56); neither were they linked to the religious aspects of the social structure as in Tenochtitlán.

It is important to recall that the conquest of the New World, especially Tenochtitlán, led to the reconquest of urban space: entire Spanish cities were constructed over existing indigenous edifices and sacred sites. For example, in Tenochtitlán, or Mexico City, the Catholic cathedral was erected near the Templo Mayor and the National Palace was constructed atop the living quarters of Moctezuma II (Low 1995:757). In the New World, as in San Antonio during the late nineteenth century, spatial dis-solution and displacement was a key element of political conquest, as the subsequent respatialization of conquered terrains served to fortify the norms, values, and cultural practices of the dominant group.

## THE SPANISH-MEXICAN COLONIAL PERIOD

The area around San Antonio was selected by the Franciscan friars as a suitable place to launch their missionary activity in Texas, mostly because of the presence of a modest but bountiful waterway, today known as the San Antonio River. Five missions were established along a short stretch of the river, with Mission San Antonio de Valero—or the Alamo—estab-lished in 1718. It was not until 1731, however, that the urban design of the city was established. Equipped with "Crown-bestowed advantages" (Poyo and Hinojosa 1991:42), families from the Canary Islands arrived and founded the town of San Fernando de Béxar across the river from Mission San Antonio de Valero and its attached presidio, San Antonio de Béxar.

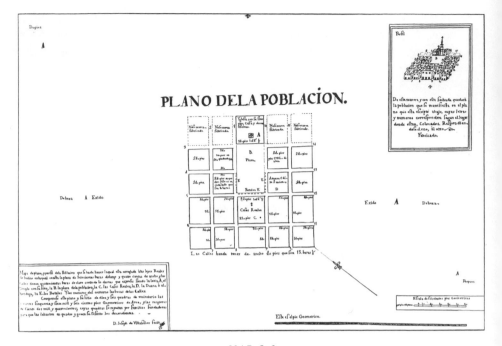

MAP 3.1
*Plan of San Antonio if the original design had been followed.*
SOURCE: *Center for American History, University of Texas at Austin, CN #01626*

The urban design of San Fernando de Béxar was informed by the 1573 Laws of the Indies (see Map 3.1). The strict implementation of this traditional plaza-grid form was hindered by the river, however, and as a result, the presidio captain, Juan Antonio Pérez de Almazán, under the instructions of the viceroy, measured and marked the boundaries of San Fernando de Béxar in July 1731 so as to amend the traditional square to provide for this waterway (see Map 3.2).

By the 1820s the mission, its attached presidio, and the town of San Fernando de Béxar had merged into four distinct wards to form the town of San Antonio de Béxar (see Map 3.3). The descendants of the Canary Islanders, who inherited their forebears' elite position and royal land grants, controlled the most fertile land and town governance and, in keeping with Spanish custom, lived near or on Plaza de las Yslas, or Main Plaza, which served as the center of town. The ward to the east of Plaza de las Yslas and across the river, identified by Jesús F. de la Teja and John Wheat (1985:9–10) as the "Barrio de Valero," was a military enclave that housed Spanish

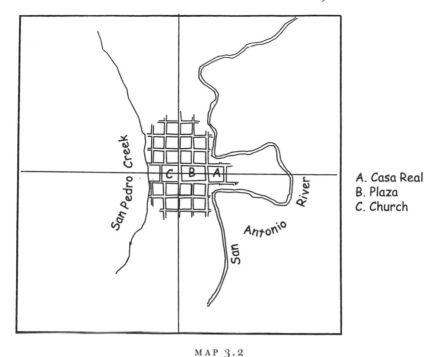

A. Casa Real
B. Plaza
C. Church

MAP 3.2
*The plaza and grid design of La Villa de San Fernando de Béxar set against the*
*San Antonio River in 1731. Redrawn from information in Cruz 1988.*

and Mexican cavalry after the secularization laws closed the missions between 1793 and 1794. Still, in 1820, San Antonio maintained the plaza-grid
design familiar to all Spanish towns in the New World.[2]

During the Mexican era, Plaza de las Yslas and its adjoining area, Plaza
de Armas (Military Plaza), were the social and commercial heart of the city
(see Map 3.4). As Miguel A. Rojas-Mix writes, the plaza "is the key to urban organization" during this period, functioning like "the patio of a large
house[,] . . . the spot where everyone met" (1978: 60, 115; my translation).
Separated only by the cathedral, these two plazas met very different needs.
Plaza de las Yslas, in the shadow of the cathedral, was the social center
where citizens met to talk and hold political rallies and religious festivities.
In the 1830s, for example, during *la temporada de fiestas,* or the festi-
val season, several important religious holidays, including Our Lady of
Guadalupe on December 12, were celebrated there with public games and
booths (Matovina 1995b:21). On September 15, 1829, the eve of Mexican
Independence Day, plaza festivities included gun salutes, musical proces-

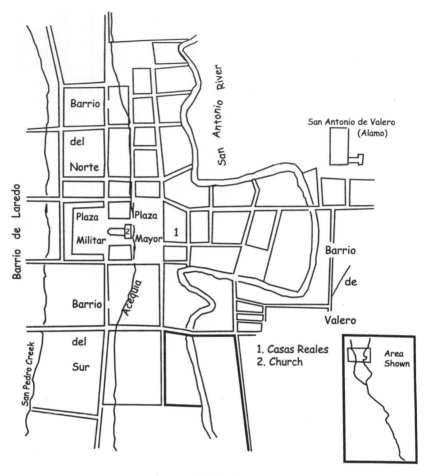

MAP 3.3
*San Antonio de Béxar from the 1820s. Redrawn from information in
de la Teja and Wheat 1985.*

sions, and the ringing of church bells. On September 16 Mass was held
at the cathedral, followed by political speeches and dances (Matovina
1995b : 22).

Plaza de Armas served as a garrison and training ground for the Spanish and Mexican military. But after 1830 it was increasingly surrounded by
residences, and its open, public space was used as a meat and produce
market and commercial center, both for trading goods and slaughtering

and selling goats and other small livestock. Residential and commercial use was strictly regulated by town officials during the Mexican period, allowing fifteen varas for residential properties and only five varas for commercial use (San Antonio, January 1824–April 1827:48). It is important to underscore that through their regulatory efforts town officials codified an understanding of the plaza that placed more weight on its residential and social aspects and less on its commercial advantages. Even into the early years of the American period, city officials made attempts to curb commercial activities on the plaza, continuing to emphasize its residential and social functions. For example, on July 25, 1845, the council forbade "the selling of fruits and meats on Military Plaza except on holidays and feast days" (San Antonio, April 15, 1844–December 3, 1848:173); and as late as 1847 city officials ruled that "peddlars of cigaritos and sweetmeats absent themselves from the plaza during the day" (San Antonio, March 1, 1839–April 5, 1844:280).

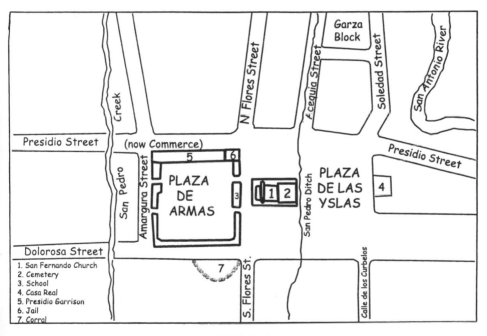

MAP 3.4
*San Antonio de Béxar and its two plazas in the early 1800s.*
*Redrawn from information in Cook and MacMillan 1976.*

## THE CATTLE DRIVE PERIOD

Between 1836 and 1848, hindered by the lack of economic activity, resources, and political stability, San Antonio saw a decline in its population (Johnson 1990:34). But economic stagnation gave way to more prosperous times after 1848 as the town became a central terminal in the developing cattle industry of Texas. Both the Chisholm Trail, which ran from the Rio Grande to points north, and the Chihuahua Trail, which connected East Texas to northeastern Mexico, passed through San Antonio. The trails required a network of local ranchers and suppliers of cattle goods and hardware, not to mention saloons and gambling houses, for the hundreds of trail riders and exporters that passed through the city (Remy 1960:5). In 1850 as much as 25 percent of San Antonio's labor force worked in transportation, holding jobs as wagon drivers and cartmen (Stewart and De León 1993:25).

The rise of ranching and the increased opportunities for distribution in the American period were aided by a "peace structure," as Montejano (1987:34) explains it, that maintained a certain level of continuity in the changing social order of Texas. This peace structure evolved as Anglo elites usurped the positions of the ruling Mexican families. While subordination of the Mexican population in general and the lower classes in particular was taking hold, elite Anglos and Mexicans often intermarried and contributed to the continuation of a cattle society, mostly in rural South Texas.

The emergence of a cattle industry in Texas facilitated the rise of mercantile ranching, a form of economic exchange that extended beyond subsistence pastoralism or regional market distribution of cattle to one engaged in long-distance trade supported by political and military institutions.[3] While there were still remnants of earlier economic forms, specifically, an estate system based on local rule, exemplified by the ranching baron Richard King, even these were dependent on the state and the military, in the form of the Texas Rangers, to enforce their economic dominion. While a broader economic analysis is beyond the scope of this work, I refrain from referring to this economic situation as capitalist production, since ranch and cattle owners did not yet purchase the labor power of their cattle hands in an open market, nor did they control the actual labor process itself (Wolf 1982:87). This would soon change.

The burgeoning cattle industry led to the establishment of small hotels, boardinghouses, and saloons on Main Plaza, among them the Hord Hotel (renamed the Southern in 1884) and the San Antonio Bar Room (Steinfeldt 1978:42). Two other hotels that were popular among cattlemen and ranchers were the Central and the St. Leonard (Prassel 1961:45). Plaza de las Yslas, now referred to in English as Main Plaza, continued to serve as an important location for public religious events and festivities associated with the cathedral (although at this time religious events were no longer organized by city officials as they had been during the Mexican period but by local citizens and the clergy) (Matovina 1995b:52). In spite of efforts by town officials to keep Plaza de Armas, now referred to as Military Plaza, free of commercial activity, the rise of the cattle industry and San Antonio's place as a hub on the cattle trails created a set of conditions that promoted the development of the plaza as the new commercial center. Between 1855 and 1875 Military Plaza served as a temporary holding station for small herds, a public lot for the trading of goods, and an ideal location for overnight stays of covered wagons (Steinfeldt 1978:46–47, pl. 1). Vendors sold their wares, wools, and hides there, and it continued to serve as the unofficial meat market for the town (see Rogers 1968).

Nightlife also flourished. "Bar rooms and businesses surrounded the plaza and nestled beneath the imposing walls of the Cathedral. The proximity of the imposing edifice did not inhibit the establishment of saloons and gambling houses, and 'fandangos,' a native Mexican dance, occurred nightly" (Steinfeldt 1978:44). For trail riders and vaqueros, the exuberant nightlife of the plazas—enhanced by a "fiery beverage distilled from the *agave* plant" (Rogers 1968:19)—offered relief from the tedious task of driving cattle. Although many of the Mexican elite still lived on the plazas in the 1850s, their homes were gradually bought and used by entrepreneurs for the selling of dry goods and hardware that supported the burgeoning cattle industry.

The expansion of commercial enterprises on the plazas shifted their earlier use as sites of civic, religious, and military activities. They remained public places, open venues that served the social and economic interests of the community, but the face of the public was more ethnically diverse, economically stratified, and Protestant. By the 1870s San Antonio was, according to Alwyn Barr (1971:14), "the most diverse and cosmopolitan city, the largest military depot in the state, the commercial center for South Texas cattle and sheep raisers, and the staging point for trade with Mexico." The first phase in the respatialization of San Antonio from a Spanish-Mexican town to a city on the western frontier of the United States had been completed.

But other areas of San Antonio were also in transition. In 1850 Samuel A. Maverick built his family home on property that occupied the northwest corner of the original mission grounds of the Alamo. Mary Maverick, his wife, writes in her memoirs: "I felt that I could not live any longer at the old place [on Main Plaza], and Mr. Maverick, too, did not want to live there. We concluded the high ground on the Alamo Plaza would be a more healthful location" (Green 1989:101).[4] Little else occupied this area until 1855, when William Menger constructed his home on the southwest corner (Smith 1966:33–34). The Mengers also ran a boardinghouse and a brewery from this property, which they expanded into the Menger Hotel in 1859. As the *San Antonio Daily Herald* reported on February 2, the day of its opening, "The Menger Hotel is a monument to the enterprise of the proprietor, and we trust will prove him a valuable investment, as we feel sure it will be the means of benefiting our city, especially that portion of it in which it is located" (quoted in Smith 1966:35).

At this time the physical structure of the Alamo was changing as well. Soon after the Treaty of Guadalupe Hidalgo in 1848, San Antonio was selected as the home of the Eighth Military District under the command of Maj. E. B. Babbitt, who established his headquarters in the Alamo. Because of its poor physical and structural condition, Babbitt had to spend $5,800 to rehabilitate the Alamo, including the construction of its famous facade (Fox, Bass, and Hester 1976:15). According to Strong, it was the military, during the intervening years, 1848 to 1875, that not only rebuilt the Alamo but also rescued the plaza from further decline. "Alamo Plaza," she states, "has been a panorama of shifting scenes. The role of the United States Military . . . was one of rescue[,] . . . of rebuilding where there had been destruction and resettling where there had been abandonment" (1987:81).

The outlying property, initially part of Mission San Antonio de Valero, was also changing. Before 1865 the open space fronting the Alamo encompassed two separately identifiable spaces: Alamo Plaza and the Plaza de Valero (see Map 3.5), which were separated by the Galera buildings, remnants of the original barracks, and a gate from the mission period (see Fig. 3.1). After several years of legal battles over ownership—the city in the end purchased the property from the Catholic Church for $2,500— these ruins, "standing like a grim phantom" (*San Antonio Daily Express,* March 7, 1869, cited in Fox, Bass, and Hester 1976:22), were destroyed, making way for future development of the area.

The peace structure that proved quite effective in the rural areas did not extend to small urban areas like San Antonio. Still, relations among elite Anglo-American, German, and Mexican families during this period were cordial but growing more strained in the lower echelons of San Antonio society. Until this time, the city was poised on the edge of the fron-

MAP 3.5
*Alamo Plaza as it appeared in the late 1860s. Redrawn from information in*
*Fox, Bass, and Hester 1976*

tier at the crossroads of the cattle trails. Although the Mexican community slowly diminished in status and became increasingly segregated, their labor was critical to the success of the transportation industry and small-scale mercantile trading in the area. According to Stewart and De León (1993:27), in 1850, 22.7 percent of all trade and transportation workers in the Mexican settlement region were Mexicans, and they made up 35.3 percent of all manufacturing and mechanical workers. While the majority of Mexican workers in Texas were employed in agricultural labor, 41.1 per-

FIGURE 3.1
*Alamo Plaza, looking northeast, ca. 1880.*
SOURCE: *Institute of Texan Cultures, San Antonio Light Collection, negative no. 1226-S.*

cent in 1850, these numbers could not hold for San Antonio's *mexicano* urban laborers.

### EARLY MODERN SAN ANTONIO

Between 1870 and the late 1880s, Reconstruction fostered the dispersal of new technologies and brought into the region an influx of Anglo-American and German entrepreneurs with little knowledge of Mexican Texas. The result was the eventual erosion of the peace structure by the establishment of new social and economic practices and a different attitude about cattle and land.[5]

Two technological innovations that greatly affected rural life in Texas were the introduction of barbed wire and the railroad. Barbed wire and the fencing of vast ranch lands effectively ended the great cattle drives that saw thousands of head of cattle transported from Texas to Kansas City and other points north. After 1875 the closing of the open range also left landless or small ranchers without this valuable resource to sustain their herds. While all cattle owners suffered, the burden on Mexican ranchers was disproportionately high, because few of them possessed the financial resources or legal connections that allowed many of the Anglo elites to amass and enclose large tracts of land. For example, Richard King had, by 1874, enclosed more than seventy thousand acres south of San Antonio (Remy 1960:9). As Montejano explains:

> The enclosure movement during the 1870s and 1880s was one in a series of innovations that eliminated the landless cattlemen and sheepmen as well as those with land but with few financial resources. . . . [T]he character of ranching had been completely transformed. (1987:58)

Economically distressed and with few resources available to them, small ranchers were also vulnerable to the fluctuating price of cattle. While prices were stable and strong in the early 1880s, the combination of severe droughts and several blizzards reduced cattle holdings, and, more important, the integration of cattle production into the international market resulted in a drop in beef prices from $35 to $5 a head by 1887 (Montejano 1987:60).

Fencing, and the closing of the range, was made possible by advances in transportation, particularly the railroad, which provided access to broader shipping venues and new markets. It also resulted in the dismissal of cattle workers from employment rosters, their services made obsolete by the termination of cattle drives. In this Anglo workers were affected more than Mexican vaqueros, since the latter could be hired for lower wages and housed and fed more poorly. Railroads also created new possibilities for agriculture by ensuring faster delivery service and safer and more secure transportation. Farm goods could now be transported hundreds of miles in the same time it had taken to ship them to local or regional vendors. For example, rail freight could reach New York City from San Antonio in fifteen days, while it took goods transported by wagon forty-five days to travel from San Antonio to El Paso (Remy 1960:30).

In essence, the economic and industrial face of Texas changed dramatically between 1875 and 1900, affecting Anglo and Mexican workers in harsh yet disproportionate ways. San Antonio was not immune to the economic vectors that were reshaping the social and cultural contours of Texas in the last quarter of the nineteenth century. And, like the state itself, it was the introduction of the railroad in 1875 that transformed the city and influenced the social place of its inhabitants. The arrival of the Southern Pacific and the closing of the cattle trails resulted in the displacement of local and regional markets that served as an infrastructure for the cattle driving industry. The economic place of local transportation workers, market representatives, buyers, and sellers was restructured by an influx of new goods, wider and nationally controlled markets, and the arrival of new capital. Elite *mexicanos,* mostly descendants of the Canary Islanders, saw their wealth and influence dwindle as new Anglo settlers with capital to invest influenced the local socioeconomic structure. "With Reconstruction (1865–77)," Richard García (1991:21) states, "the non-Mexican community increased in numbers and slowly began to replace the Spanish Mexican upper class as the new elite. . . . People such as the Mavericks and the Callaghans began to replace the Seguíns, the Herreras, and the Urrutias as the political leaders of the community." After 1875 the Mexican community lost its economic base and diminished in numbers. According to the *General Directory of the City,* in 1879 San Antonio had 7,800 Americans, English, and Irish, 7,610 Germans and Alsatians, and about 3,700 Mexicans and 2,075 blacks (Remy 1960:55).

A minority in terms of power, prestige, and population, Mexicans experienced residential segregation and cultural marginalization. By the 1870s San Pedro Creek, west of Military Plaza, served as the dividing line between "Laredito" and "Chihuahua," where the Mexican population lived, and the area to the east containing the majority of the residential area and business district, including Main and Military Plazas (Remy 1960:58). Another factor that led to the downward mobility of San Antonio's *mexicano* population was the stagnation of emigration from Mexico between 1880 and 1900 (R. García 1991:22). Still other factors included "increased American population, the industrial progress of the city, Anglo ingenuity, the financial resources of Anglos, the increases of military bases, and the fact that San Antonio had become a boom town that contracted Eastern monies" (R. García 1991:22).

Although it is difficult to point to any single factor that led to the segregation of Mexicans, it is clear that socioeconomic displacement worked in conjunction with a growing anti-Mexican sentiment that became a public discourse against Mexicans. The words of De León (1982:22), who states that after 1836 Tejanos were imputed to have a "childlike mentality" and to be "satisfied with grinding poverty," gain semantic weight when read alongside *The Great South,* by Edward King, published in 1875. "The Mexican," King writes, "is hard-headed, and terribly prejudiced; he cannot be made to see that his slow, primitive ways, his filth and lack of comfort, are not better than the frugal decency and the careful home management of the Germans and Americans who surround him" (p. 163). As I have argued elsewhere (Flores 1993), narratives like King's serve as "strategies of containment" that give credence to social and hierarchical differences that legitimize and naturalize differences that lead to segregated living arrangements and various levels of racial and economic exploitation.

In response to their increased social and economic isolation, Mexicans in San Antonio organized against local segregation efforts, such as ordinances that restricted them from socializing in public parks. They also sought increased political representation and, in the 1880s, organized to pressure the Democratic Party to give their concerns a place on the local party platform (De León 1982:32).

The marginalized place of Mexicans, however, did not keep them from their long-standing cultural practice of socializing on the plazas, nor did it keep others from participating in the social life long associated with San Antonio's public squares. As the *San Antonio Daily Express* described on June 29, 1877:

> There is not a second Military Plaza in the United States of America.... The Colonial with his pigtail, the Turk, the Russian, the Pole, the Irishman, the Englishman, the German, the Frenchman, the Italian, and dozens of representatives of other races who have found their way to this section of our "land of God and Liberty," following the advance guard of Americans who came here about forty years ago and "lifted" the yoke of Mexican tyranny, are all here, and the original Mexican is also here, and maintains the same customs that his fathers held in the days of Montexuma's [*sic*] supremacy.

But the social scene of San Antonio's plazas was different. As the story in the local paper demonstrates, life on the plazas continued, but the politics of participation had shifted. The labor and transportation services provided by the Mexican community up until 1875 ensured them a place in the local and regional economy, but the transition from a mercantile ranching economy to one organized around capitalist production and the emerging state bureaucracy changed not only the place of Mexican workers in the local and regional market but also perceptions about them. What once was a daily cultural practice for the Mexican community was now seen as spectacle by the dominant classes.

"And this place is in the United States!" an 1879 story in the *San Antonio Express* begins.

> Adobe buildings, Spanish plazas, foreign tongues, strange customs, and picturesque people. How novel this old cathedral, the light of the

moon and stars surveyed from the open market place, the flare of gas-jets, the noise of many vehicles, the sounds of music, and the applause and laughter issuing from the theatre. . . . To-night off in one corner a band of fantastically dressed Mexicans, are discoursing in loud strains a kind of wild music to the infinite delight of a medley crowd of unkept Mexicans, fun loving darkeys and admiring boot-blacks. (March 2, 1879)

The inscription of Mexicans as crude, primitive, fantastical, wild, and tyrannous cannot be dismissed. It serves as the narrative analogue of the changing social and cultural relations as Mexicans were increasingly expelled from the key arenas of San Antonio's public life. These constructions clearly advance a modern project whereby various groups of people are strategically segregated and stigmatized by elites whose own social, economic and cultural place is served thereby. As Harvey (1985:52) states, narratives such as these serve to rupture the "binding links" of a previous social reality, facilitating the implementation of a new social order.

One signpost of the new social order is the emergence of an ethnically stratified class system. By 1900 more than half of all Mexican workers in Texas were in unskilled jobs established in the transition to wage labor. The Mexican settlement region of South Texas experienced a rise in agricultural work during this period that saw an increase in unskilled and unspecialized labor that was five times the rate found in other parts of the state (Stewart and De León 1993:26). This shift to unskilled labor in South Texas affected Mexican workers most severely, increasing their representation in the unskilled workforce from 0.3 percent in 1850 to 54.5 percent in 1900, while Anglo unskilled workers increased from only 0.1 percent to 19.0 percent during the same period (Stewart and De León 1993:27). As De León and Stewart conclude,

> To say that service and general-labor roles became the "niche" of Tejanos in the Mexican settlement region is to say that they became an ephemeral, unskilled working underclass. As demand for skilled labor waned, Anglo workers dominated the available supply of specialized occupations in agriculture, the professions, trade, transportation, and manufacturing. Tejanos, on the other hand, fended for themselves in unspecialized day labor and in a variety of menial, personal-servant capacities. (1993:28)

The rapid and intense social changes in San Antonio between 1875 and 1900 are the result of increased labor specialization, the introduction of wage labor, the transition to industrialization, and the emergence of capitalism as the dominant economic mode. Of course, the move to capitalism began long before 1875 in San Antonio; the first national bank was opened there in 1866 (Remy 1960:97), already a clear indicator that capital was in full swing. But my point is threefold. First, by the 1880s there is a major downward shift in the economic position of San Antonio's Mexicans as they are incorporated as wage laborers in a capitalist economy. Second, the spatial segregation of Mexicans, specifically, the prohibitive laws and practices used to control their public presence, serves as a clear sign that class, ethnic, and racial notions of civic participation are entering the public consciousness of the polity. And third, as I demonstrate shortly, the displacement of Mexicans is expressed not only in public discursive forms like the writings of King and the local press, but was also embedded in the spatial topography of the city between 1875 and 1900.

## THE RESPATIALIZATION OF ALAMO PLAZA

San Antonio was originally a Spanish-Mexican town in terms of urban geography, forged from a historically and culturally specific relationship among the Church, the Crown, and the military that operated in the public sphere. While the initial stages of the American period put an end to this arrangement, the social relations endemic to a mercantile cattle society still required public places for economic and social transactions that replicated those of the Spanish-Mexican period. In 1877 Harriet Prescott Spofford, in an article written for *Harper's New Monthly Magazine*, describes San Antonio's Spanish-Mexican urban ethos as a quality that was apparent to most visitors. Quoting one of her informants, she says, "San Antonio is, in fact, a Spanish town . . . and the only one where any considerable remnant of Spanish life exists in the United States" (pp. 838–839). But this description would not hold true for long. Due in part to the railroad and the emergence of capitalism after 1875, San Antonio underwent a deep spatial restructuring whereby the commercial center shifted from Main and Military Plazas to the area around the Alamo. This relocation had important social and spatial consequences: it marked the transition of San Antonio from a Spanish-Mexican town to an American city.

If the railroad was a major factor in the transition to modernity in Texas, local public transportation was a critical element in the development of Alamo Plaza. In 1878 the San Antonio Street Railroad Company began to operate its mule-drawn cars from this location, extending two miles out to San Pedro Springs. Its success—it carried more than one hundred thousand passengers in the first six months—led to the addition of several other lines, allowing citizens and tourists to patronize this growing commercial area, including any of the seven saloons, and transforming it into the "commercial hub of the city" (Smith 1966:39).

Adding to the importance of Alamo Plaza, the Grand Opera House was opened there in 1886 and soon gained a reputation as one of the finest opera houses in the region. It attracted visitors from throughout the country and led to increased efforts on the part of city officials to refurbish the plaza. In spring 1889 the San Antonio City Council allocated funds to pave the plaza with mesquite blocks and, more important, to plant a garden in the center (Smith 1966:40). The garden, along with sixty-foot-wide streets around it, respatialized the plaza from an open, free-flowing area to one cordoned off by trees, shrubs, grass, and, the following year, a fountain. If the commercial interest of these improvements are in doubt, the local business community was certain of the advantages these changes would bring. In March 1890 A. F. Wulff, the alderman responsible for these efforts, was awarded an ebony, gold-headed cane for his work. As the local newspaper reported, he was congratulated for having given "a poem amidst the prose of the city improvements, and it will be the beginning, it is hoped, of other improvements intended to beautify our city and gladden the eye and heart of the humblest" (quoted in Smith 1966:41).

Between 1878 and 1890 a number of commercial enterprises moved to Alamo Plaza, including five dressmakers, two retail druggists, three liquor stores, three meat stores, a physician, an attorney, a dentist, a bank, an undertaker, and two real estate offices. In the same period, the number of boardinghouses and hotels on the plaza decreased from six to four. General merchandise stores remained the same, at four, while the number of transportation agencies, such as ticket agents for railroad and stagecoach lines, numbered ten in 1878. Between 1877 and 1878 San Antonio listed sixty-two saloons, eight of them on Alamo Plaza. On December 22, 1877, the new post office was relocated to a plot of land on the southeast end of Alamo Plaza, a move that city officials undertook, like its beautification projects, with the expectation of attracting more commercial ventures to the area. And in 1890 the post office moved to the north end of the square when the construction of a new federal building was completed.

These developments on Alamo Plaza are significant markers of change. First, the new mercantile and tourist enterprises are important infrastructural and commercial anchors that facilitate the growing needs of the city. Second, and perhaps more important, these changes map "centrality with power" (Zukin 1992:231) as Alamo Plaza emerges as the new icon of San

Antonio's modern identity.[6] Cecilia Steinfeldt nicely summarizes the cumulative effects of these changes:

> During the late 1870s and the decade of the 1880s, the dusty, drab, unattractive area in front of the Alamo underwent a radical change. Alamo Plaza began to blossom and flourish and change in character. The Menger Hotel had become the finest hostelry in town, renowned for its cuisine and comfort. Julius Joske and Sons became Joske Brothers Department Store and moved from Austin Street to a new location on Alamo Plaza. The United States Post Office moved from the corner of Soledad and Veramendi Streets to the first floor of the newly erected Gallagher Building on the corner of North Alamo and Blum Streets. Business firms shifted away from Main and Military Plazas or opened branch offices in the newly activated areas. (1978:54)

The rise of commercial investment on Alamo Plaza accompanied the state's interest in the Alamo property as well. In the 1890s Adina De Zavala began her efforts on behalf of the Daughters of the Republic of Texas to purchase the Alamo and the original mission property, which was then partially owned by the Hugo-Schmeltzer Company. The purchase and preservation of the Alamo entailed a series of complex and politically and racially charged events that are the subject of the next chapter. Suffice it to say here that it was not until 1905 that the Twenty-ninth Legislature of the State of Texas appropriated $65,000 for the purchase of the Alamo.

But Alamo Plaza was not the only plaza commercialized and "improved" during this period. In 1888 Military Plaza was officially designated the public market for the city, a move that not only codified what had already been the local custom but also gave jurisdiction of the plaza to the city market master (Rogers 1968:32). But the plaza was changed beyond recognition in 1889 with the construction of a new city hall in the middle of the square. City Hall, concretely, changed forever the flow of the plaza even if vendors, at least until the 1890s, in an act of resistance, simply relocated their wagons to the surrounding sidewalks and continued to sell their wares.

Main Plaza was also the site of new construction. The south end was selected as the location for a new county courthouse. Beautification efforts were also planned for this site, but not all citizens were pleased to see them actualized. A letter to the *San Antonio Express* on March 20, 1887, states, "With all due respect . . . I look upon this [the planting of a garden in the middle of the plaza], so far as Main Plaza is concerned, as childish in the extreme. . . . Is it right to destroy the business property on this square to make a park of it." Despite the criticism, the garden was planted and the courthouse soon dominated the space in the area.

The shift I have just described is not a benign occurrence but serves as a material signifier of a more complex and dynamic process by which changing modes of material production, social and cultural organization, state control, and public cultural forms emerge. Beginning with the Maverick house and the Menger Hotel and ending with the state's purchase of the Alamo itself, San Antonio's Mexican and Spanish urban landscape underwent a spatial transformation as the original plaza grid was dissolved, giving way to a distinctively new use of space.

#### BETWEEN APPROPRIATED AND DOMINATED SPACE

Montejano (1987), speaking of rural Texas, and Robert J. Rosenbaum (1981), discussing New Mexico, show how attitudes toward land differ markedly among Mexicans and Anglos. During the colonial and early cattle period, Mexicans used land for subsistence farming and ranching and patrimonial inheritance, while Anglos saw land as a resource for producing income. This same kind of distinction can be made with regard to the use of land in the Spanish-Mexican plaza tradition and later uses, especially post-1875. Beginning with the Menger Hotel and Brewery, property on Alamo Plaza served as a means of securing income for its proprietors, signaling a restructuring of the use of property. What Dora F. Crouch, Daniel J. Garr, and Axel I. Mundigo (1982:172) claim for the plaza of Los Angeles can be applied equally to San Antonio: "When the Anglos took over the government . . . they perceived the plaza to be like any other piece of real estate, something to be put to practical use." This break was so distinctive, I suggest, that it required an entirely new geographic location—the high ground of Alamo Plaza—and not merely the reorganization of the Mexican plazas (although this eventually did occur).[7]

By way of untangling the spatial and social differences between Alamo Plaza in the late nineteenth century and Main and Military Plazas during the Mexican colonial period, I want to juxtapose their formal features for further scrutiny. I have already discussed how the socioeconomic changes that occurred in San Antonio between 1836 and 1900 affected the general spatial occupation and social practices affiliated with plaza life. The transition I have noted is the result of social agents participating in a technologically different social order through which they actualize a new spatial logic. What I am suggesting is that this new spatial logic, when examined formally, is made visible as one's focus shifts between the distinctive formal features of these two plazas' spatializations.[8]

Plazas in the Spanish-Mexican tradition are public places: locations where men and women gather for their evening *paseos,* or promenades, where potential suitors direct discreet glances at their intended, where debates over political and social issues of the time are held, and where festive celebrations are enacted (see Map 3.4). A conjuncture of civic, ecclesial, and public forums, these places are sites of religious processions and ritual dramas, news from colonial agents, dueling *decimeros,* musical events, *fiestas patrias,* and mercantile trading. The formal features of the plaza consist of a rectangular, if not square, opening circumscribed by public and private dwellings. The central area of the plaza is a blank, open space. The emptiness of the form, therefore, connotes a spatial openness whose contours are determined by the dynamics and actions of specific social actors. On any day religious, economic, social, or any combination of these events could shape the content of these plazas. They operate, in Lefebvre's (1991:165) terms, as "appropriated" space, a site that is modified to "serve the needs and possibilities of a group." Not coincidentally, such spaces, Lefebvre (1991:165) continues, are associated with "a square or a street." This does not suggest that individuals relinquish their rights to property — in fact, property in the sense of possession is a necessary precondition for the appropriation of space — but highlights the underlying public organization of plaza life. Public life, for early-nineteenth-century San Antonio, references a type of social interaction whereby individuals experience a sense of sociability among nonfamilial others (see Sennett 1974:17). Unlike sixteenth- and seventeenth-century aristocratic practices, plaza life during this period reveals a spectrum of society that includes ethnic and economic diversity.

Viewed from above, the formal features of the plaza show an open, blank space filled by the daily interactions of the public. The plaza is open in its configuration and provides a place for the public body to organize for personal and social interactions. However, lest we romance this form, it must also be stated that these plazas, more in the interior of Mexico than in San Antonio, were also crucial sites of power and ideology. In the colonial city, Rojas-Mix says, "main plazas play an important ideological role of the first order, exercising political control over the Indian" (1978:103; my translation). Still, the claim holds that plazas are "centers of sociability" that signify a system of social and economic exchange based on a face-to-face way of life (Bonet Correa 1982:69).

Turning to Alamo Plaza, we see a different configuration and use of

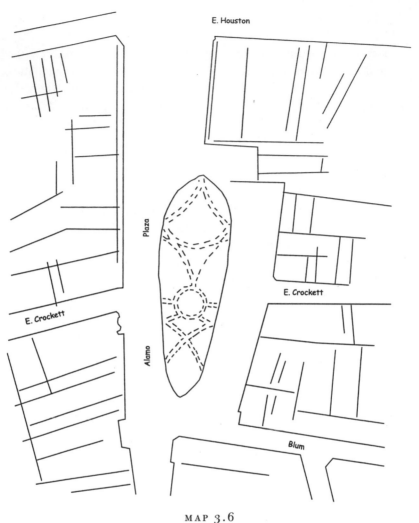

MAP 3.6

*Alamo Plaza in 1904. Redrawn from information in Fox, Bass, and Hester 1976.*

space (see Map 3.6). While it has a center—one constructed by city officials anxious to improve the physical condition of the area—its narrow,
elongated form landscaped with gardens and walkways forces the public
body to the perimeter.[9] There one finds hotels, breweries, an opera house,
stores, saloons, public rail cars, and government offices where the conduct of social life occurs in private. Continuing Lefebvre's (1991:165) com-
parison, Alamo Plaza, by the late nineteenth century, is a "dominated"

space, one that has been transformed by technology as it introduces a "new form into a pre-existing space." Alamo Plaza reconstitutes the earlier plaza form through the presence of the railroad, government offices, and commercial enterprises associated with the technological advances of modernity. I want to emphasize, however, that Lefebvre's categories of appropriated and dominated space are interpenetrating categories where one form seldomly overtakes another.

The constitution of Alamo Plaza dissolves the earlier social and spatial rubrics of Main and Military Plazas in several ways. First, it provides income-producing property, revealing a fundamental shift in the social content and spatial logic of the earlier plaza tradition. Although this space is constructed and revived "as a plaza," the social practices it affords are limited to those that are conducted by individual consumers housed in private business facilities. The development of Alamo Plaza is the result not only of a transformation in the social relations as refigured in spatial forms but also of a break in the cultural logic of spatial production made possible, in part, by the various regulatory initiatives passed by local officials after 1875 aimed at attracting commercial investors. Whereas Main and Military Plazas are public, open, and accessible, Alamo Plaza is reconfigured by capital into a chain of commercial, privately owned storefronts that negates the public character of the early Spanish-Mexican plaza tradition (see Fig. 3.2).

The formal features of Main and Alamo Plazas (see Map 3.7) reveal how the public, social interaction of the Mexican plazas has been refashioned and privatized. The respatialization of the Mexican plazas, especially evi-

FIGURE 3.2
*Alamo Plaza with the Hugo-Schmeltzer Company on the left, ca. 1910.*
SOURCE: *Institute of Texan Cultures, Ayres Collection, negative no. 83-484.*

FIGURE 3.3
*Aerial view of City Hall as it occupies what was once Military Plaza
and San Fernando Cathedral, 1927.*
SOURCE: *Institute of Texan Cultures, Ayres Collection, negative no. 83-979.*

denced by the construction of City Hall in 1889, results in the "pulveriza-
tion" (Harvey 1985:13) of the Spanish-Mexican tradition into a plaza form
emptied of its earlier social qualities (see Fig. 3.3). In my previous discussion of how Alamo Plaza emerged from commercial and government intervention I described how the plot of land fronting the Alamo was "re-
suscitated" by capital: a space barely inhabited at the time of Olmsted's
visit—in fact, his description of "burnt bricks and brown idlers" reads
like a postmortem of the area—is renewed by mercantile and early capitalist entrepreneurs.

But the making of Alamo Plaza—the emergence of a new place configured through a different social rubric—merits another query. Why here?
Although it is true that capital transforms the use of property and, subse-
quently, reorganizes the dynamics of social interaction on the plazas, it
does not answer the more telling, albeit difficult, question: why San Antonio's commercial and tourist economy was relocated to Alamo Plaza. Recall that in the 1890s the Alamo proper was still in disrepair, partly in the

MAP 3.7
*A bird's-eye view showing the differential use of space in Alamo Plaza and Main Plaza
(Plaza de las Yslas).*

59

hands of private entrepreneurs and not yet an official site of public history and culture. Why, then, this shift?

I put off my full discussion of this issue until the conclusion, where the accumulated evidence of the intervening chapters allows me to provide a more sustained argument. At this point, however, let me make the following claim. The reshifting of San Antonio's center from the Mexican plazas to that of the Alamo, even with the dilapidated condition and private ownership of the physical structures of the Alamo buildings, fixes in the built environment a nondiscursive reference point that validates the changing relations between Anglos and Mexicans in the 1890s. In San Antonio the assembly of sociospatial relations that gave rise to the Spanish-Mexican plaza tradition were dissolved and replaced by a more pragmatic, commercially informed, spatial rubric. While Alamo Plaza is constructed in the Mexican plaza tradition, it is one made possible by the dissolution and reconquest of a former social and spatial practice. But the emergence of the Alamo and its plaza as the new hub of the city entails a double conquest: first, the dissolution of a public, Mexican, spatial logic; second, a conquest over those whose practice actualizes that logic, the Mexican community. The struggle over and usurpation of one spatial rubric over another cannot be understood without also attending to the social actors whose cultural practices shape and are shaped by these practices, since to control spatial organization is to wield power over social reproduction.

The respatialization of Alamo Plaza signals the emergence of a new social order that revalues property as capital, privatizes the conduct of commerce and leisure, and redefines the public from a social collectivity to one based on class location and privilege. One effect of this respatialization is to recode the former, Mexican, cultural world, as King does, as primitive, childlike, and prejudiced. But the respatialization of San Antonio occurs at the Alamo. As such, the Alamo serves as a material sign that spatially registers a cultural memory of Anglo-American heroism and Mexican tyranny (associated with the "Battle of the Alamo") that advances the socioeconomic system of capital. The emergence of Alamo Plaza as the heart of the Alamo City serves as a spatial unconscious of power and class formation whose undergirding logic is found in the emergence of the Alamo and its symbolic utility for the project of the Texas Modern.

# 4

⊢═ ═⊣

## FROM PRIVATE VISIONS
## TO PUBLIC CULTURE
### THE MAKING OF THE ALAMO

The Alamo is the most visited site in the state of Texas. As a place dedicated to the brave men who fought and died within its walls, this shrine remembers the "Battle of the Alamo" between "Texans" and "Mexicans" in 1836. However, unlike Gettysburg, the Alamo did not become a site of public culture soon after the battle. Instead, the physical structures of this former Spanish mission, already in ruins at the time of the battle, were used as a grain facility for the U.S. Quartermaster's Depot, as a supply store, and as a saloon, to name several of its purposes after 1836. It was not until the late 1890s that two women, Adina De Zavala and Clara Driscoll, collaborated to preserve the Alamo and then disputed quite openly over their different visions of how to save it as a site of public history and culture.

Recent studies concerning the formation of places of public culture, especially locations connected to power, identity, and community, have received critical attention in anthropology (Friedman 1992; Karp and Lavine 1991; Karp, Kreamer, and Lavine 1992; Lass 1988). These efforts explore the dynamic and processual relations between the past and its objectification in the present. And, when these reproductions concern the making and establishment of national, regional, or cultural identities, along with their concomitant asymmetries of power, as does the Alamo, it behooves us to explore and understand the social processes and conditions that transform private visions into public places.

Sites like the Alamo emerge from specific sociohistorical conditions, and the need to uncover the initial impulses and desires that influence their making is critical for understanding how places of public culture reproduce partial visions of the past. How, then, do we map the coordinates of places of public culture in ways that reveal the social traces of their making? Because these traces are not readily evident—they are repressed and embedded in the politically volatile work of public history and culture—where and how do we detect the unspoken and unformulated provocations that shape the formation and establishment of places of cultural memory like the Alamo?

The response I propose in this chapter is twofold. First, because the Alamo is produced as a place of history in history, any attempt to understand the contemporary evocations of this place must consider these antecedent concerns. Therefore, I examine the writings of Clara Driscoll and Adina De Zavala as a means of detecting the unspoken motivations these women have concerning the significance of the Alamo and its place in turn-of-the-century South Texas. I read Driscoll's and De Zavala's narratives for traces of the social processes and conflicts occurring in Texas and in which the making of the Alamo as a public place is a critical factor. It is no coincidence that during this time of social and economic transformation these two women focus on the Alamo as a means of publicly representing modern-day Texas. Juxtaposing Driscoll's and De Zavala's efforts at cultural preservation and their literary writings on the subject allows me to explore how and why their private visions inform their efforts of making the Alamo a public place.

Second, I have argued thus far that the Alamo operates as a multiply inflected sign that serves the social, political, and economic interests of the dominant Anglo population. But such service on the part of the Alamo must also be rendered personally, working on the practical lives of individuals as they make their way through the social maze of early modern San Antonio. For reasons that will become clear, De Zavala serves my interpretive needs in this capacity as well. Not only is she instrumental in the effort to preserve the Alamo, but her mixed ethnic ancestry, Mexican and Irish on her father's side and Irish on her mother's, and her strong allegiance to the memory of her grandfather, Lorenzo de Zavala, who served as Mexico's ambassador to France and the first unofficial vice president of the Texas republic, allows us to witness the turmoil and contradictions between the Alamo as a sign and the life as lived. I do not wish to imply that all Mexicans of De Zavala's generation experienced the shrine of the Alamo as she did; hers was a unique conjuncture of biography and history. But I am suggesting that the emergence of the Alamo in the early 1900s serves a social meaning negotiated at the subjective level.

The original mission complex of the Alamo consisted of a church, a *convento,* a granary, workshops, storerooms, and housing for the native Indians. The famous facade recognized as the Alamo—not constructed until the mid-nineteenth century—is actually the front of the mission church, completed in 1744. In the 1750s the roof of the church collapsed because of poor construction materials and workmanship. Still in shambles, Mission San Antonio de Valero was secularized along with all other Texas missions in 1793.

The mission fell into disuse and, left to the perils of abandonment, total disrepair until 1802, when it was occupied by a Spanish cavalry unit, the Segunda Compañía Volante de San Carlos de Parras del Alamo, from which the name "Alamo" stems. This occupation marked the last use of the Alamo as a church, since it was again abandoned in 1810 and remained so until it was used as a fort by the Mexican army from 1821 to 1835. By the time of the Battle of the Alamo in 1836, the mission complex covered two to three acres, and the roofless chapel was 75 feet long and 62 feet wide, with stone walls 22 feet high and 4 feet thick. Attached to the northwest end of the church lay the *convento,* which was 186 feet long and 18 feet wide and high. The upper floor contained an infirmary, and the first floor was soldiers' quarters (Ables 1967:376).

In 1841 the Republic of Texas returned the Alamo mission church, along with the other local missions, to the Roman Catholic Church. And in 1848 the Alamo mission was leased to the United States as a quartermaster's depot. The U.S. government renovated the church in 1849, adding the now-famous top center gable and new upper windows. After the Civil War the Alamo was again used as a grain reception facility. The *convento* was sold to Honoré Grenet in 1877, who proceeded to construct wooden porticos above the stone walls. In 1883 Grenet's lease to the mission church was purchased by the state of Texas, placing that portion of the Alamo in the hands of the city of San Antonio. On Grenet's death, an advertisement for the sale of the Alamo in 1882 read:

FOR LEASE OR FOR SALE,
to the purchaser of its valuable and constantly kept-up stock of Goods,
together with the lease of the ALAMO, and the goodwill of the business,
so long and so profitably enjoyed by its deservedly popular founder.
(Gould 1882:16b)

A buyer for the Grenet business was found in the Hugo-Schmeltzer Company in 1886. From the activities of Grenet and the Hugo-Schmeltzer Company during the 1880s, it is clear that this portion of the Alamo mission was used primarily for commercial reasons, being described as a "modernized and . . . mammoth business house," and only secondarily evoked interest as a historical site (Gould 1882).[1]

## MAKING VISIONS PUBLIC: TEXAS WOMEN AND THE ALAMO

Adina De Zavala's pursuits in restoring the mission church of the Alamo led to a promise from Gustav Schmeltzer "not to sell or offer the property [of the Alamo] to anyone else without . . . giving the Chapter [of the DRT] the opportunity to acquire it" (Ables 1967:378). By this time De Zavala had been quite active, not only in her chapter of the DRT, but in establishing herself as a dynamic and bold leader, which resulted in her 1902 election to the executive committee of the DRT.

De Zavala's initial agreement with Schmeltzer stated that the De Zavala Chapter of the DRT would have the first option on purchasing the appurtenance of the Alamo mission that housed the Hugo-Schmeltzer Company. This would give the DRT time to raise $75,000, the agreed-on price. However, early in 1903 De Zavala received word from her close friend, the Italian sculptor Pompeo Coppini, then living in San Antonio, that a commercial enterprise from the eastern United States was interested in the Hugo-Schmeltzer property. Devising a strategy for raising the necessary money, De Zavala heard of a "prominent, rich and very ambitious young woman who may be of some help" (Ables 1967:381). This was Clara Driscoll.

Driscoll was the daughter of Robert Driscoll, Sr., a wealthy railroad and ranching entrepreneur who lived near Corpus Christi, Texas. Clara Driscoll attended private schools in San Antonio, New York, and France, and after her mother's death in May 1899, she traveled throughout Europe, to return to Texas in 1903. Before her departure in 1899, however, she wrote a letter to the *San Antonio Express* in which she stated her grave concern over the "hideous" buildings surrounding the Alamo (Ables 1967:379). Once back in Texas, she acted on her concerns and in February 1903 joined the DRT.

De Zavala approached Driscoll about the Alamo, and the two met with Charles Hugo in March 1903 concerning the purchase of the Hugo-Schmeltzer property. After the meeting, Driscoll paid $500 for a thirty-day option on the building, after which an additional sum of $4,500 would extend the option to February 10, 1904, giving the DRT enough time to raise the remaining $70,000. It was further agreed that the property was "to be purchased for the use and benefit of the Daughters of the Republic of Texas and [was] to be used by them for the purpose of making a park about the Alamo, for no other purposes whatever" (Colquitt 1913:91). By 1904 the DRT had collected little more than $7,000, at which time Driscoll advanced another $17,812.02 to complete an initial $25,000 down payment that was due in February 1904. After a year of campaigning, on January 26, 1905, the Twenty-ninth Legislature of the State of Texas appropriated $65,000 to purchase the Alamo.[2]

After acquiring the property, the state, as agreed, transferred custodianship of the Alamo to the DRT. On their part, the DRT initially agreed to have the De Zavala Chapter care for the Alamo, based on De Zavala's initial and continuing efforts; however, this action was blocked by the executive committee of the DRT until the state had officially entrusted them with the property. Then, on receiving the property, the executive committee gave custodianship of the Alamo to Driscoll and not the De Zavala Chapter, recognizing her financial contributions to this effort. This led to the first clash between the De Zavala Chapter and the DRT.

Since Clara Driscoll was scheduled to be out of town until December, she appointed her close friend Florence Eager to serve as custodian in her place. But before the mayor of the city presented Eager with the keys, De Zavala claimed them and took possession of the Alamo (for the first time). According to De Zavala, she was ready to deliver the keys to Driscoll "but not to anyone else" (Ables 1967:387). Adding to the confusion and bitter tension of the moment, the DRT filed suit against De Zavala, demanding that she return all relics to the Alamo and refrain from interfering with future DRT efforts. The legal complaint against De Zavala read as follows:

> Plaintiff [DRT] alleges that on Oct 4, 1905, the State of Texas, acting through S. W. T. Lanham, Governor, did convey the custody of the Alamo Church property to plaintiff; that defendant [Adina De Zavala] claiming to act for plaintiff took possession of said church, and afterwards about Nov. 1st, 1905, repudiated the right of plaintiff to the possession thereof, and refuses to deliver said property or the relics contained therein to plaintiff.[3]

The DRT withdrew its suit when De Zavala returned the Alamo to their care.

The following April, at its annual convention and with De Zavala's followers in clear control of the meeting, a motion giving custody of the Alamo to the De Zavala Chapter on November 11, 1906, was made. When a motion to substitute Clara Driscoll's name for the De Zavala Chapter failed, Driscoll offered her resignation, which was refused (Ables 1967:390). With this, De Zavala moved that Driscoll be appointed custodian until November, and when Driscoll refused, she continued, "In further compliment to Miss Driscoll, I move that this convention bestow the honor upon the young lady she has expressed the desire should be the actual custodian, her friend, Miss Florence Eager." [4] While Eager accepted this temporary post, De Zavala's courtesy extended no longer than November 11, for on that day she drafted the following telegram to Eager:

> The time having arrived at which the Convention of the DRT held at Goliad April 20 and 21, 1906, directed the De Zavala Chapter to assume control of the Alamo, I desire to inform you that De Zavala Chapter is ready to take immediate charge. Are you ready to deliver Custodianship according to said order? [5]

Although it seemed that Adina De Zavala and her supporters had succeeded in winning the day, they were on their way to losing the Alamo. At the April convention Driscoll and her supporters established a second San Antonio chapter of the DRT named the Alamo Mission Chapter. It took until 1910 for Driscoll and her colleagues to legally force the De Zavala Chapter from the DRT; before then, however, De Zavala was to garner national attention as the woman who rescued the Alamo—again.

In February 1908, as the Hugo-Schmeltzer building lay vacant, the DRT arranged to temporarily lease the building until efforts could be organized to remove the *convento* structure entirely and beautify the area so as to highlight the mission church. Their rationale was that the Hugo-Schmeltzer building was not part of the original Alamo mission but constructed at a later date. Outraged by such a desecration and total disregard for historical fact, De Zavala, presenting "authorized" letters from the DRT, received the keys to the building from local authorities and enlisted three men to prevent access to the building. While De Zavala acted out of moral indignation, the tumultuous politics inside the DRT precipitated this incident. As L. Robert Ables (1967) has adeptly shown, internal conflicts and legal chicanery within the DRT resulted in the election of two different sets of officers: those that supported Driscoll and those siding with De Zavala. When De Zavala claimed the keys to the Hugo-Schmeltzer building, she was charged with a letter, dated February 2, 1908, from Miss Mary Briscoe, secretary-general, and Mrs. Wharton Bates, first vice president and acting president of the DRT, stating that she, as president of the De Zavala

Chapter, was "the Agent for the Daughters of the Republic of Texas, and [had] authority to directly receive the keys."[6] Briscoe and Bates were indeed officers of the DRT—at least of the faction supporting De Zavala. Either local authorities were unaware of both sets of officers, or if they were, they believed they were in no position to determine the legalities of either side's claims.

On February 10 De Zavala was met by the sheriff and other officials carrying an injunction against her for occupying the premises without authorization. In a move that made headlines across the country, De Zavala quickly sealed off the building and barricaded herself within its walls, where she remained for three days, being refused water or food by the local officials. On February 13 De Zavala, under duress but willing to negotiate with state authorities, relinquished the Hugo-Schmeltzer portion of the Alamo to the state superintendent of buildings. Reeling from the negative publicity, the DRT formally denied they were planning to destroy any original structures of the Alamo. However, court papers filed by the DRT revealed their belief that the Hugo-Schmeltzer building was not part of the original Alamo mission complex as well as their plan to "remove this unsightly building and place in lieu thereof a park, museum, or something else."[7]

It appears that De Zavala's effort to preserve the Alamo from destruction, while impassioned, was premeditated and calculated. In a letter to an attorney representing the De Zavala Chapter dated January 10, 1908, she wrote:

I have also my original idea in vein & that is to take possession bodily of the Alamo building rom [*sic*] to be vacated by the Hugo & Schmeltzer Co. That is by putting an agent in charge & holding the fort. This could be done by me in person as president of De Zavala C. The H[ugo] S[chmeltzer] people are afraid to deliver the keys to us, for fear they may be held liable or responsible for the rents or for damages etc. So we would have to *take* it. Mrs. Bates writes me just what you told me before—Writes that you say for us to "act as though there has been no injunction, for it was really void," & should they try to hold us in contempt of Court to say you told me to go ahead. So I really believe I shall be brave enough to go ahead and take possession—that is—step in when the Hugo S[chmeltzer] people step out unless you advise me to the contrary, for though the H[ugo] S[chmeltzer] people may *not* deliver to us the keys—we can stay inside & make our own keys. What do you think of it?

. . . We want the Alamo—nothing *else*—nothing less will do. We would prefer that it all be under *our* management Church & Alamo proper but the Church is not as important—nor in much danger as the Alamo proper (the building now occupied by the Hugo & S[chmeltzer] people).[8]

Adina De Zavala found the strength to carry out her plan, and the news of her exploits traveled across the country. In *Human Life for June,* published in 1908, De Zavala is featured centrally as a defender of the Alamo:

The young woman, highly cultured, thoroughly educated, aristocratic—a descendent from the best Spanish blood—is making her fight against business men, mercenaries, who, she says "care nothing for historic association nor for glorious tradition." She maintains that they would put the old mission to commercial uses; while they claim that they are but practical business men, and want to make good use of only part of the building and enclosure.

Last February, however, these men, who had enlisted the aid of a deputy sheriff and others, found that the American girl of Spanish origin was not to be bluffed, nor even starved out. Miss De Zavala had placed guards about the Alamo, but for these the deputy sheriff and his companions did not seem to care. It was the young woman herself whom they hesitated to encounter. About eight o'clock one evening, being assured that the "defender of the Alamo" had left for the night, they demanded admission in the name of the law—to which occurrence Miss De Zavala refers with scorn. They broke down one set of doors, but they found the girl on guard duty, and they retreated.

For three days and nights Miss De Zavala remained on post, in the Alamo, alone. Those in intrigue against her, she says, prevented her watchmen and friends from bringing her food. A sister patriot, Miss Lytle, poured coffee through a pipe which she slipped under a window, and in this way the young woman sustained strength to resist the invaders until Governor Campbell took a hand. During the siege all means of communication, telephone wires, etc., were cut off. At night Miss De Zavala was in darkness, for the electric light wires were also cut.

The girl certainly displayed the fighting spirit born in her. De Zavalas fought for the liberty of the people in Spain, Portugal, Ecuador, Bolivia, Mexico, Texas! It is no wonder that she is courageous.

The Alamo tangle bids fair to be soon legally adjusted.[9]

Wasting little time to regain support for the DRT's beautification plans of the Alamo, Driscoll petitioned friends to contribute money for the refurbishment (and destruction) of the Hugo-Schmeltzer building. She writes:

To All Texans:

As legal custodians of the Alamo, The Daughters of the Republic of Texas request your signature in endorsement of their plan for the beautifying of the Alamo Mission grounds adjoining the Chapel of the Alamo, more generally known as the Hugo-Schmeltzer property.

It is their [the DRT's] desire to convert this property into a beautiful park filled with swaying palms and tropical verdure, enclosed by a low way, with arched gateway of Spanish architecture. They also wish to restore the roof of the Chapel of the Alamo, and have a replica of the original doors placed at the entrance to the Church.

The Daughters of the Republic of Texas ask for your support in their honest endeavor to be worthy of the obligation imposed upon them by the Twenty-ninth Legislature of the State of Texas.

Clara Driscoll Sevier

Chairman Alamo Auxiliary Committee

Menger Hotel, San Antonio, Texas

or

37 Madison Avenue, New York City [10]

But De Zavala and her associates were adamant about preserving the Hugo-Schmeltzer building, erected on the original Alamo mission walls. It was not until December 28, 1911, at a special meeting convened by Gov. Oscar B. Colquitt, that the issue was fully addressed. At this session, held at the St. Anthony Hotel in San Antonio, De Zavala submitted her plats, maps, and other evidence showing that at the time of the battle the chapel was in ruins and that "the walls now standing and known as the Hugo-Schmeltzer building, the convent or the monastery, are the original walls of the fortress" (Colquitt 1913:137).[11]

The Driscoll faction contended that the convent walls were unimportant and favored a plan that would remove them entirely from the property to provide space for a park and a monument. During this debate, Colquitt claimed, "The walls which were then standing, we want to preserve," to which Driscoll replied, "You don't mean to restore it as it was built by the Franciscan fathers before the battle?" (Colquitt 1913:137). The governor concluded that the wooden frame of the Hugo-Schmeltzer building should be removed but that the two-story stone walls were part of the original Alamo structure and should be preserved and restored. However, to the

DRT's delight, funds were extinguished before the work could be completed, and in 1913, while Colquitt was out of the state, his lieutenant governor ordered the demolition of the upper-story walls.

Years later, in her late eighties, De Zavala would reflect back on her effort to influence Colquitt's decision to save the Hugo-Schmeltzer building, recalling the trouble she supposedly had sending Colquitt important documentation.

> Tapped my telephone during "war" to save the Alamo (to get my views and names). Things, documents and pictures, historical matter sent to Gov. Colquitt disappeared after being mailed in P.O. and Gov Campbell Colquitt *never* received my letters nor *historical* documents nor any material from me. Either they disappeared from P.O. here or by some means at Austin before the Gov. received his mail. . . . [A] man connected with the one most interested in tearing down the Alamo property was arrested by Federal authorities for taking mail from P.O. (so I was told) and served a prison sentence (so I was told). I always suspected that he may have had something to do with the disappearance of my historical pictures and documents. They were a great loss.[12]

While her official alliance with the DRT ended as a result of this ordeal, De Zavala's interest, passion, and vision to protect the Alamo never did. She constantly wrote letters to the governor, the mayor, and the local papers in which she beseeched the DRT to change their plans to alter the grounds in any fashion. As of 1935, her greatest dream, she said, was "to see the main building of the Alamo Mission restored. Historically, the church of the Alamo is not of such great importance. It was the building adjoining the long barracks, which witnessed the slaughter of our Texas heroes. But we still have the lower walls of the long barrack and of the arcades facing the patio."[13]

De Zavala's relationship with the DRT never mended. She became the organization's most vocal critic, constantly reminding the public of its failure to adhere to historical accuracy and its myopic vision of the Alamo's historical significance. For its part, the DRT never fully acknowledged De Zavala's contribution, instead giving Driscoll full credit for saving the Alamo. One example is found in a pamphlet published by the DRT Library Committee in 1960 and written by Jack C. Butterfield, titled, "Women of the Alamo." Butterfield rightly credits the DRT and Driscoll for their efforts in preserving the Alamo but makes no reference to De Zavala—in fact, her name fails to appear anywhere in the pamphlet.[14] The irony is that Butterfield was well aware of De Zavala and her vast knowledge of the Alamo and Texas history, as is clear from the following note he wrote to her in 1902:

> I am preparing a little story, the scene of which is laid in San Antonio de Bexar in 1835. . . . Knowing your interest in all things pertaining to Texas history, I thought perhaps you might be able to assist me.[15]

After leaving the DRT, De Zavala continued to work ceaselessly for the restoration of historical places. In 1912 she organized the Texas Historical Landmarks Association (THLA), a group that would remain active until soon after her death in 1955. The objectives of the THLA, according to its charter, were

> 1) to work for the repair, restoration, and preservation of all the missions of Texas; 2) and for the use of the main building of the Alamo — the long two-story Fort (north of the Church of the Alamo [the Hugo-Schmeltzer property]) as a Texas Hall of Fame and a Museum of History, Art, Relics and Literature.

The THLA is credited with identifying a number of historical buildings and sites throughout the state, including its most celebrated, the Spanish Governor's Palace in San Antonio. She was a charter member and fellow of the Texas State Historical Society, an organization that, on numerous occasions, used her as an expert reference for questions on the Alamo. De Zavala was an active member of the Texas Folk-lore Society. She served as vice president in 1926–1927 and presented a paper at the annual meeting in Austin that year titled, "How the Huisache Came to Bloom." Her article "Belief of the Tejas Indians" appeared in the first publication of the Texas Folk-lore Society, edited by the eminent folklorist, Stith Thompson.[16]

### CLARA DRISCOLL AND THE POETICS OF SENTIMENTALITY

Driscoll's efforts to preserve the Alamo have been highly acclaimed, both by the DRT and by Texas state officials. There is no doubt that she brought financial resources to bear at a critical moment in the Alamo preservation movement. At one level, there is even less doubt as to why: she was motivated by a sense of responsibility and stewardship, taking great care and pride in the Texas traditions she was preserving and, in many ways, shaping. But to admit this is to recognize other influences, other social conditions that were, at another level, very much part of the historical milieu of Clara Driscoll.

While still a young woman, Driscoll wrote two novels and a comedic three-part opera that was produced on Broadway. While two of these works, the opera known as "Mexicana" (Driscoll and Smith 1905) and her first book of fiction, *The Girl of La Gloria* (1905), are important in developing a more extensive grasp of Driscoll's writings, it is her book, *In the Shadow of the Alamo* (1906), that I will emphasize here. I read Driscoll's narratives alongside her preservation efforts as two instances, both occupying relatively the same chronological space, of the broader social reality in which she participated.

*In the Shadow of the Alamo* is a collection of seven short stories. Each story is a brief vignette or encounter with myriad characters, including Anglos, Mexicans, Indians, Spaniards, nuns, priests, soldiers, and street vendors. The stories are tragically sentimental, recalling in many instances the same theme: the restlessness of the human condition is only calmed by the affection of one's beloved. In these narratives romance is the fulfillment of all desire while its loss results in social and personal disfigurement. Losing or attaining romantic love is the critical element that either rescues Driscoll's characters from the depths of isolation and tragedy or plunges them into a condition of psychological and social agony. The human condition is depicted as dependent on romantic love; one is unable to maintain even the most mundane social existence without it. Such a position is a privatized rendition of the Romantic wherein the meaning of human existence is found only in one's beloved, partitioned from all other facets of the social world. While all the stories repeat the same theme, I focus on two in particular, "The Custodian of the Alamo" and "Juana of the Mission de la Concepción."

"The Custodian of the Alamo" is written in two parts. The first, subtitled "The Past," is a historical reconstruction of the Alamo. Besides a few brief dates that refer to the founding of the missions in Texas, it is a partisan telling of the events that led to the "Battle of the Alamo," scattered with anecdotes, legend, and unsubstantiated historical "facts." The narrative makes no attempt to present the complexities of the past in relation to Texan and Mexican social history and assumes, quite incorrectly, that the defenders of the Alamo were all U.S. citizens or "Texans." In structure, Driscoll's account follows the same binary logic of the official Alamo narrative that continues to infuse the public presentation of history even today.

The past, in this account, is not the construction of a historical narrative but of historical memory, imbued with the ideological cadence such discourses promulgate. By her own admission, Driscoll's discussion of the past has little to do with understanding the ambiguities of the movement of history but with establishing a place where a particular vision of the past ensures the future of a select few.

> By the honoring of a glorious past we strengthen our present, and by the care of our eloquent but voiceless monuments we are preparing a noble inspiration for our future. (1906:25)

In part 2, "The Present," the story shifts dramatically, telling of a wealthy visitor to the Alamo who encounters a beautiful, demure young woman who works as the custodian or official guide of this historic place. After receiving a personal tour of the Alamo during which the woman's passion for narrating the events of the battle inflame the man's heart, he is smitten with love. Later that evening, at closing time, he returns to ask the woman to marry him when he next comes to San Antonio.

> "Ah—if you only knew how much I needed you. There are many who can tell of the valor of these dead heroes, but there is only one who can satisfy this living being. Say you want me to come for you. I shall never leave unless you do . . ."
>
> In the darkness of the chapel his eyes burned into hers, his warm breath fanned her cheek.
>
> "If you love me," he replied, "you will come with me."
>
> Closer she nestled in his arms, and with her mouth against his she breathed the words:
>
> "Yes, I will come." (1906:51–52)

Here we find the displacement of romanticism by sentimentalism. Instead of a narrative that celebrates the triumph of the human spirit, even that of the individual Romantic Hero, the story collapses in on itself through a narrative of "sentimentalist self-absorption" (Douglas 1977:255). As Ann Douglas (1977:255) states, whatever else the Romantic may be, it is "a genuinely political and historical sense[,] . . . an antidote and an alternative to the forces of modernizing society." This is clearly not the case in Driscoll's text. In her story social life is disengaged from history—from quotidian events and the conditions from which these events emerge—providing a self-absorbed reading of both the past and the present. In Driscoll's text the past is not the fullness of all previous occurrences (as we find in De Zavala's writing) but a single incident that is made to represent all previous events. While Driscoll's narrative uses historical language, it is completely ahistorical. It makes no attempt at engaging the forces and conditions of its making but instead articulates a position that valorizes her present social location. The complex, multifaceted events and social conditions that brought Anglo-Americans to Texas, that influenced Mexico's initial acceptance of U.S. settlers into its provinces, that led Mexicans in Texas to join forces against Santa Anna, have all been erased from Driscoll's narrative. In its place is a chronology of the events of 1836, uncoupled from the complexity of the situation and rewritten as a narrative that fosters a feeling of sentimentalism that denies the hidden "dynamics of development" (Douglas 1977:13).

The second part of this story further signals how Driscoll's social world has been privatized, displaced from its social ground, and sentimentalized as the consummate love of individuals. The custodian, in choosing to leave with the visitor, forgoes all social relations, including familial ones. This is not a Romantic text—one born from and expressed in the context of one's social world—but a privatized one: that which is ultimately a social affair, the joining and making of kin, is expressed as the doing of individual persons. The past and the present have been displaced from their social moorings and rewritten as the product of individual subjectivities, a process effected through the poetics of sentimentality. For Driscoll, sentimental love serves as the benchmark of subjectivity.

"Juana of the Mission de la Concepción," while it repeats the basic tenet of romantic love, is significant for another reason. It begins with a man who wanders up the bell tower of Mission Concepción, built in San Antonio by the Franciscan priests during the Spanish colonial period. At the top of the tower the man encounters a young woman whose "eyes were lustrous-black, filled with a wild unrest" with "the look of madness in their depths" (1906:88). Startled, he returns to the church, where he finds an old Mexican woman who divulges the story of Juana, an Indian woman gone mad after her husband, a Mexican musician, commits suicide in the tower.

While Driscoll writes the woman as an Indian, I suggest that she is a mestiza, that is, someone of Spanish and Indian descent. Texas Indians, for the most part, assimilated with the Mexican population in South Texas. And, in many cases, Mexicans with phenotypic Indian features are called "indios," even by their mestizo kin. Furthermore, Indians and mestizos were often grouped together by the Anglo-American social categories of the time.

The old woman narrates how Juana went mad from having loved too much. "She was a good girl Juana—but she loved, and when a woman loves it is always like that" (1906:91).

Her husband, Andres, was a musician who played at local dances. On one occasion a "fair-haired woman" attended the dance and Andres fell passionately in love with her. He is found dead with his knife at his side, a flower from the dress of the fair-haired woman in his hand. "Men sometimes go mad like that for love," the old Mexican woman claims (1906:97).

Besides the tragedy of romantic love found in this story, this text reveals another facet of Driscoll's character—her attitude toward Mexicans. In every story Driscoll depicts Mexicans as deeply flawed. They have either gone mad with love, committed suicide, or found themselves trapped in a world of agony and pain as a result of their romantic failures. While Anglo men and women are present in these narratives, none are depicted as maligned as are Andres, Juana, and all the other Mexican characters. Driscoll's Mexican figures are not whole persons, in either a psychological or a social sense, but individuals who are skewed, off balance, and lacking.

In these texts Mexicans are flawed because of their romantic failures. For Driscoll, the Mexican self is not constructed from the dialectical engagement of an individual life within the social arena; instead, and like her understanding of the past, Mexicans are displaced from the social field and constructed from private, sentimental affairs. By writing Mexicans as romantically unaccomplished, Driscoll displaces responsibility for their beleaguered plight from the realm of the social to that of personal nonachievement in matters of the heart. And when the social is hinted at later in this book, it is a realm insulated from Anglo-American influence and expressed as a cultural flaw, that is, stemming from the Mexicans' way of life.

There is another, more biographical reading of this portrayal. Driscoll and her family were deeply involved in the social and economic restructuring of South Texas. Driscoll's family business interests in railroads were responsible, in large measure, for the economic displacement of Mexicans in South Texas. To see Mexicans as socially maligned by the socioeconomic reorganization that she and her family contributed to would implicate her and her family. However, in perceiving Mexicans as personally responsible for their own social demise, Driscoll absolves herself and others of her class from any responsibility.

### ADINA DE ZAVALA AND THE POETICS OF RESTORATION

In 1917, several years after her chapter was voted out of the Daughters of the Republic of Texas, De Zavala privately published *History and Legends of the Alamo and Other Missions in and around San Antonio.* A work consisting of varied narrative forms, it is in many ways the magnum opus of De Zavala's career as a writer of Texas history and folklore. Why it was published privately, I have yet to discover. It may have been because of her intense desire to control its content and details. It is uncertain how many copies were printed, but it was issued in both cloth and paper binding, selling for $1.50 and $1.00 respectively, and was available from De Zavala's Taylor Street address in San Antonio.[17]

Judging from her personal communication, the book sold well. In 1925 the secretary of the Texas Folk-lore Society wrote her asking for ten more copies of the book, because the society had exhausted its supply.[18] And on March 3, 1936, she received a letter from G. B. Dealey of the *Dallas Morning News* saying that he was unable to find a copy of the book and that when he attempted to receive a copy from the Methodist Publishing House, he was told it was out of print and a new edition was being considered.[19]

While there is little information on how the book was received, the jacket of the cloth edition has the following quote from the *San Antonio Express:*

> There is a wealth of romance and history and folklore in the neatly-printed, well-bound volume of more than 200 pages, making it a real addition to the works on the history of the Southwest.[20]

We can further infer the reception of the book by De Zavala's growing reputation. As noted earlier, it was the custom of the Texas State Historical Society to refer questions on the Alamo and Texas missions to her, a recognition that accrued, in part, from the quality and accuracy of the book.

*History and Legends of the Alamo* begins with an extensive and strikingly comprehensive historical survey of the Alamo. De Zavala reconstructs the history of Mission San Antonio de Valero, or the Alamo, beginning with its founding as a Spanish mission. She includes Spanish documents portraying the allotment of mission lands as well as excerpts from church records from this period. She details how the Secularization Laws of 1793 led to the abandonment of the missions and their occupation by Spanish and Mexican cavalry as frontier outposts.

De Zavala portrays the Battle of the Alamo, the events that precipitated it, and its final outcome using diary entries of Fannin's soldiers and the letters of Sam Houston, William Travis, and others. She incorporates most of the available published work on the Alamo, including Reuben M. Potter's *The Fall of the Alamo* (1878), H. Yoakum's *History of Texas* (1855), and

George Garrison's *Texas* (1906). She also draws from baptismal records from the missions and the cathedral and includes artists' sketches and plats of the Alamo from Mexican sources. With these early documents, De Zavala provides information on the location of the mission structures, their dimensions, their design, and their condition during the Alamo battle.

De Zavala concludes her historical chapter with a record of postbattle events and describes the mission's structural decline and its use by the U.S. Army and the Hugo-Schmeltzer Company. She also recounts her efforts to purchase and restore the property. Overall, De Zavala weaves a clear and putatively accurate narrative that chronicles the Indian, Spanish, Mexican, Texan, and U.S. presence at the Alamo.

## History and Legends of the Alamo: *The Legends*

Immediately following the historical section, De Zavala switches genres and provides a series of legends related to the Alamo and other San Antonio missions. But unlike the numerous stories that speak of Bowie, Travis, or Crockett, these portray a different understanding of turn-of-the-century Texas.

The first legend she recounts tells of ghosts with flaming torches that appear to anyone who attempts to tamper with the walls and physical structure of the Alamo. There follows a legend about the statue of Saint Anthony, the patron of Mission San Antonio de Valero. Accordingly, all statues were removed from the mission after the Franciscans departed, except for that of Saint Anthony, which could not be dislodged. The legend claims that "Saint Anthony held his statue there, because he wished his church to be repaired and placed again at the service of the people he loved, whose mission and town had been given his name, and whom he was still anxious to serve!" (De Zavala 1917:57). The statue was present during the battle in 1836, and years later when St. Joseph's Church was built only a few blocks away, "all ideas of the use of the Alamo church for religious purposes was abandoned, and the statue of St. Anthony gave no more trouble, and was easily moved" (1917:57).

It is the next series of legends that interest me more, because they form a triptych of tales bound with a singular motif. Each narrative under the heading "The Folk of the Underground Passages" depicts the presence of mysterious characters who emerge from the "enchanted city" to which underground passages of the Alamo are connected.

The first tale, "The Padre's Gift," concerns a man who appears to unsuspecting people and gives them a special gift. According to this legend, the padre is one of the "good people who have power . . . to pass from the enchanted city of Tejas by way of the underground passages of the Alamo" (1917:59). After providing some brief contextual material, the author, identifying herself as the narrator of the legend, recalls her own encounter with an old man dressed in a religious habit while she was riding outside the city as a young girl. On greeting him, she is presented with a thick book written in Spanish. The one condition of receiving the gift is that no one else is to touch it until she presents it to someone else under the same conditions of privacy. Agreeing, the narrator states, "I have always regretted that I did not ask the old man's name—but I thought, then, only of the precious old treasures and my wonderful good fortune in receiving them" (1917:60).

The second legend concerns the mysterious woman in blue who ascends from the underground passages of the Alamo to seek out a native Texan woman, "pure and good, well-bred, intelligent, spiritual and patriotic," on whom she will bestow a gift. "What is her gift? The gift of seeing to the heart of things! She sees . . . all that may vitally affect, for good or ill, the people of her city and state whom she ardently loves with a strange devotion" (1917:61). This woman, the legend continues, is ready to help "the rich, the poor, the artist, the artisan, the writer, the children—the whole people of her beloved Texas land" (1917:62).

The third legend describes Ursula, a young girl, missing after playing with friends around the Alamo. Ursula's parents are faced with difficult financial problems because of the father's ill health, and when she fails to come home a search is organized by the townspeople. Fearing Ursula has been taken by Indians, the search party is relieved when they find her in a heavy sleep amid the ruins of the Alamo. On her safe return home she recounts how, while playing hide-and-seek, she helped a woman who had stumbled and fallen. After aiding the woman, she continued to hide from her friends and fell into a deep sleep, awakening only after being found by the search party. The woman she helped had given her a small wrapped package and told her to stow it in her pocket. "The mother, realizing her daughter had met the 'good woman' of the underground," examines the package and finds "several very old Spanish gold coins, two diamonds and three pearls[,] . . . and her first thought was that now, Joseph [her husband], could go to consult and secure the eminent specialists" who could cure his ailing health (1917:65).

These stories are linked by their motif of gift-giving. However, in place of operating as a form of exchange, this motif serves as an articulation of hope, or more specifically, the nostalgic hope for social restoration. Gift-giving in these legends serves to restore elements of a world displaced by the radical changes instituted by the social and economic reordering of South Texas.

In the first legend, the gift presented is a thick book written in Spanish from a man who comes from the enchanted city of "Tejas." In light of the Anglo-Americans' "repudiation of the Spanish past" for their own "self-identity" (Weber 1992:430), the use of the referent "Tejas" is instructive. It is derived from a Caddo word adapted by the Spanish as a name for the area and was later kept by the Mexican government as the name of the province. Its presence indexes a world of Indian, Spanish, and Mexican influence, further implied by the gift of the book, a prototypical literary and cultural document, written in the Spanish language. The woman in the legend, whom the author claims is herself, makes an intriguing comment on receiving the book: "I am sure it is wonderful, but it appears well nigh undecipherable [*sic*] with age, and besides, you see, I do not know the Spanish language well." On hearing this, the padre responds, "No, use what you can, and pass it on" (De Zavala 1917:60). The woman's comment seems to contradict the historical figure of De Zavala who, born into a Mexican family, was accustomed to communicating with her Mexican relatives in Spanish.[21] This legend, therefore, is not autobiographical but a sentimental narrative in which history gives way to hope. By encountering the man from the enchanted and underground city, a place embedded in the unseen reaches of unconscious desire, the young woman in the legend receives a gift that calls attention to and seeks to restore a Spanish and Mexican social and cultural world now lost.

In the "Mysterious Woman in Blue," the recipient of the gift is always a "native Texan woman . . . eyes of gray . . . not black" who is intelligent and good-hearted (De Zavala 1917:61). The description of gray eyes is not a common feature: *mexicanas* are usually described as having dark, often black or brown eyes while Anglo-American women have blue or light eyes. Gray eyes are an amalgam. The woman who receives the gift, I suggest, is identified as neither Mexican nor American but one who can claim that "[a]ll the children are her children—all the people are to her friends, and brothers and sisters!" (1917:61).

The issue of social restoration is more apparent in her gift of seeing. The woman in possession of the gift sees "to the heart of things" with the "clear-eyed vision of Joan of Arc," fighting for "justice" for the "whole people of her beloved Texas land" (1917:61-62). To see to the heart of things is to see beyond the personal and sentimental, beyond the isolated events of every day. The woman's gift of sight restores the unity of experience and vision lost to the reductive processes that render the social world a personal and private affair.

The third legend is that of the lost girl who, after helping an old woman, opens a gift of gold coins, diamonds, and pearls. This gift signifies another form of restoration by enabling the father to visit a medical specialist to cure his health. It is consistent with this reading that the gifts offered are forms of wealth and not, strictly speaking, money. That is, the coins and jewels are actually precapitalist forms of wealth and exchange and not, as Max Weber (1946:331) would have it, the money-form—the most reified of all forms of exchange.

The gift of wealth serves to restore the father's health and thereby the economic and social health of the family, as its economic troubles stem from his inability to work. As in the previous legends, the gift bestowed is not meant for personal use, even when given to an individual, but for the good of the "whole people of Texas," as in the gift of seeing—or as in this last text, for the restoration of the family, because the gift of health is really that of economic restoration and stability.

### SENTIMENTALITY, REIFICATION, AND PUBLIC CULTURE

While Clara Driscoll and Adina De Zavala disagreed openly about their visions of the Alamo, the question remains as to why. It is clear that both women were informed by a patriotic spirit and desire to preserve the past. But how could such committed allies in their early quests arrive at such a disjuncture in their common project? And, more important, how did their private visions inform the public image of the Alamo? My initial response is that traces of their private visions—those of sentimentality and Utopian restoration—are found in their historical and fictive writings: De Zavala's legends of restoration are the Janus-faced other of Driscoll's sentimental stories. However, the poetics of sentimentality and restoration serve not as causes but as organizational codes that inform these texts. The relationship between the poetics of sentimentality and restoration and their social ground is complex, and any effort to reduce one to the other denies the processual and dialectical relationship between art and society. Symbolic processes, even the most creative and seemingly idiosyncratic, emerge from the same conditions of possibility as daily life, which constitutes an analytic horizon that cannot be dismissed.

Along these lines, the work of Fredric Jameson is instructive. Building on various literary and critical traditions, including the structuralism of Lévi-Strauss, he demonstrates how narratives function as "symbolic resolution(s) of real political and social contradictions" (Jameson 1981:80). Taking Jameson's critical perspective alongside Douglas's (1977) keen reading of the role of nineteenth-century women in literary and cultural practice lends credence to the poetics of sentimentality and restoration. The "problem" a poetics of sentimentality and of restoration seeks to resolve, as socially symbolic narratives, is the impact of "laissez-faire industrial expansion" and its "inevitable rationalization of the economic order" (Douglas 1977:12). It is crucial to remember that the preservation of the Alamo and the writings of Driscoll and De Zavala are coterminous with capitalist expansion and modernization in South Texas. The effect of capitalist expansion in Texas was the dismantling of *mexicano* traditional society and its subsequent reorganization by capitalist entrepreneurs into a more efficient and pragmatic economic form.[22] As demonstrated in chapter 1, the railroad and large-scale commercial agriculture were two activities that eroded the traditional, family-based, cattle ranching society of South Texas and reshaped it to the needs and logic of a market economy.

This is the social environment of Driscoll's and De Zavala's narratives. However, the poetics of sentimentality and of restoration inform not only these women's narrative efforts but their work of cultural preservation—as distinct articulations of the same social formation—as well. Driscoll's response to Governor Colquitt's intention to restore the Alamo to its original "mission" form acquires special significance. For her, the preservation of the Alamo is neither an act of restoration nor an effort to recapture or reestablish a link to a Spanish and Mexican past but to remember the past through a particular heroic code. But Driscoll's sense of the heroic is not that of the Romantics. In place of fending off the forces of modernity, as Douglas suggests of Romantic writers, Driscoll's heroic intent lends discursive weight to the economic reorganization of South Texas. Her bifurcation of the past as events between "Texans" and "Mexicans" and the uncoupling of the "Battle of the Alamo" from it social and political ground legitimates the place of Anglo-Americans in the emerging class structure of South Texas. By projecting Mexicans as inferior, socially disfigured, and tyrannical followers of Santa Anna, Driscoll promotes the Alamo as a public icon that represents Texans, and concomitantly, Anglo-Americans, as morally, politically, and socially superior.[23] Only here Driscoll's efforts are expressed not solely in narrative form, but are objectified in the public place of the Alamo.

Driscoll's sentimental view of the world uncouples the "past" and the "heroic individual" from the wider social field and rewrites them as "natural" qualities of Anglo-American society. For example, her celebration of the Alamo fighters Bowie, Travis, and Crockett is a vehicle through which heroism is reconfigured to the needs of individualism and liberalism. Driscoll's private vision reconfigures the social scene as a place where Texans reign supreme over those "swarthy-skinned neighbors," as she refers to them, from south of the border (Driscoll 1906:5).

How are we to make sense of De Zavala's two different narratives about the Alamo? What is the relationship between her historical text and collected legends? Here, I turn to Paul Ricoeur's (1980) discussion of historical narrativity, which I find instructive on these points.

Ricoeur states that every narrative "combines two dimensions in various proportions, one chronological and the other nonchronological." By "chronological," Ricoeur means the "episodic" aspects of narratives that "characterize the story made out of events"; by "nonchronological," he means how plots configure "wholes out of scattered events" (Ricoeur 1980:178). While Ricoeur refers to the dialectical relationship between chronology and nonchronology in the same text, it is quite clear that he understands texts to be weighted in one direction or another. Finally, as Ricoeur (1980:171) states, a historical event is more than a single occurrence and contributes "to the development of a plot." As such, a historical text is one that not only provides a chronology but also situates this chronology within a processual frame. My concern is, first, to see how De Zavala's narratives are weighted in different directions; and second, to demonstrate how the meaning of these two texts can be more fully appreciated through Ricoeur's dialectical relationship: that is, De Zavala's historical narrative is only historical when paired with her collected legends, and these legends make interpretive sense when contrasted with the historical texts.

Equipped with these briefly stated notions of Ricoeur, I now return to De Zavala's writings. I understand her chapter on the history of the Alamo as a chronological narrative that tells an "episodic" story. But this chapter, replete with "data" and "facts," is only a partial history and must be read alongside her nonchronological legendry, since it is there that we find the "plot" of this story. De Zavala's collected legends allow us to understand the "historical" significance of the Alamo, not as a place with a chronology, but as an event whose meaning is situated within the larger process of Texas social life. That De Zavala's legends are dialogically responsive to the social and economic displacement experienced by *mexicanos* at the turn of the century is fairly clear. These Utopian narratives seek to "fix" the problem of socioeconomic displacement by pointing to various forms of restoration and recalling the "enchanted city of Tejas" where social and racial cleavage is unknown.

## DE ZAVALA, SUBJECTIVITY, AND THE ALAMO

My concern thus far has been the struggle between De Zavala and Driscoll over the inscription of the Alamo as a public marker. At this point, however, De Zavala merits further scrutiny as a woman whose own life offers an insight into the relationship between the Alamo as a sign of the dominant and the formation of Mexican subjectivity in the early 1900s.

De Zavala was a complex woman, ruled by her passion for all things historical. Of Mexican and Irish ancestry, she was devotedly American. A preserver of Mexican and Spanish material culture, she gave seemingly negligible attention to the contemporary heirs of these artifacts. At one level we must recognize and admire the portrait her deeds and words have painted; on another, we must probe beneath the multitextured surface of this complex image and pose a series of questions, for De Zavala was both an acute chronicler of the past and a person shaped by its particular modality.

It is important to recall that during De Zavala's battle to save the Alamo from capitalist entrepreneurs, rural Mexicans in Texas were being economically displaced in the dwindling cattle industry and transformed into wage laborers in the emerging agricultural industry (De León and Stewart 1985; Montejano 1987). Accompanying this transformation were the various discourses, or "strategies of containment" (Jameson 1981:10), that rationalized and supported that social displacement. For one who studied, collected, and prided herself in the knowledge of all things Texan and Mexican, it is difficult to imagine De Zavala being wholly unfamiliar with the social conditions of this period. Could she have missed the growing anti-Mexican sentiment experienced by the émigrés to Texas and San Antonio as they fled the revolutionary turmoil of Mexico? Much of the conflict between Texans and Mexicans was heralded in the local *corridos,* a genre of folklore about which she seemed to have some knowledge: not only did she lecture on a particular text, but I found scribbled among her papers a quatrain, written in Spanish, under which she wrote "Corrido is a running rhyme." [24] Contemporary scholarship on the Texas-Mexican *corrido* is quite extensive and demonstrates how the years between 1860 and 1920 were a high point of *corrido* production, especially of those ballads that sang of the conflict between Mexicans and Texans (e.g., Flores 1992; Limón 1983; Paredes 1958). Even if De Zavala was unfamiliar with the political elements expressed through these texts, she could hardly escape the events of 1901 concerning the search, chase, arrest, and trial of Gregorio Cortez, or the events of 1915 connected with the border skirmishes between the Texas Rangers and Los Sediciosos (Flores 1992). Why, in the midst of such social and economic upheaval, does Adina De Zavala fixate on the Alamo? It is here, I suggest, that further discussion of De Zavala's sense of Mexicanness is warranted, including some remarks on her own sense of ethnic identity.

De Zavala clearly celebrates all things Texan: historical places, characters, and folklore. But she is equally adamant about the Mexican and Spanish roots of Texas. She continues to search the state for evidence and artifacts from these historical periods and construes history as a summation of the past, influenced by social actors from both sides of the border. And yet it is De Zavala's intense effort to understand, interpret, and restore the Alamo both as a Spanish mission and as a place of battle that distinguishes her understanding of this place from that of Clara Driscoll and the DRT.

But ambiguity remains. While she may have had an inclusive sense of history when it came to Mexican Texas, what were her thoughts about Mexicans as a people, not as places or things? And, likewise, how did she meld her Mexican ancestry, however partial, with her larger sense of self? These are not easy issues to examine, but De Zavala provides us with a few ideas that lead in interesting directions. In 1949, already in her late eighties, she addresses a letter to Paul Adams regarding a text written for schoolchildren about the *San Antonio Story*. Its relevance to this discussion is apparent, and I reproduce it here in its entirety.

Dear Friends:

It seemed to me that the youth or adult who reads the *San Antonio Story* should be given an overall understanding of how San Antonio came to be, therefore, I sent in the suggestive sketch.

I did not re-read my notes as they were sent in and I am wondering if I have made myself thoroughly understood as to objections to certain terms as "Anglos," "Anglo-Americans," "Latin-Americans," "Yankees," etc.

In a book intended for our schools we should be truthful—accurate in what we say, and try not to offend anyone by our expressions. However, we MUST hold fast to the truth—notwithstanding uninformed and prejudiced opposition. We should set a standard! Other writers should be able, confidently, to take this history as a model—a criterion. We should not copy others' mistakes even if considered popular. It

MUST be done! And what a splendid advertisement this would be for our city and schools!

If a German [25] becomes naturalized in the United States, he is a citizen of the United States of America—and entitled to the designation "American"—though born in Europe. And should he be asked in England who he is—he could and should truthfully answer: "I am an American of the United States." This is what our highest authority on Emigration and Naturalization says.

After Mexico won her independence from Spain, and before—there were so many uprisings, revolutions and changes in administrations, and these early settlers were always reaching out and hoping for a stable government. However, they never felt that they really "belonged" until Texas became an independent Republic, March 2, 1836! Then, of course, when Anson Jones, the last President of the Republic of Texas, lowered the Texas flag February 19, 1846, and raised the Stars and Stripes in its stead—they felt that they, too, "belonged" and were citizens of the United States!

Unfortunately, we, in Texas, in the early days of Statehood—and later—have often placed in power persons who carelessly or heartlessly permitted neglect and abuse of our early settlers and their descendants: the real owners of the soil before our arrival. They have been for the most part, for years, a confused and "hurt" people. These underprivileged citizens—many descendants of early settlers—know they are NOT Mexicans, for to be one they would have to have been born in Mexico and now hold citizenship there, or have acquired it—yet, when they are questioned as to their citizenship and pressed for an answer they generally say "Mexican," because they have been told continually that they *are* "Mexican." Though puzzled—knowing that they are expected to give that answer—they obligingly do so.

On account of ways and other serious troubles, many of these early settlers and their children were not able to obtain the educational advantages of our citizens elsewhere, though there were many educated people in the early days, and many naturally superior citizens who were looked to for leadership. (See authors of the Memorial to the Mexican Government in 1832. Also Gil Y'Barbo etc.) These people are "Americans" in every sense of the word—and if we still have descendants of our aborigines—and there were some quite gifted ones here—not so long ago they, too, are preeminently "Americans."

Should we not begin at once to let these under-privileged citizens know that we recognize them as Texans and fellow citizens and fellow

Americans? Should we not strive to teach and inculcate a feeling of love, loyalty and pride in our city, state, nation and in all our citizens and young people? And try to instill a sense of responsibility and a desire and determination to work whole heartedly and unselfishly foe [*sic*] the good of all. We, as well as they, are suffering from our short sightedness—from our neglect in meeting our responsibility! Should we not, at once, try to repair our mistakes? It is LATE—but with God's help we may not be TOO LATE![26]

De Zavala's letter is revealing on several counts. First, note that she speaks of Mexicans in the third person and includes herself among the list of citizenry, Texans and Americans. Second, De Zavala accurately places responsibility for the social demise of Mexicans on "*our* neglect from meeting *our* responsibility" (my emphasis). Mistakes have been made, she writes, and amends must clearly be made. Furthermore, although these people were not born in Mexico, it is the dominant, Anglo-American, class that "continually" reminds these people that they are "Mexicans."

In one of her more telling phrases, De Zavala clearly claims that it is "we, in Texas" who have been abusive and neglectful toward "the real owners of the soil before our arrival." The issue here is land. Like those heroic defenders, not of the Alamo but of the *corridos* of border conflict, ownership of land and the economic resources it provides for those who control it are her concern. Mexicans, because of the abuses inflicted on them by Texans, have been "confused and 'hurt'" and exist as "underprivileged citizens." De Zavala pleads that we recognize Mexicans as "Texans and fellow citizens and fellow Americans"; she requests that Mexicans not be treated as second-class members of society but as full participants. While the rhetoric of cultural nationalism is clearly absent from her writing, the goals of shared responsibility and equality, the issues of class displacement and racial abuse, and the subsequent outcome of social and psychological disvaluation are clearly a concern of hers.

De Zavala's letter displays a keen sense of the inequities of the past that perhaps was not present in her earlier writings. I do not believe these are the musings of an elderly woman who—as a result of the privileges of old age—now speaks her mind; De Zavala always spoke her mind. Instead, this text is the product of experience, reflection, and knowledge that resulted, perhaps, in a kind of personal and textual reconciliation of her Mexican past and American present.

But what does she make of her Mexican-Irish-Spanish self? To the extent that language serves as an important marker in discussions of ethnic

formation and identity, I invoke the following example. In a recent article
for the tourist magazine *Texas Highways,* Frank Jennings (1995:16)
claims, "Despite her Spanish surname, she [De Zavala] never learned the
language." The evidence for Jennings's claim, I suggest, is not so clear;
and, judging from De Zavala's papers, there is more cause to believe that
she was a dedicated student of the language, if not nearly fluent in the written text.

An assiduous keeper of records, De Zavala left a handwritten and typed
record of her personal library holdings.[27] Listed as part of her collection
are a number of works on Mexican history, written in Spanish, as well as
texts for learning Spanish. Furthermore, it is known that De Zavala traveled through Mexico on more than one occasion and received correspondence in Spanish from a number of people. While some of her Mexican
correspondents may not have known English, her Uncle Lorenzo, Jr., did,
and on more than one occasion he wrote to her in Spanish.

Another source that suggests she was knowledgeable in Spanish is her
copious notes and papers. In more than several places she jotted down
phrases, notes, and book titles in Spanish. Although it is not clear if she
copied this material directly from other sources, Ables (1967:373) quotes
De Zavala as stating that, near her resignation as a teacher, she had been
studying "Mexican history in Mexico."

While De Zavala's knowledge of Spanish is of interest in and of itself,
this issue serves as a marker for her sense of ethnic self. There is no doubt
that she considered herself an American and, more important, a Texan.
But did her clear sense of Texan identity require a rejection of her Mexican heritage? If anything, De Zavala was devoted to remembering, restoring, and recollecting the entire past of Texas, including its Spanish and
Mexican roots. I cannot imagine she would think otherwise about herself;
and yet, based on her letter to Adams, she would not call herself a "Mexican." This is why De Zavala's knowledge of Spanish is significant. I believe Jennings is incorrect in stating that she never learned the language:
not only do her personal papers demonstrate a clear effort to do just that,
but they further indicate a certain proficiency in reading it. Jennings's discussion of this topic leads one to think that De Zavala was Mexican in
name only, alienated from her Mexican heritage. Perhaps her unflinching
sense of "Texanness" moves him to claim such a position; I believe another set of factors must be considered on this issue.

It is here, I suggest, that we bring into sharp focus the twin passions
that consumed De Zavala's life—places and stories of the past. De Zavala
is acutely aware, going back to her letter to Adams, of the treatment Mex-

icans experienced at the hands of Americans. She claims that any sense of self that is rooted in a "Mexican" identity is the result of its imposition on people who otherwise seek to be "American." From this statement, we can glean the following possibilities. At one level, De Zavala's identification as an American and a Texan appears as a form of ethnic abandonment and reattachment. Instead of accepting her Mexican, lower-status identity, she reattaches herself to her Texan ancestry, one rightly accorded through her Irish lineage. But, even as I suggest this explanation, let me also claim that I do not think this approach answers enough questions. For one, ethnic reattachments are found not only on the part of Mexicans claiming a Texan identity, but are foisted on "good" Mexicans by local discourses. In an example resulting from De Zavala's own efforts, we have the local San Antonio newspaper referring to Enrique Esparza, De Zavala's eyewitness informant on the Battle of the Alamo, in the following way: "Esparza tells a straight story. Although he is a Mexican, his gentleness and unassuming frankness are like the typical old Texan" (Matovina 1995a:67).

Reading this description of Esparza alongside De Zavala's celebratory Texan identification serves as a critical reminder of how the hegemonic forces of this period worked their way into local representations of Mexicans, as well as Mexicans' self-references. This leads me to suggest that ethnic reattachments—like that exhibited by De Zavala—while at one level must be considered for their referential content must also be evaluated in terms of personal repression arising from ethnic hostility and racism. At this level, De Zavala's insistence and fervent declaration of "Texanness" must be seen as a form of personal repression whereby her ethnic self—informed by the same racial sensibilities that turned Esparza into an "old Texan"—has been displaced onto another level of practice. Here I draw on De Zavala's politically unconscious work, both material and discursive, that reveals an embedded political posture that cannot be dismissed. My suggestion, and the crux of my thesis on De Zavala, is that her deep interest in the material and social restoration of a Spanish and Mexican past, expressed through her work of artifactual preservation and historical legendry, results from the displacement of her "Mexican" self onto these other levels of identification.

In an acutely perceptive work, Peter Stallybrass and Allon White (1986:196) argue a similar notion of displacement when they claim that "sentimentality for 'lost' realms can be avoided by mapping the inner articulation of semantic domains/sites of discourse within the historical formation of class subjectivities." Their claim is that displacements, or the discursive shifting of meanings and subjects, are not neutral practices but ones invested with the social modalities of their time. Instrumental for Stallybrass and White, as well as for my own interpretive claims, are the hierarchical relations that emerge from particular historical configurations that lead to the validation of "one set of social practices over against others" (Stallybrass and White 1986:197). De Zavala's passion for Spanish and Mexican places, I contend, emerges, in part, from the anti-Mexican atmosphere of early-twentieth-century Texas. In place of validating her own mestizoness—a unique conjuncture of Spanish, Mexican, and Irish ancestry—she forges a unified Texan subjectivity that displaces her "cultural otherness" onto historical places. Her life is spent in search of the "lost realms" of Spanish and Mexican Texas precisely because her ethnic sense of self has been displaced by a Texan subjectivity. Displacement, in this case, is linked to the Freudian notion of sublimation, which sheds further light on this discussion.

Ricoeur's groundbreaking work, *Freud and Philosophy* (1970), allows us to read Freud not just as an interpreter of the human mind but of the sociocultural world as well. According to Ricoeur, Freud's notion of sublimation is a "displacement of energy and an innovation of meaning" (1970:514) that is marked by a profound "unity of disguise and disclosure" (1970:519). De Zavala's celebration of her Texan identity serves as a disguise, I contend, while her Utopian legends disclose an embedded political critique. But sublimation is itself a mechanism, a response; here Stallybrass and White (1986:197) offer a particular rationale, since for them sublimation is inseparable from "cultural domination," of which ethnic hostility and racism is, I believe, a particular form. Sublimation— the displacement of energy that leads to various shades of disguising and disclosing—is a response to certain forms of social and cultural hegemonic practices. The paradox that leads De Zavala to empathize with Mexicans while celebrating Americanism, to work unceasingly for the historical preservation of Spain and Mexico's artifactual past while simultaneously holding little value for her partial Mexican heritage, occurs from repressing the depth of the social, cultural, and economic domination experienced by Mexicans at this time. Personal displacements such as this are not unheard of for Mexican women of this period. Writing about De Zavala's colleague and associate in the Texas Folklore Society, José Limón's comments concerning Jovita González are appropriate for De Zavala as well.[28] She was, he says, "unsupported by the luxury of a 'growing ethnic-feminist consciousness,' who perhaps only appears 'to turn a blind eye' on her role as a historical writing subject with respect to her native community" (Limón 1994:74). But in the case of De Zavala, it was not a lack of sight but a displaced sense of ethnic self that affected her. The letter to Adams demonstrates her particular vision where, like her Woman in Blue, she too saw "to the heart of things."[29] However, it is only through a critical reading of her Utopian legends that the (dialectical) other registers of her sublimated voice can be heard. The social restoration semantically keyed in De Zavala's legends serves as the muted and displaced critical voice of De Zavala's subjective speech. Unable to confront directly the sources that socially and economically displaced Mexicans, she emplotted them as the historical rationale of the Alamo; stymied by the racial hierarchies of the period, she displaced her ethnic self onto a Texan identity and a passion for the material past.

Although it is not clear to what extent De Zavala experienced, first-hand, the anti-Mexican climate of this era, she could not escape knowing it, as the following example from her papers demonstrates. On September 13, 1929, she received a letter from the Reverend Charles Taylor, OMI, of Sacred Heart Church in Crystal City, Texas, requesting money for his church. His letter begins: "Mexicans, non-Catholics, rural life—are these not the three great problems that confront the Church in America today? . . . People here need no authority to tell you that their [Mexicans'] name is legion."[30] And yet, even as some members of the Texas Catholic clergy held views like Taylor's, De Zavala's own sense of Catholicism—buried beneath layers of Texas pride—manifests itself in her religious practice, for also among her papers is a worn holy card, printed in Spanish, of Our Lady of Guadalupe. If not by self-referentiality, and disguised as it may be, Adina De Zavala was in certain culturally gendered ways a *mexicana.*[31]

The apparent contradictions surrounding De Zavala are many: a romantic defender of the Alamo, she is forced out of the DRT and her contributions are ignored; a woman of mixed ethnic ancestry, she embraces her own sense of Americanness and Texanness; a romantic chronicler of Texas, she emplots a Utopian vision for a restored "Tejas"; a writer and collector of all matters historical, her accomplishments have been mainly ignored in the present. It is only by historicizing De Zavala herself that these contradictions make interpretive sense. While much of this chapter has in fact historicized De Zavala, let me add the following distinction. As a subject and social actor, De Zavala's ouster from the DRT and her romantic views of Texas are quite understandable: she spoke loudly and vehemently about her own historical knowledge and the makers of the past.[32]

But as a social agent, one who occupies a particular structural position, her life is less clear. To what extent does her ethnic structural slot color the view of the DRT's understanding of her? No doubt they reacted in many ways to De Zavala the actor: brash, confident, outspoken, she was clearly a force to be considered. But as an "ethnic other," in a period when such social positions were more rigid and confining, we see little of her enemy's views. It would be misleading to suggest that De Zavala was treated *only* as an "ethnic other," for she was not; but the level of ethnic prejudice and racism cannot be dismissed. While it is clear that De Zavala's own personal characteristics and historical vision gave the DRT much to wrangle with, the deep social, ethnic, and gender repression of the period were clearly prescriptive forces in her life.

For all her accomplishments, it was the Alamo that remained the singularly most important aspect of her public life. While much that precedes this conclusion has gone to suggest why, let me summarize by stating the following. By 1905 the Alamo served as the most salient and ambiguous symbol of Texas. Its semantic imprint dominated the social landscape between Texans and Mexicans, even as its full disclosure revealed deep racial and class fissures between the two. De Zavala lived, paradoxically, in the canyon (arroyo is perhaps more accurate) between the past as a romantic history of "Tejas" and the present as a Utopian longing for its social restoration. She worked diligently and energetically to restore the Alamo as a shrine of Texas liberty — a bastion, in many cases, of anti-Mexican sentiment. And yet, in spite of all her colonial interests — that is, her concern for "things" and "places" of the past with seemingly little or no concern for their social effect — there remains a critique, a critical discourse, embedded, even repressed, in her work. For we find that the historical frame De Zavala constructs for the Alamo, the plot in which she embeds its story, is the social displacement of Mexicans stemming from the forces of modernity. According to this plot, the fictive restoration of Mexicans is necessary, since their real condition is one of degradation brought forth by the cultural, economic, and social reorganization of Texas as an industrialized state. The historical narrative De Zavala provides of the Alamo configures a past for a place, but as a narrative whose plot has itself been displaced, embedded in her collected legends, we find a historical text that prescribes a social place for a people. It is not surprising, following the deep, resistive role that *mexicano* expressive culture has played in Texas, to find De Zavala's critical practice portrayed in such a way.[33] This reading of De Zavala's work serves to counter the monological discourse of the DRT and the growing sentiment surrounding the Alamo in the early

1900s. Her legends that call for a return to "Tejas," precisely *because* of their Utopian impulse, express an allegorical unity that emplots a very different kind of Alamo in a rather unheroic historical narrative.

The efforts of Clara Driscoll and Adina De Zavala are important for understanding the contested and negotiated processes that construct places of public history and culture. But the discord between these two women reveals another critical moment: the emergence of the Alamo as symbol. James Fernandez (1986:31) defines symbols as "abstracted sign-images which have lost their direct link with the subjects on which they were first predicated." I explore the significance of the Alamo as symbol more fully below; here I want to underscore the historical emergence of this occurrence. De Zavala, in her attempt to emphasize the mission and battle history of the Alamo, clearly attempted to maintain a link between the place of the Alamo and its entire historical context. Driscoll did not. Her efforts, as well as those of her followers in the DRT, have led to the enshrinement of one moment of history that is rewritten into the values, practices, and notions of a developing American identity at the time.

The significance of De Zavala's and Driscoll's disagreements rests not solely on whose vision of the past will come to define the Alamo, although this certainly has had repercussions for contemporary identity politics,[34] but the very elements of their conflict reveals a deep fissure between history as a discussion of the past and history in the service of the modern nation-state. The story of De Zavala and Driscoll gives credence to Homi Bhabha's (1990b:5) claim that in "'foundational fictions' the origins of national traditions turn out to be as much acts of affiliation and establishment as they are moments of disavowal, displacement, exclusion, and cultural contestations." No more accurate description can be had for how and why the Alamo is remembered.

# Part Two

⊬ ⊣

## THE ALAMO AS PROJECT,
## 1890–1960

What is needed is . . . to dissolve the reification of the
great modernistic works, and to return these artistic and
academic "monuments" to their original reality as private
languages of isolated individuals in a reified society.
— FREDRIC JAMESON
*Modernism and Its Repressed*

Thus only when the theoretical primacy of "facts" has
been broken, only when every phenomenon is recognized
to be a process, will it be understood that what we are
wont to call "facts" consists of processes.
— GEORG LUKÁCS
*History and Class Consciousness*

# 5

⊬— —⊬

## CINEMATIC IMAGES

### FRONTIERS, NATIONALISM,
### AND THE MEXICAN QUESTION

The changing state of relations between Anglos and Mexicans in 1915 required the formation of new strategies to support the emerging racial culture of the Texas Modern. The story of the Alamo, stripped of the tensions and historical ambiguities of 1836, played a strategic role in this process. Between dime-store novels, early tourist and trade books about San Antonio and Texas, and oral legendry, the Alamo now occupied a foundational place in the production of frontier mythology. While the weight of these efforts led to the dissemination of the Alamo story beyond the confines of Texas, it is the emergence of motion pictures, with their visual texture and iconic density, that best exemplifies the linkages between the Alamo as historical event and its emerging cultural memory made real through the project of modernity. Not only is the Alamo story retold through cinema—what Leo Charney and Vanessa R. Schwartz (1995:1) consider the "fullest expression" of modernity—but more critically, it provides a cognitive and visual projection of the displacing practices characteristic of the Texas Modern.

My discussion here is not intended to be a survey or exegesis of all cinematic representations of the Battle of the Alamo. Not only have others already provided this invaluable work, but such an effort fails to serve the central thesis of this project.[1] I am principally concerned with two Alamo films: *Martyrs of the Alamo, or the Birth of Texas,* released in 1915, and John Wayne's 1960 rendition, *The Alamo.* These films represent the earliest and latest "modern" cinematic productions of the 1836 battle. They are two very distinct films, and their differences are informative for understanding the shifting image of Mexican Americans in American society in the forty-five years between them. Although a series of films after 1960 are important for rethinking the Alamo through historical correction and parody, *Viva Max* (1969) being perhaps the most well known, these films emerge from a different, postmodern if you want, era and are produced through a different sociohistorical lens.

Between 1911 and 1915 four films depicting the 1836 battle were made, of which only the latest has survived. Of the three lost films, it is *The Immortal Alamo* (1911) about which any substantive information is available. Virtually nothing is known about the other two, *The Siege and Fall of the Alamo* (1914) and *The Fall of the Alamo* (1914). The oldest extant film is the 1915 production, *Martyrs of the Alamo, or the Birth of Texas,* which I will shortly address. The production of four films in four years erases any uncertainty about when the Alamo emerges as a national reference point. Only the period between 1955 and 1960, the years of Walt Disney's *Davy Crockett* and John Wayne's *The Alamo,* are comparable.

*The Immortal Alamo* is the work of Gaston Méliès, brother of early cinema's influential practitioner, Georges Méliès. In January 1910 Gaston moved his film production and distribution unit, Star Film Company, to San Antonio from New York and immediately made plans to produce what he promised would be a historically "correct" representation of the 1836 battle. Méliès released his brief production on May 25, 1911. Directed by William Haddock, it starred Francis Ford (brother of John Ford), William Carrol, Méliès himself, and cadets from the local Peacock Military Academy. Col. Wesley Peacock, who was fourteen at the time of the shooting and son of the commander of the school, recalls Méliès using "real Mexicans," more than likely Mexican Americans, with uniforms from the Peacock cadets meant to "represent those of the era." [2] Despite its claim to historical accuracy and its supposed footage of the actual structure of the Alamo (although without copies of the film, this cannot be verified), the movie's plot reproduces the already formulaic narrative of a "pretty girl, a shy hero, and a villain." Specifically, the film's story revolves around the characters of Señor Navarre, a supposed "Mexican spy," Lucy Dickenson, and her husband, Lieutenant Dickenson (Thompson 1996).

The real plot of the film begins when, in the midst of the siege, Lieutenant Dickenson answers Travis's call for a volunteer to carry a message to Sam Houston. Soon after his departure, Señor Navarre makes a play for Lucy, who refuses his sexual advances and is rescued by Colonel Travis. Expelled from the Alamo, Navarre makes contact with Santa Anna and provides him with strategic information on how to overtake the Texans and the Alamo. In exchange, Navarre convinces Santa Anna to allow him to choose a bride from among the survivors of the battle. When the siege is over Santa Anna makes good on his promise and gives Navarre permission to marry Lucy. The next morning, moments before the marriage ceremony is to begin, Dickenson arrives on the scene and reclaims his wife, defending her honor from the disgraceful union with Navarre (Thompson 1996).

*The Immortal Alamo,* only ten minutes long according to Thompson, is illuminating on a number of accounts. First, it is clear from the length of the film that there could have been no significant portrayal of the battle. Second, in terms of historical resonance, there was a Lt. Almeron Dickenson[3] who fought and died at the Alamo, and his wife, Suzanna (not Lucy) Dickenson, along with their infant daughter, did survive. However, there is no evidence of a Mexican spy or of an attempted marriage between Mrs. Dickenson and any of Santa Anna's men. After the battle, the now-widowed Suzanna was released by Santa Anna and sent north to relay the details of the Mexican victory to Sam Houston. Of note, *The Immortal Alamo* anticipates its successor, *Martyrs of the Alamo,* in the way it collapses, and thereby negates, the sociohistorical events of 1836 into the sexual desire of Anglo women by Mexican men. I develop this point in more detail below in my discussion of *Martyrs of the Alamo.*

Third, Gaston Méliès, after his stay in San Antonio, went on to produce no less than sixty-four films that Fatimah Tobing Rony (1996:85) describes as a hybrid of "documentary and fantasy." From 1912 to 1913 Méliès traveled to Tahiti, New Zealand, Australia, Java, Cambodia, and Japan shooting films under the tutelage of Round the World Films in which he created "on film what he failed to find in reality": the savage (Rony 1996:85). Rony (1986:85) highlights how indigenous people in the Méliès films of this period were "target[s] of humor." I suggest, however, that the juxtaposition of primitive innocence and worldly traveler implies other referents. Méliès ceaselessly searched the globe for the paradigmatic savage as a blend of fantasy and fact that revealed a lifeway of primitive innocence, unspoiled by the ravages of modern life (Rony 1996:85). *The Immortal Alamo,* I suggest, serves as an important precursor to this effort in two ways. His wish to produce a historically accurate film makes *The Immortal Alamo* an early attempt at historical documentary. His concern for authentically representing the decorum and physical atmosphere of the battle serves as but one example. More important, I believe his interest in the battle of 1836 serves to underscore, if not the loss of innocence, then certainly its threat. Here, Lucy serves as a key trope of Utopian innocence threatened by the conniving activity of the Mexican. The slots occupied by Méliès's later savages, then, follow closely those outlined by Trouillot in his discussion of Utopia and savagery. For Trouillot (1991:28), the figure of the savage only emerges in relation to the Utopian projection of the West, a West represented under siege in *The Immortal Alamo*. Once the West is firmly established and secure from the threat of outsiders (i.e., after the Mexicans are defeated at the Alamo), a Utopic elsewhere could be imagined as the material place of future colonizations. Méliès's Alamo film, then, anticipates and explores his later cinematic motifs where the Mexican Other serves as both a threat to the West and an aggressive savage in need of rule.

By 1915 the cinematic projection of Mexicans as the "savage" Other had arrived full blown. It is then that William Christy Cabanne, a little-known actor and assistant of D. W. Griffith, cowrote and directed the earliest extant film on the Alamo, *Martyrs of the Alamo, or the Birth of Texas.* Appearing only several months after Griffith's *The Birth of a Nation,* Cabanne's film—which the credits state was supervised by Griffith—was deeply influenced by his mentor's effort. Released through Triangle Film Corporation, a joint filmmaking venture of Griffith, Harry Aitken, and others, *Martyrs* is one of several films made in 1915–1916 under the "supervision" of Griffith. While Griffith oversaw the work of his directors, it was the policy of the corporation to give individual filmmakers the fullest possible freedom, making the direct influence of Griffith tangential at best.

Regardless of Griffith's personal involvement, *Martyrs* takes its cinematic inspiration from *The Birth of a Nation.* Cabanne had worked with Griffith for five years as an assistant director and occasional actor, making his directoral debut in 1913; and he continued to make films, mostly B westerns, until his death in 1950. But Griffith's involvement marks another factor in my discussion: the emergence of modernity. *Martyrs of the Alamo* was made in 1915, the same time that a "certain space was shattered," according to Lefebvre (1991:25), leaving in its wake a different set of codes and markers in which the visual plays a significant role. While Griffith contributed little, at least in terms of intellectual momentum, to this emerging aesthetic, and in fact he purposefully sought subjects for his films from the Romantic era of the nineteenth century, his technical and formal contributions to filmmaking were part of the new modern order.

*Martyrs of the Alamo,* then, as a cultural product of this period, even as a poor imitation of Griffith's own style, participates in a logic of the early modern period whereby the partialities of the visually projected are taken as complete or whole truths (Lefebvre 1991:286). Thus I have two principal concerns with cinematic projections such as *Martyrs of the Alamo*. First, they represent the complexities of the past only partially and in ways that allow viewers to render them as complete truths. My second concern has to do with the projections themselves and the symbolic work they attempt to achieve. Partial projections treated as wholes obscure and omit critical features that serve as important counterpoints. When these visualizations are those of the past, what remains absent is history itself, that is, history as the condition that warrants these projections in the first place.

A silent film, *Martyrs of the Alamo* intersplices text with visuals. The movie is introduced as a historical drama about the events that led to the independence of Texas, making claims to historical accuracy. In the first scene, Santa Anna is already in San Antonio, giving General Cós instructions as Santa Anna prepares to journey, presumably, south to Mexico.

The film then moves to a depiction of the local Mexican population, both soldiers and civilians, as ill mannered, slovenly, drunken, and lusting after women who are passing by. We find a Mexican officer stopping an Anglo woman, verbally accosting her, and making suggestive advances. On returning home, the woman reports this to her husband, who locates the Mexican officer and, after an exchange of words, shoots him. As a result of this incident, Santa Anna confiscates all weapons from the Anglo population, except for a cache of arms hidden beneath the floor by David Crockett and Jim Bowie.

These two projections, the maltreatment of Anglo women by Mexican men and the confiscation of weapons by Santa Anna, are presented as the rationale for Crockett, Bowie, and other Anglo settlers to plot the taking of the Alamo. The opportunity to enact such a plan arises when, in the wake of Santa Anna's departure, the local Mexican population, including the military, take to the streets in wild debauchery (see Fig. 5.1). Finding this an opportune moment, Crockett, Bowie, and their followers gather the concealed weapons, storm the streets, take the Mexican army by surprise, and seize control of the city. With the Anglos in charge, the local Mexican citizenry comport themselves very differently. After a text that reads "Under the new regime . . . ," there is a scene in which Mexicans are taking off their hats in deference to women strolling by, greeting each other and Anglos in a sober and respectful manner, and generally acting in a "civilized" fashion.

I must underscore that up to this moment in the film, and continuing throughout, the movie depicts an ethnic and racial divide between Texans and Mexicans. As we have seen, those who fought on the Texas side were

FIGURE 5.1
*Mexicans before a cockfight. Scene from* **Martyrs of the Alamo.**
SOURCE: *Wisconsin Center for Film and Theatre Research, negative no. 10672mp.*

immigrants from the United States and Europe as well as Mexican citizens. According to *Martyrs of the Alamo,* however, all Texans were "white" while the Mexicans were "brown." The one exception is Bowie's "slave," portrayed by a blackface actor, who dutifully sits by the ailing defender.

Once the Texans take charge of the town, they expel General Cós in a scene that already reproduces specific body features of dominance and subordination. Cós strikes a passive and grateful pose as he is allowed to leave with sword in hand, an act drawing attention to the fairness and magnanimity of the Texans. But throughout this interaction, Cós is represented in a cowering and lamely submissive, eyes-cast-down posture in relation to the direct-looking, erect-standing, and serious Texans. And as the Mexican troops depart, they do so with little show of their earlier bravado but as a beaten and docile group.

Cós reconnects with his superior, Santa Anna, who is, expectedly, incensed and calls his generals together to plan an attack on the Alamo. However, unknown to the Mexicans, "Deaf" Smith, one of the Texan leaders, is hiding in the bush, from where he hears the entire plan. Carrying this information back to the Alamo, Bowie, Crockett, and now Travis, sent by Sam Houston to take charge of the former mission, prepare for Santa Anna's arrival and battle. (See Fig. 5.2.)

When Santa Anna arrives and the actual siege of the Alamo begins, the Mexicans are portrayed as the more powerful, impersonal, villainous, and, at times, even inept force. Perhaps one of the more disturbing images appears when the Mexicans have made their way into the Alamo. During a scene of hand-to-hand fighting, the screen shifts to a small, unarmed boy cowering behind a cannon, taking cover from the fighting around him. From nowhere appears the arm of a Mexican soldier grabbing the youth by his neck and pulling him out of camera view. The next frame shows the dead corpse of the boy flying across the room, landing against the far wall.

At several points the film draws attention to the tension between the soldiers of Crockett, Bowie, and Travis. For example, in the midst of battle two men haggle about whose followers are the bravest. In each of these cases, tension between the Texans is dissolved as they return to their common foe, the Mexicans, and their common cause, liberty.

In the midst of battle, Travis sends Smith to carry a written message to Houston. Here again is one of the many incongruities between the film and the event of 1836. It is known that Travis used several couriers during the siege, mostly Mexican Texans, like Juan Seguín, because he believed they could maneuver through the Mexican forces less conspicuously. Since *Martyrs* does not portray Mexicans fighting alongside the Texan forces, it has Smith serving in this role.

After reading Travis's letter, Houston hastens his forces as there is dire need for them at the Alamo. But the Alamo falls before they arrive. Already in this film we see Travis drawing the legendary line in the sand when he realizes no reinforcements will be arriving. As the film shows, even Bowie, ailing and near death, crosses the line, choosing to stay and die.

After the battle, Santa Anna, admiring Smith's blond female companion, releases all the surviving women but her. Among those to leave is Suzanna Dickenson, who heads north and relays the news of the defeat to Houston and Smith. At this point, Houston decides to relocate his forces to San Jacinto where he plans to make his assault on the Mexican forces. Smith, however, concerned about the fate of his "girl," decides to spy once again on Santa Anna's army. This time, however, he is captured overhearing a meeting between Santa Anna and his generals. In a display of keen slyness, Smith convincingly feigns deafness and is released by the Mexicans and allowed free rein of the camp. On finding the tent where his girl is being held, he frees her and returns to Houston with his newly acquired Mexican battle plans.

FIGURE 5.2
*Santa Anna played by Walter Long in* **Martyrs of the Alamo.**
SOURCE: *Wisconsin Center for Film and Theatre Research, negative no. 8455mp.*

The last scene I want to briefly address is one in which Santa Anna is camping near San Jacinto just before Houston's forces arrive. It shows the Mexicans in their tents, sleeping, drinking, and totally unprepared for battle. The text makes note of Santa Anna as a "drug fiend" who also engages in "orgies." With this, the film cuts to Santa Anna in his tent surrounded by scantily clad dancing women in a drug-induced stupor. After spending several minutes on this image, the forces of Sam Houston arrive and Santa Anna, too inebriated to hold his sword, flees for his life.

With Houston's forces shouting "Remember the Alamo," Santa Anna, hiding in a row of shrubs, is captured. Houston, deciding the Mexican general is more valuable alive than dead, stops several soldiers from placing a noose around his neck and proceeds to sign a treaty with him that frees Texas from Mexican rule.

The final frame of the film is a series of flags — the Mexican, Lone Star, Confederate, and then the Stars and Stripes — blowing in the breeze.

How do we understand this early film on the Alamo? In *Martyrs,* the impetus for Texas to secede from the Mexican union is portrayed not as a political act but a social one, based on the projection of Mexicans as disrespectful, uncivil, promiscuous, and sexually dangerous to Anglo women. Like the depiction of arrogant Reconstruction-era blacks in *Birth of a Nation,* Mexicans, both citizens and soldiers, are presented as morally reprehensible. Their comportment, in terms of social and sexual behavior, is projected as flawed, threatening, and in need of control by the new Anglo regime.[4] This results in the negation of history and culture as political difference is collapsed into social comportment and sexual desire. This representation stigmatizes Mexicans but also circumscribes their participation in the emerging social order of 1915.

This projection is directly referenced in the representation of gender in two ways. First, as witnessed both in the opening scene and in the scene in Santa Anna's tent, Mexicans are to be feared in terms of miscegenation. Women's sexuality, in particular the pristine state (as opposed to the loose morals of the dancing Mexican women in the tent) of Anglo women, must be protected from the lascivious Mexican male. The baseness and unrestrained manner through which Mexican desire is portrayed marks them with a wild, even primitive sexuality. It is this sexuality that must be contained "under the new regime," a not so latent reference to civilized modernity. (See Fig. 5.3.)

The need to control Mexican sexuality not only stigmatizes Mexicans but also validates the construction of the patriarchal, heroic Anglo male. This is, in effect, a variation of Michael Taussig's (1993:65–66) "colonial

FIGURE 5.3
*"Deaf" Smith, "his girl," and her father in **Martyrs of the Alamo**.*
SOURCE: *Wisconsin Center for Film and Theatre Research, negative no. 10673pm.*

mirror of production" whereby the dominant impute savagery to the native so as to legitimate their civilized violence against them. In this case, the dominant (male) social order imputes a sexual obsession with white women to Mexican men as a way of legitimating their need to protect, hence control, Anglo women's sexuality. The male hero not only rescues the Anglo woman from Mexican defilement, but in doing so upholds (reproduces) the necessary alibi of patriarchy. This double troping of race and gender is experienced full force, as one might expect, on Mexican women as projected in the scene in Santa Anna's tent. Here several Mexican women, dancing before the general's bulging eyes, are circumscribed by sexual desire and the patriarchal gaze. *Martyrs of the Alamo,* therefore, negates the events of 1836 by collapsing political allegiance and historical ambiguity into a gendered and racialized discourse objectified through the female body.

The fear of Mexicans is not limited to miscegenation but extends to their behavior within the norms of "civil" warfare. The case of the murder of the young boy cowering behind the cannon serves as a critical example of this position. Contrast this with the sparing of Santa Anna's life by Houston as well as Cós's departure with sword in hand, and the noble character of the Anglo emerges quite clearly. The portrayal of Mexicans as fully incapable of civil behavior—in regard to sexuality, social comportment, or honoring the civil practices of warfare—posits their difference as the result of *their* social and cultural practice. It is Mexicans, we conclude from this film, who are responsible for their plight in Texas. By imputing a radical alterity to Mexicans, *Martyrs of the Alamo* advances a position of ascribed dominance whereby Anglo superiority is manifestly destined in the emerging social order of the Texas Modern.

It is here that Daniel Bernardi's (1996) work on D. W. Griffith's construction of "whiteness" is instructive. Although Griffith had little technical input in the making of *Martyrs of the Alamo* and Cabanne was not a filmmaker with Griffith's status or technical skill and vision, Cabanne's perspective on race followed very closely the contours of Griffith's work, especially *Birth of a Nation.*

In his discussion of Griffith's construction and projection of whiteness, Bernardi, borrowing from the earlier work of Tom Gunning (1991), discusses three aspects of Griffith's narrative system: tense, mood, and voice. "Tense" looks at flashbacks and ellipses as well as the continuity built into spatial setups across time; "mood" refers to the perspective one finds in the narration, the "point of view"; "voice" is the "ideology of the narrator," that sense of a narrator's presenting the film to an audience (Bernardi 1996:112).

According to Bernardi (1996:112), voice is most central to the production of whiteness. Whiteness references the presence of racial privilege that has been used to systematically reproduce hierarchical divisions in society (Bernardi 1996:104). White privilege has not been used exclusively against Mexicans but references a series of practices, actions, attitudes, and values that have reproduced whiteness and thus the identities of those who fall in and out of such a category and their concomitant privileges and displacements (see Hale 1998; Lipsitz 1998).

Film serves as an important genre for promulgating whiteness. For Bernardi (1996:112), three intermixed genres in particular are noted for their utility in constructing the voice of whiteness: "1) stories of non-white servitude; 2) stories of colonial love; and 3) stories of the divinity of the white family and serenity of the white woman." Each is found in *Martyrs of the Alamo.*

The presence of nonwhite servitude represents a critical outcome of the Battle of the Alamo. The early scenes with San Antonio under Mexican control, displaying the drunken and wild debauchery, quickly give way to civility "under the new regime." The lesson here is clear: the only way Mexicans will comport themselves in a civilized manner is when they are kept in place by the white, dominant social order. The Texans are justified, then, not only in their actions here but also in their general discourse of Manifest Destiny, since their dominance is required to keep the nonwhite savages under control and under thumb. Servitude, either formalized as in slave relations or practiced through various forms of Jim Crow segregation, promotes a social order.

The genre of colonial love, collapsed or intermixed with the third genre concerning the serenity of the white woman, also finds its place in *Martyrs of the Alamo*. The subplot of Deaf Smith and his beloved that runs alongside that of Suzanna Dickenson and the death of her husband serves to add an element of pathos, loss, and, more important, gender to the production of whiteness. Recall that *Martyrs of the Alamo* begins with a Mexican soldier making verbal advances to a white woman. Refusing those advances and seeking protection from her husband, it is the protection of women and the whiteness engendered by keeping them safe from miscegenation that initiates the early conflict in this film. But this theme recurs when Santa Anna takes the fair-haired love interest of Deaf Smith captive after the defeat of the Texans in the Alamo. This is no small feature for this film, for it is in rescuing her from the confinement of Santa Anna that Smith hears of the Mexicans' military plans and returns to Sam Houston with the information.

It is clear that political tension between Texans and Mexicans serves as the impetus for the Battle of the Alamo. *Martyrs of the Alamo,* on the other hand, extends this portrayal in ways that highlight the ideology of whiteness and male supremacy as the proper attitude toward a fabricated miscegenistic and tyrannous Mexican threat.

By aesthetically depicting Mexicans as Other, *Martyrs of the Alamo* maps the relationship between Mexicans and Anglos as one marked by radical difference, implicitly negating the historical past and the social present. This renders what otherwise cannot be stated, namely, an understanding and comprehension of the historically contingent political economy of the Mexican. This film serves as a visual manifestation of alterity, which itself conceals the class differentiation and social displacements being "worked out" during this period. Thus *Martyrs* is much more concerned with 1915 than 1836. It is by now clear that in 1915 the world map was changing radically, induced by foreign trade and investment, imperial conquest, and emerging technologies. But how does this international process relate to the projection of Mexicans?

Mexico was itself in the midst of an agrarian-based revolution in 1915, and while it was hardly in a position to threaten the national sovereignty of the United States, the revolution had the potential to affect the emerging international economy. Moreover, there are the various conflicts and disputes associated with the Texas Modern discussed earlier.

What, then, is the relationship between *Martyrs of the Alamo* and these issues? I contend that in this film we have a series of cinematic projections that mediate local, national, and international concerns. At the local level, the cinematic collapsing of the historical relationship between the United States and Mexico, in which the Battle of the Alamo plays a key role, into one of social and cultural difference serves to render Mexicans as radically Other. This projection places the burden and responsibility of the socioeconomic displacement of Mexicans on Mexicans themselves and posits their "uncivilized, inhuman, and socially threatening behavior" as the cause. But this rendering of Mexicans, and by default, Mexico, as radically Other serves a second purpose. It provides a visual code for the advancement of modernity whereby the need to control what is culturally foreign and socially different legitimates the imperial project itself. The production of the Mexican as uncivilized serves, as Trouillot (1991:32) reminds us, as an imaginary effort through which the West, by means of the trope of the West, constitutes its legitimacy.

One of the means through which *Martyrs* produces its own legitimacy is its petition to historical accuracy even as it negates the contours of the past. At issue is the manner in which this film is read by an audience as "historically real." "There is a thrill from opening to close," *Variety* reported in its review of October 1915.

> The Mexican Army and its handling, the stockade scenes, the rangers, the warfare, everything in connection with this frontier picture appears faithful, to the last detail, including Bowie's slow death by consumption and his last act of killing a Mexican with a knife he invented. (Quoted in Rimmer 1978:27)

Or, as the *New York Dramatic Review* wrote, "The picture is historically correct in every detail with each and every one of the well-known characters who took part in this memorable event, faithfully portrayed" (quoted in Rimmer 1978:27).

The film was met with much the same sentiment when it opened in San Antonio. The *San Antonio Express* reported on January 5, 1916:

> When D. W. Griffith conceived and directed [*sic*] the action of the "Birth of Texas or Martyrs of the Alamo" he had in mind not only historical data in detail and event that were highly dramatic, but he acquired an understanding of the motives, the very souls of the Texans who lived in San Antonio of old. . . . The theatre was filled to capacity last night by throngs who were moved to the very center of their beings by the stirring events which led to the Texans seizing the Alamo.

This intense and widespread reading of *Martyrs* in realist fashion is instructive, not for the way it accomplished its task, but for the way in which the real is shaped. Reading this film as historically accurate renders other interpretations of the Alamo story fictitious at best; it promulgates an understanding of the past even as it negates it. Such a project amplifies the narrative terrain for new ideas, values, and practices. The "hypothesis of realism," as Jameson (1992b:166) claims, "and its specific narrative forms construct their new world by *programming* their readers; by training them in new habits and practices, which amount to whole new subject-positions in a new kind of space" (emphasis in original).

In *Martyrs,* as in *Birth of a Nation* before it, the subject-position of the dominant is constructed over that of the racialized Other through the multiple negations of the past and the political economy of the present. The new habits, practices, and spaces are those of the Texas Modern that reproduce a socially constructed hierarchy of Anglo dominance and Mexican alterity that, in turn, legitimates the radical displacement of Mexican social life. Hidden in these various projections and displacements is that liberty and freedom, espoused by the now-formulaic cultural narrative of the Alamo, serve as the necessary fiction for the stigmatizing practices and ideologies actualized through the birth of the Texas Modern and the Alamo.

#### BEYOND THE MEXICAN QUESTION: MINOR FILMS, 1926 – 1956

If *Martyrs of the Alamo* serves to advance a new regime of control over the Mexican, later films reproduced this same element but through an increased projection of nationalist ideologies. That is, while every film on the Alamo rendered Mexicans through a particular Othering lens, films after 1915 expanded the nationalistic discourse of the United States through the trope of the Alamo. In effect, I want to articulate two moments of subject formation concerning the Alamo. The first, and here I depend on

Homi Bhabha's discussion of the stereotype and its regime of truth production, is found in *Martyrs of the Alamo*. This film sets the visual image
of the Mexican Other "as a population of degenerate types on the basis of
racial origin, in order to justify conquest and to establish systems of administration [the Texas Modern] and instruction [wage labor]" (Bhabha
1994:70). Such efforts, Bhabha rightly claims, attempt to situate the Other
in a state of fixity, suppressing other semic possibilities. This fixity of discourse denies the "play of difference" (Bhabha 1994:75) that might move
beyond the ordered representation, beyond the "always already" image of
the treacherous Mexican that under certain conditions may produce other
images or possibilities.

But there is a second moment that comes into being after 1915. As discursive tropes of the Other are fixed, as the always already overdetermined image of the treacherous Mexican is rendered "natural" through its
repetitious fashionings, the fixed image of the Mexican Other serves as a
foundation for other representations. With the semic divide between Anglos and Mexicans well established, later films are no longer solely concerned with the referent of the Mexican Other but reproduce various
other meanings through the play of this seme with other images and discourses.[5] That is, once the image of the Mexican Other at the Alamo is set,
once the historical "truth" of the event is "known," the Alamo—and its
Othering apparatus—serves as a discursive springboard for other issues.
It is as if the gaze of the dominant could focus solely on one subject at a
time: with the Mexican Other safely bound, the eyes shift to other subjects
and the making of other meanings. In this move, the treacherous Mexican
stereotype serves as the seemingly absent but always necessary ground for
other discursive formations.

Lest I be mistaken, let me reiterate that the Alamo always *is* a construction of the dominant that must use the Mexican as its vehicle for semic
production. But films after *Martyrs of the Alamo* used the image of the
Mexican Other to explore other issues. I do not mean to suggest that Mexicans, either native or foreign-born, were no longer in need of "administration and instruction." This is always the first-level reference of the
Alamo. What I *am* proposing is that by the 1920s the Mexican population
was fully incorporated, perhaps hegemonized, into the American social
structure and no longer required the same level of ideological containment
that they did earlier. Once fixed, the image of the treacherous Mexican became a matter of "fact," not ideology. The cultural revolution set off by the
Texas Modern—that tenuous moment of structural reconfiguration and
invention of new habits and practices between 1880 and 1920—had

prescibed the participation of Mexicans as mostly powerless, segregated, and wage-poor so as to no longer be a direct threat to American society and culture. At least not until the 1950s.

Between 1920 and 1956 five major films were made of the Alamo battle: *Davy Crockett at the Fall of the Alamo* (1926); *Heroes of the Alamo* (1937); *The Man from the Alamo* (1953); *Davy Crockett: King of the Wild Frontier* (1955); and *The Last Command* (1956). According to Brian Huberman and Ed Hugetz (1985), in a work highly congruent with mine, these films concerned a series of nationalist issues unique to their particular moment.[6] For example, *Heroes of the Alamo*, besides being planned in connection with the centenary of the Alamo battle, speaks to depression-era concerns; *The Man from the Alamo*, McCarthyism; *Davy Crockett: King of the Wild Frontier*, post–World War II disillusionment; and *The Last Command*, the military-industrial state.

*Davy Crockett at the Fall of the Alamo*, which survives only in fragmented form, was made by Anthony J. Xydia through his film company, Sunset Productions. Xydia was born in Tinos, Greece, in 1880, emigrated to the United States, and began working in the movie industry, forming Sunset Productions in 1921. In 1925 he initiated an effort to produce films based on well-known historical events, one of which was the Alamo. While Frank Thompson (1991: 31, 32) believes *Davy Crockett at the Fall of the Alamo* was aimed "at the lowest standards of a juvenile action audience," he also considers it "the best of a bad lot" of Xydia productions.

In 1931 Xydia retired from filmmaking, citing ill health as the reason, only to return to it a few years later to remake several of his earlier historical productions with sound. The first remake was *Heroes of the Alamo*. His intent was to premiere the film in 1936, to coincide with the centenary of the battle, but delays pushed the opening to September 1937. On its release, *Heroes of the Alamo* garnered wide praise, including accolades from James V. Allred, governor of Texas, and Leita Small, custodian of the Alamo for the DRT (Graham 1985).

Not much better than Xydia's earlier films, *Heroes of the Alamo* does provide a unique plot line—Don Graham (1985: 49) refers to it as one of the more "original" among Alamo films—by focusing on Almeron Dickenson instead of Bowie, Crockett, or Travis. Another peculiar twist is the seeming disinterest in the death scenes of the three heroes. While Bowie, Travis, and Crockett succumb in battle, there is nothing particularly triumphant or notable about their deaths. The result is that the "common man" is made central to the story, "thereby accomplishing . . . a democratic presentation of death: all defenders of the Alamo are equal" (Graham 1985:49). As Thompson (1991:39) states, although in other Alamo films the heroes die for Liberty and Freedom, in *Heroes of the Alamo* they "want only to preserve their homes and families," not unlike depression-era sentiments. One interesting anomaly of the film occurs the evening before the final siege when the Alamo defenders sing "The Yellow Rose of Texas" as they sit around the campfire. The song had not been written in 1836 and refers to a mythical figure associated with the Battle of San Jacinto (which had not yet been fought), not the Alamo.

The next film on the Alamo appeared in the early 1950s, one of three released during this decade. *The Man from the Alamo,* which premiered in July 1953, takes its initial plot from the legend of Moses Rose, the one man who supposedly abandoned the Alamo when given a chance by Travis. The legend of Rose stems from an 1873 article in the *Texas Almanac* titled "An Escape from the Alamo." According to the author of the article, William Zuber, Moses Rose was a native of France who resided in Nacogdoches. Zuber's father, Abraham Zuber, became acquainted with Rose around 1827. Supposedly, Rose was about forty-five in 1830, therefore about fifty-one in 1836. In Zuber's story Rose left the Alamo when Travis gave the defenders an opportunity to leave before the final assault. Rose then made his way to East Texas and the Zuber family cabin, where he was cared for after his arduous flight.

According to J. Frank Dobie, until the publication of Zuber's story in 1873 there had been no discussion of someone escaping from the Alamo (Dobie, Boatright, and Ransom 1939:9). Nor had there been any information on Travis's final speech or of the line drawn in the Texas sand that has become such a critical element of the Alamo myth. Yet Paul Hutton (1986:13), who has written extensively on the Alamo, states that Zuber's claim (of the line and the speech), denied by most academic historians while blindly accepted by popular writers, was seemingly verified by R. B. Blake in 1939 after he discovered Rose's 1838 testimony in Nacogdoches court records. Hutton also reports that Walter Lord, author of *A Time to Stand,* discovered an 1876 interview with Suzanna Dickenson in which she recalls one man, named Ross (could it be Rose?), who left the mission when given the opportunity by Travis.[7] The Zuber story provides one of the more interesting contradictions of the Alamo myth. Clearly, if Hutton is correct, the entire mythology of the line drawn in the sand comes to us from Rose through Zuber through Blake.[8] And yet it is only because of Rose's supposed cowardice, leaving his comrades behind to die, that we have this story at all.

Before *A Man from the Alamo* was made, news that a film about Rose was being considered drew the ire of many in Texas. Velma Vandervoort, speaking for the DRT, responded, "I am very distressed that the Motion Picture fraternity has scraped the barrel to the point that they have to use Moses Rose as the hero of the picture" (quoted in Graham 1985:52). But *A Man from the Alamo* uses the Alamo only as a springboard for another story. The Rose-like character, John Stroud, played by Glenn Ford, is selected by the drawing of a black bean to return to his town of Oxbow to protect local families from marauding Mexican bandits. On his arrival, Stroud discovers that the "Mexicans" are actually Anglo Texans disguised as Mexicans and he quickly maneuvers his way to their capture. With this task accomplished, he journeys to San Jacinto to join the forces of Sam Houston. The film, then, despite its early connection to Rose, used the backdrop of the Alamo to tell another story of bravery and patriotism.

The most well known of the minor films on the Alamo is Walt Disney's *Davy Crockett: King of the Wild Frontier.* Its portrayal of the Alamo story, both romantic and mythic, inspired a generation of coonskin hat wearers with heroic images of martyrdom. The movie was originally made in three segments, each depicting a phase of Crockett's life, and broadcast on Disney's new television series. The first segment, broadcast on December 5, 1954, portrayed Crockett's adventures in the Creek Indian War; the second installment, shown in January 1955, covered his tenure in Congress; and the final episode, "Davy Crockett at the Alamo," was televised on February 23, 1955.

The shows were an immediate success, making Fess Parker, the actor who portrayed Crockett, an overnight celebrity. The one regret of the many followers was that Walt Disney broadcast the Alamo segment showing the death of Crockett before preparing other episodes of the show. But Disney could not have anticipated the furor the show would create. By spring 1955 Crockett fever was so strong that Disney had the three episodes edited into one feature film, releasing it on June 5 as *Davy Crockett: King of the Wild Frontier.* Perhaps because of Parker's slow yet stately manner, Crockett became an instant icon. No longer "half-horse and half-alligator," Crockett emerged as "the highest ideal of American heroism and virtue" (Thompson 1991:51).

There is little that is historical in this film; instead, it builds on the mythic and heroic qualities of the Crockett legend. Even in relation to the battle, there are no women featured, and an occasional Mexican appears but only during the fighting. The most famous scene occurs at the close of the movie. Filmed several times over, the fadeout shot depicts Crockett, the last of the heroes still alive, standing tall above a horde of Mexicans, swinging his rifle, Ol' Betsy, at the attacking soldiers.

For Huberman and Hugetz, this film speaks to the social and political disillusionment initiated by the post–World War II, McCarthy-era mood. At some level they are correct. Crockett, as portrayed by Parker, is an optimistic fellow less concerned about his ego and leadership and serving "primarily as a much-needed symbol of hope and morale" (Thompson 1991:55–56).

The last Alamo film of this decade, released on August 3, 1955, in the midst of the Crockett furor, is *The Last Command*. This film owes much of its presence, in several ways, to John Wayne, although he did not produce it. For a number of years, at least since the 1940s, Wayne had wanted to make a film about the Alamo. While still under contract with Republic Studios, whose president was Herbert J. Yates, Wayne began investigating locations in Mexico, Central America, and the United States. He even enlisted the support of his colleague and friend James Edward Grant, a Republic screenwriter, to produce a script. But Yates refused to give Wayne money to make the film, and when Wayne's contract expired in 1951, he left Republic Studios. Grant's script remained the property of Republic, however, and Yates soon made *The Last Command* from Wayne's initial effort.

*The Last Command* features Sterling Hayden as Jim Bowie and, like earlier productions, returns to portraying the Alamo story from the perspective of Bowie, Travis, and Crockett. Although Hayden's performance was "solemn" and "wooden" (Graham 1985:54; Hutton 1986:16), it was called "the best of the Alamo films" (Hutton 1986:16). A striking feature of the film is the role of Santa Anna, played by J. Carrol Naish, who is portrayed not as a "blustering cartoon" but someone Bowie could "respect, talk to, and finally disagree with strongly enough to oppose in combat" (Graham 1985:54).

*The Last Command* was directed by Frank Lloyd, who made the original *Mutiny on the Bounty,* with Grant's script rewritten by Warren Duff. Its $2 million budget resulted in an impressive film. The film is influenced by Amelia Williams's portrait of Travis as "impetuous, hot headed and arrogant" (Hutton 1986:16). Interestingly, publicity concerning the film barely mentioned the Alamo, except for those releases targeted for Texas audiences (Thompson 1991). The rationale may have been that the film focuses more on the events leading up to the battle than the actual siege. In fact, a major portion of the film depicts Bowie's growing involvement with Texas politics, including an early friendship with Santa Anna. *The Last*

*Command,* in part because of its lack of flair and one-dimensional portrait of the Alamo events, played and faded from public view with little fanfare. But by 1955 John Wayne was already enmeshed in preproduction activities and script revisions, along with Grant who left Republic Studios with Wayne, on his own Alamo film.

## JOHN WAYNE'S *The Alamo*

Wayne's *The Alamo* is the apex in Alamo film production. Not only was it the most extravagant and expensive Alamo production to date, it was also the last attempt to portray the 1836 battle in modernist terms. The decade before the release of *The Alamo* was marked by the craze over Davy Crockett as well as the release of *The Last Command.* Such intense and persistent interest in the Alamo, albeit with different ideological emphases, signals a deep crisis in the American social and political scene. While Wayne's film certainly evolved from his own political vision, that vision was founded on the social currents of the 1950s. Any discussion of *The Alamo,* therefore, cannot ignore its twin formative elements: Wayne's politics and the sociopolitical moment from which it emerges.

Wayne's devotion to the Alamo, verging on religious obsession (Wills 1997), dates back to the late 1940s. When Wayne left Republic Studios, he and his associate, Robert Fellows, formed Wayne-Fellows Productions. After only two years Fellows left the partnership, and Wayne formed his own company, Batjac Productions. Although he made more than nine pictures in the 1950s, Wayne was primarily occupied with arranging the financing, location, and personnel for *The Alamo.*

One of the biggest decisions facing Wayne was where to shoot his movie. Realizing money was a major factor, he scouted locations in Mexico, Panama, and Peru. During this period, news of Wayne's plans to shoot *The Alamo* in Mexico was spreading. This outraged some in Texas, including the DRT, which let it be known that if the film were made in Mexico it would be boycotted in Texas (Huberman 1992). It appears they had forgotten that at the time of the 1836 battle the Alamo was located in Mexican territory. In the end, Wayne decided to make his movie in Texas on the 22,000-acre ranch of James T. "Happy" Shahan, six miles north of Brackettville and about ninety miles west of San Antonio. The Shahan ranch proved to be an ideal site, especially when Shahan offered his services as contractor for the construction of the sets.

Wayne's goal was to make the most authentic film he could. And although it is better than most, it accomplished this goal in only one way, set design. The liberties taken by the script, in particular, the relationship between Bowie, Travis, and Crockett and the character of Flaca, the love interest of Crockett, as well as several major blunders in terms of Texas history and geography (the Río Bravo does not run through San Antonio de Béxar as the film states), resulted in a highly fictionalized telling of the story.

The crew reconstructed, nearly in total, the Alamo mission. Alfred Ybarra, Wayne's art director, designed the mission church to scale and its surrounding buildings and walls to 75 percent of their size. It is estimated that the mission complex alone used nearly four hundred thousand adobe bricks, not including those for constructing the sets of the town. Such a task took the coordinated efforts of the town of Brackettville and, in an ironic twist of fate, required the importation of Mexican laborers to produce more bricks since American workers did not have the requisite skills to do so (Clark and Andersen 1995:29).

Filming *The Alamo* was a major task. Wayne served as director and producer and portrayed Davy Crockett as well (see Fig. 5.4). His original plan was to take the innocuous role of Sam Houston, but United Artists insisted that he appear in a starring role if they were to be a major financial contributor. Shooting began in September 1959 and lasted until mid-December of that year. Despite delays—weather, fire, and the murder of one of the extras by a jealous boyfriend—the film proceeded relatively on schedule.

The production was, in some ways, a community event. Workers from Brackettville and Eagle Pass, on the U.S.-Mexico border, were used as support staff, and local Mexican personalities from San Antonio were used as extras in the film. The cantina scene in particular drew on the talent of Mexican-American artists: it featured Rosita Fernandez, a well-known singer; Willie and Teresa Champion, who had already garnered an international reputation for their flamenco dancing and guitar playing; and a troupe of Mexican dancers featuring Alma Reyes (see Fig. 5.5). Bill Daniel, brother of the Texas governor, was also given a role and listed in the credits. The arrival of the key actors—Lawrence Harvey as Travis, Richard Widmark as Bowie, and Richard Boone as Sam Houston, along with Frankie Avalon, Chill Wills, Linda Cristal, and others—was celebrated with parades, parties, and, in the case of Harvey, honorary sheriff awards in seven Texas counties.

The release of the film was even more of an occasion. It was premiered at the Woodlawn Theatre in San Antonio on October 24, 1960. Attended by nearly all the major actors involved, it also included governors from seven states, a U.S. senator, numerous mayors, and motion picture executives. Most of San Antonio was carried away with the enthusiasm of the moment, spurred on by the interviews and parties arranged by the public

FIGURE 5.4

*John Wayne as Davy Crockett, Joseph Calleia as Juan Seguín, and Linda Cristal as Flaca. Photograph courtesy of Brian Huberman from his personal collection.*

relations people. Included in the events was a citation given Wayne by the DRT, a thirty-foot cake in the shape of the Alamo, a square dance with twenty thousand in attendance, ceremonies to honor the Alamo heroes, and numerous parades. The press kit alone was 184 pages.

Realizing this film would require special attention, Wayne hired the publicist Russell Birdwell, who had managed the publicity for *Gone with the Wind,* to work on this project. Birdwell did a masterful, yet controversial, job, including an advertisement in *Life* magazine titled "There Were No Ghost Writers at the Alamo," that coincided with that year's elections and preached the virtues of liberty and personal freedom. He had two other ideas: the United States would posthumously award the Medal of Honor to those who died at the Alamo; and a major summit of the world

FIGURE 5.5
*Alma Reyes with John Wayne after the cantina scene. Photograph courtesy of Alma Reyes from her personal collection.*

powers would be convened within the Alamo walls (Clark and Andersen 1995:115). Fortunately, neither of these plans was received well or came to fruition.

While the opening was a huge success, the film did not fare so well. Reviews were mixed, although in some cases predictable. The DRT praised the film for its message, representation, and authenticity; film critics considered it too long—it was more than three hours—and boring. Its various subplots and tangential scenes—the romantic encounter between Crockett and Flaca, played by Linda Cristal, that allowed Wayne to pursue his leading lady; and the birthday party scene for Lisa Dickenson, portrayed by Wayne's daughter, Aisa—took away from the breadth of the more interesting battle shots. A goal of Wayne's, from at least 1948, *The Alamo* was a Hollywood production of the first order but had little cinematic creativity. The expense of its production and the vastness of its publicity—even knocking on the doors of the Academy Award nominators suggesting that a vote against the Alamo was a vote against patriotism (Wills 1997:227)—fell flat and resulted in great disappointment. In the end, *The Alamo,* nominated for seven Academy Awards, including best picture, received only one, a technical award for sound.

In terms of content, the film has little to do with 1836 and more to do with Wayne's vision of Cold War nationalism told through the idiom of the Alamo. From this perspective, the movie is instructive for understanding the height and vastness of the Alamo's range of meanings as well as for anticipating the demise of the Alamo as trope.

### PATRIOTISM, COMMIES, AND THE MEXICAN OTHER

Forty-five years had passed between Cabanne's film and Wayne's. During this period, the United States had suffered through two world wars, a depression, and a war in Korea and was on the brink of another war in Vietnam. If *The Martyrs of the Alamo* was concerned primarily with the Mexican Other, Wayne's projection of Mexicans is less clear. *The Alamo* required the idiom of the 1836 battle, but Wayne's cinematic narrative no longer concerned itself principally with the "instruction and administration" of the Mexican as much as with the character and quality of liberty, democracy, and nationalism. This is not to say that Wayne's film is neutral concerning the projection of Mexicans. It is not. What I suggest is that his movie is shot through a bifocal lens: one that allows Wayne to explore a number of issues that lay at some length from the putative events of the Battle of the Alamo while at the same time remain focused on the characters and social actors that appear on the Texas stage in 1836. This is possible, I believe, because the Alamo story is by this time a formulaic narrative that Wayne fills with his own ideological concerns. While he claims to be concerned with reproducing an "authentic" version of the story, it is a reproduction forged from his understanding of the ideological struggles of his moment.

If Garry Wills (1997:302) can claim that John Wayne embodies the American myth, then the Alamo serves as one of the primal scenes of American birth. It had become a master symbol. Like all polysemic structures, the Alamo, born from the overdetermined desire to write Mexicans as tyrannous and Other, now reached beyond this initial, but always present, text to inform other tales through this now-classic narrative. And while Wayne's rendition of this tale went to great lengths to represent Mexicans in a much better light than did his predecessors, the tropic and binary structure of this primal scene could not be overcome, as I will shortly demonstrate.

For Wayne, the Alamo was an archetypal American tale. He used it to preach his views on patriotism and anticommunism. For instance, speaking through the character of Crockett, Wayne says the following when he meets Travis for the first time.

> Republic. I like the sound of the word. Means people can live free, talk free, go or come, buy or sell. . . . Some words give you a feeling. Republic is one of those words that makes me tight in the throat.

For Huberman and Hugetz (1985), the Alamo allows Wayne to express his understanding of freedom, responsibility, and the relationship of leaders to those they lead. Travis, the educated and sophisticated high-class southerner, is a step above the rest: he frowns on his men and the citizens of the town, claiming, "I am better than that rabble"; and he is disgusted by Bowie's drunkenness in the early part of the film. Bowie, for his part, is the tough, hard-minded leader. While serious like Travis, his leadership style depends on the rugged qualities of his persona. Crockett, on the other hand, is both the country populist who can outpunch and outdrink any of his followers and, in his city clothes, the streetwise, smart-thinking former congressman who can talk his way through any situation. He mediates between Travis's superior attitude and Bowie's stubbornness by seeking a common ground that can unite each of them. At various points in the film, conflict erupts between Travis and Bowie only to have Crockett intervene, understanding their positions and values and at the same time providing a perspective that underscores their commonality (Huberman and Hugetz 1985).

Through these figures Wayne addresses the tension between the freedom of the individual and one's responsibility to the collective. Freedom,
for Wayne, is the freedom to be oneself. But such freedom is tenuous, open
to infringement by more powerful forces. As the narrator in Brian Huberman's (1992) documentary on the making of the Alamo states:

> The question of Wayne's capacity to be a leader coincides with the film's
> portrayal of Crockett as a man torn between the responsibility of lead-
> ership and the desire to be one of the men. Crockett's changing costume
> reflects this contradictory position. The frontier outfit suggests a belief
> in the rugged individual; the fancy city clothes are an expression of
> Crockett's social and political beliefs. Wayne's shifting position regard-
> ing the relationship of the people to their leaders reflects a major con-
> cern of Americans in the 1950s, of how big business and government
> might control their lives.

I believe Huberman is correct in his interpretation of leadership, but what
if we move from understanding these characters as representative of leadership styles to one that explores their social location in a democratic society? It was no secret that Wayne understood the true American patriot
to be an anticommunist. So deep were his convictions that when the
movie failed to receive the critical praise he believed it merited, Wayne
blamed the "Commies" (Wills 1997:227). If Wayne's *Alamo* is a statement
against communism, then the class structure endemic to a capitalist democratic society merits serious consideration as a subtext of this film.

Consider Travis. While he claims to have come to Texas with just
two uniforms, it is quite clear that he sees himself as a member of the elite
class, better than the common "rabble" who serve under him (his finely
starched and tailored uniform, while perhaps limited to two, further be-
speaks his social position). Bowie's class markings are equally visible. He
is one of the landed elite, and his comportment is much different from
Travis's. In some ways one can sense the conflict between Travis and
Bowie as emerging from their different social locations. Travis, the consummate aristocrat and educated southerner, signifies a very different relationship to wealth and land than the old ranching elite that Bowie represents (this tension does indeed have historical resonances in Texas as I
described in my discussion of the Texas Modern). Crockett, quite apart
from Travis and Bowie, serves as the fast-thinking individual who has
achieved a level of stature, not from education or land, but from his own
ingenuity (see chap. 6). He is the idealized version of the common man

who can, as he claims, "make a buck or two," as well as maneuver his way to Congress. And when the time arrives, he moves on ready to invent himself in another place. Whatever challenges he meets, Crockett overcomes them through perseverance and self-confidence; he is the epitome of the pull-yourself-up-by-the-bootstraps man. Together, Travis, Bowie, and Crockett serve as critical reminders of the dominant U.S. ideology in light of the communist threat: private property, status, and personal liberty that allow for the fullest expression of individual freedom. The united front of the three men signifies the cherished values of American capitalist democracy that most certainly had to be the object of communist desire, at least in Wayne's mind. As Wills (1997:200) writes, one of Wayne's dreams was that "the Alamo would be a knockout blow to communism." This, of course, was congruent with Wayne's personal biography.

Anticommunist activity kept Wayne in the news during his earlier career. In 1948 he served as president of the Motion Picture Alliance for the Preservation of American Ideals. It was the Alliance that invited the House Committee on Un-American Activities to Hollywood in 1944, leading to the investigations of actors and writers (Wills 1997). And his films such as *The Sands of Iwo Jima* (1949), *Flying Leathernecks* (1951), and *Big Jim McLain* (1952) cannot escape their propagandistic slant. But Will's skepticism about Wayne's patriotism serves as an interesting counterpoint to Wayne's career. All the while Wayne was making his highly charged patriotic films in the forties and fifties, Wills claims, he was busy putting "careerism" ahead of his own military service. Wayne's patriotic, anticommunist role was "to emerge after the battle" to "shoot the wounded" (Wills 1997:197).

Despite Wayne's ideological concerns, *The Alamo* is a movie that must still be shot through the lens of the 1836 battle. As such, the story of the Alamo can never escape the Mexican question, for Wayne or any other telling. While it is clear that Wayne's film is principally about liberty and nationalism in the Cold War era, the ambivalent projection of Mexicans returns full force through this film's narrative content. While on the one hand Wayne's projection of Mexicans is perhaps the most neutral of all Alamo films, it is, on the other, a projection that equally captures the ambiguous social location of Mexicans, Mexican Americans, and other ethnic groups during this period.

Wayne no longer portrays the Mexican army in general and Santa Anna in particular through the racist imagery found in Cabanne's film. Let me even suggest that Mexicans fare better in this movie than in any other, at least on its initial reception. Graham (1985:50), citing as evidence how the Mexican army was portrayed as "a marching mass of choir boys," suggests that by 1960 the cultural climate had changed, making it unfashionable to "resort to the simple racist contrasts" of earlier films. This is further attested when, in the midst of battle, the Gambler, one of Crockett's Tennesseans, turns to his compatriot and says: "I was proud of 'em [Mexican soldiers]. Speaks well for men that so many are ready to die for what they believe in." On this point, Hutton (1986:18) refers to Wayne's high regard for "Hispanic culture," including the fact that all three of his wives were Latinas. Wayne even portrays, although without character development, Mexicans fighting inside the Alamo alongside the Texans. And his depictions of Santa Anna as a "gallant gentleman" (Hutton 1986:18) took some by surprise. But Mexicans and Mexico never leave one's ideological sight at the Alamo, despite Wayne's conciliatory portrait of them.

Contrasting Wayne's depiction of Mexicans with Cabanne's in *Martyrs of the Alamo* brings into relief the vivid differences between the racial politics of 1915 and their refinement by 1960. Recall that in *Martyrs* Mexicans are scripted as sexually threatening, opium-consuming savages whose personal comportment requires the controlling presence of the Texan. Wayne's film has none of this. By 1960 the Mexican is brave, valiant, and gallant; he is no longer the ogling primitive featured by Cabanne but one whom Bowie can trust. But, as the structured slot of the Mexican in the Alamo narrative necessitates, Mexicans still signify the antithesis of the Texas defenders. Consider, for example, the actions of Jorge Ferretis, director of the Cinema Department for the government of Mexico, who denounced the film and refused to allow its release in Mexico.[9] What, then, serves as the source of this antithesis? It is here that Wayne's cinematic story line is important, since the film's portrayal of the conflict between Texans and Mexicans reveals something of the relationship between Anglos and Mexicans in 1960. If, according to Wayne's film, Mexicans do not demonstrate improper behavior, if they do not lack valor or bravery, how are we to understand the Mexican question in this production? By way of exploring this issue I want to examine the various Mexican characters present in this film: Santa Anna and his forces, Juan Seguín and his cohort, and the women in the town of San Antonio de Béxar, including Flaca and the entertainers in the cantina.

Beginning with the Mexican forces, we are indeed led to believe, with Graham, that Mexicans are portrayed almost without difference. They act bravely, die with dignity, and comport themselves, especially Santa Anna, with utmost chivalry.[10] Their habits and practices, the exterior manifestations of culture, are likened to those of the Alamo defenders. Where does difference lie? According to this film, the Mexican forces differ ideologically. As enforcers of Santa Anna's rule, they, like him, are aligned to a regime of "tyranny" that seeks to destroy freedom and liberty and oppress the citizens of his country. Recall the opening text of the movie:

> Generalissimo Santa Anna was sweeping north across Mexico toward them, crushing all who opposed his tyrannical rule. They now faced the decision that all men in all times must face[,] . . . the eternal choice of men . . . to endure oppression or resist.

That which separates Santa Anna and his men from the Texans, according to Wayne, is political ideology.

The same cannot be said for the women of the town.[11] These women appear primarily in the cantina scene, where they are "overcoded" for their cultural differences: style of music, dance, and attire. But they are equally marked by their sexuality: they are loose, close-dancing women who spend the night singing, drinking, and having their way with men. Unlike the Mexican soldiers, and in keeping with stereotypical representations of gender, these women are scripted without political sentiment. In fact, their frolicking with the Tennesseans would lead us to believe they either side with the Texans or are totally oblivious to the ensuing events. Alternatively, Flaca, with whom Crockett has a brief romantic interlude, also fits this portrayal. Her attire is demure and low-key, but her corseted body cannot be missed and quickly draws Crockett's attention. Although she is the only Mexican woman to present a political view, it is personalized through her family history and then dropped as she leaves town before Santa Anna's arrival.

The only other group of Mexican women appear when LaSoya, one of the defenders, is killed in an early skirmish outside the Alamo walls. Travis has just ordered one of his men to pass the news to the slain man's family when he notices their presence. Two elderly women, outfitted in long, dark dresses with *rebozos* covering their heads, stand silently.

Except for Flaca, the women of San Antonio are portrayed as ideologically neutral, caught between both forces with little to gain from the clash. And while this is fairly accurate in relation to the historical residents of San Antonio de Béxar, their nonpartisan portrayal leaves only cultural differences as that which distinguishes them from the Texans.

Finally, we have the character of Juan Seguín (see Fig. 5.6). The histor-

FIGURE 5.6

*Joseph Calleia as Juan Seguín. Photograph courtesy of Brian Huberman from his personal collection.*

ical Seguín served with the Texas forces inside the Alamo until he was sent by Travis as a courier to Fannin (de la Teja 1991:79). Wayne, however, depicts Seguín as a member of the Mexican landed elite, the mayor of San Antonio, and friend of Bowie.[12] Early in the film, when Seguín offers important details on the position of Santa Anna's forces, Travis explodes with suspicion:

I'm sorry, Señor Seguín, but as a civilian you cannot realize how worthless this sort of information is: some Indian told some vaquero. But anyway, thank you, sir, and good day.

BOWIE: Travis, you know the Seguíns are absolutely reliable.

SEGUÍN TO BOWIE: You'll excuse me.

TRAVIS: I make no personal affront, Señor Seguín. But I cannot make a plan of action based on third-hand rumors.

SEGUÍN: I do not take personal affront, Colonel Travis, else I should be forced to act other than to just bid you good day.

TRAVIS TO LIEUTENANT DICKENSON [later, in his quarters]: A true gentleman, Seguín. I dislike being rude to him.

There is historical precedence here as the historical Travis was mistrustful of Mexicans in town, but the idea of using Seguín, who actually served under Travis, to portray this aspect of the narrative is troublesome. It is only later when Seguín arrives with a group of volunteers from Gonzales, both Texan and Mexican, that Travis changes his views.

It is Seguín, I suggest, who manifests most clearly the ambiguous position of Mexicans in this film. The Mexican army, besides their deep ideological differences, even if they demonstrate courage, are still the "enemy." The Mexican women from San Antonio serve as an entertaining sideshow, both for Crockett's men and for viewers. (See Figs. 5.7, 5.8.) Even Flaca's romantic interlude with Crockett distracts from the main narrative. But how are we to understand Seguín? He believes in the same political principles as Travis, Crockett, and Bowie. He offers information against Santa Anna. Ideologically, he is one of the defenders (not to mention that the historical Seguín *was* a defender). But, and herein lies his major mark of difference, he is a Mexican.

I suggest that the overall portrayal of Mexicans in *The Alamo* turns on differences between culture and ideology. At one level Graham is correct. Absent are the features of radical Otherness found in earlier Alamo films. But in its place we find an equally disturbing construction that is mapped in the following manner.

|                     | *Mexican Forces* | *Mexican Women*                | *Seguín* |
|---------------------|------------------|--------------------------------|----------|
| Identity:           | Mexican          | Mexican                        | Mexican  |
| Political position: | Enemy            | Neutral                        | Texan    |
| Role in film:       | Enemy            | Subject of male Cultural gaze  | Other    |

FIGURE 5.7

*Chill Wills and one of the dancers from the cantina scene. Photograph courtesy of
Brian Huberman from his personal collection.*

At one level we can negate the depiction of Santa Anna and his soldiers simply because there is no way of telling this narrative without scripting them as the "enemy." The portrayal of Mexican women, at least in the cantina scene, is a gendered and racialized portrayal as they serve as the desired objects of Crockett's men (see Fig. 5.9). However, the male gaze of the Alamo defenders dismisses them as ideologically neutral and therefore, at some level, harmless to their cause. Seguín, on the other hand, is an issue. His only measure of difference is his Mexican identity, which, according to this film, suffices to raise suspicion. Even when Seguín sacrifices his status as a Mexican citizen by opposing Santa Anna, he remains suspect. He may share the values and ideas of the Texans, but he remains a "cultural" Other.

We learn from this film that regardless of one's comportment, regardless of one's values, regardless of one's political stance, cultural difference constitutes Otherness. I suggest that the America Wayne believes in is an America of singular identity forged from ideological and cultural conformity. There is little room, if any, in Wayne's *Alamo* for the interpellation of difference; there is little room for dissenting Americans, unpatriotic Americans, and, need I say, Mexican Americans. Despite his notions of personal liberty and individual freedom, Wayne's social vision is rooted in conformity and acquiescence to a monolithic social order that requires the abandonment of cultural markers of difference. Perhaps it is no accident that Wayne's wives were foreign-born Latinas, since to be American-born and Latina is, it appears, a contradiction for him.

John Wayne's *The Alamo* tells us little about the events of 1836. It does, however, serve as a reminder, perhaps better, a rejoinder, to the Cold War politics of the 1950s. But if communism and its threat serves as one focus of Wayne's film, why is it that cultural difference, specifically, Mexican-American cultural difference, continues to inform this film? Here my metaphor of the bifocal lens continues to serve an interpretive purpose. From

FIGURE 5.8
*Alma Reyes in the cantina scene. Photograph courtesy of Teresa Champion from her personal collection.*

FIGURE 5.9
*Teresa Champion dancing to the music of Willie "El Curo" Champion in the cantina scene. Photograph courtesy of Teresa Champion from her personal collection.*

a distance, communism, imaginary or real, is understood as a threat to capitalist democracy and the United States as a nation. There is no question that this film is deeply nationalistic in a broad, international sense. But nationalism plays an internally, close-up, normalizing role as well, which points to *The Alamo*'s deep concern with cultural difference. I am reminded of Bhabha's (1990a:297) classic statement: "The scraps, patches, and rags of daily life must be repeatedly turned into the signs of a national culture, while the very act of the narrative performance interpellates a growing circle of national subjects." Here the ragged and patched clothing of Crockett's Tennesseans and especially their mixed views and understandings of Mexican history have coalesced into a national symbol of liberty and freedom. Yet this production negates the political and cultural sentiments, the "patches" and "rags" of individual expression, within the discursive locale of the nation.

It is clear how Cold War politics informed Wayne's nationalism, but what conditions continue in the 1950s that require the circumscription of the cultural Other? This question is critical for understanding not only Wayne's *Alamo* but also the continued presence of the Alamo as an American object of cultural memory more generally from 1880 to 1960. I want to defer a sustained answer to this question until the next chapter, as

Wayne's *Alamo,* along with the entire corpus of Alamo movies, participates in a broader logic of cultural production that cannot be attended to
without specific attention to the place of "patriotism" and the "heroic" in
American society. My point is that the films discussed above are products
not only of their historical milieu as shot through the cinematic lens of
their makers but also of a history of patriotic and heroic discourse that
emerged in the nineteenth century. This brings me, as it did Wayne, to
Davy Crockett as the embodied icon of patriotism, liberty, and modern
nationalism in the United States.

# 6

## WHY DOES DAVY LIVE?

### MODERNITY AND ITS HEROICS

Since shortly before his death at the Alamo in 1836 and continuing to the present, David Crockett, former congressman from Tennessee, writer, and adventurer, has captured the imagination of people across the United States. Not one to hide from controversy in life, the exact means of his death have been disputed since 1836. The details of this debate—whether he died fighting or was executed with a handful of others after the siege had ended—are addressed more fully below. Here I want to claim that the question, How did Davy die?—suggested by the title of Dan Kilgore's (1978) book—provides only a partial understanding of the Crockett mystique. Any discussion of Crockett's death must be informed not solely by the details of the 1836 battle but equally, even fundamentally, by uncovering the social and historical conditions that gave shape to this debate as it emerged over time. Here I am concerned with two critical issues. Debates over Crockett's death already assume a heroic "Davy," the enshrinement of an individual life that is itself the result of particular historical conjunctions. Restoring these conjunctions—the "raw materials" from which Davy and heroic figures like him are constructed— is my first concern. This query entails that we move beyond the legends and formalized features of the heroic into the realm of the social so as to understand the historical conditions of hero making itself. Once done, my second concern revolves around the specific meanings of the heroic Davy. I suggest that formalized projections such as the heroic Davy, re-created over time, serve to advance a number of disparate ideological positions that require critical attention. Thus any discussion concerning how Davy died must come to terms with why, after 1836, he continued to live.

### DAVID CROCKETT: THE LIFE

Untangling the maze of facts concerning David Crockett the historical figure from Davy Crockett the legend is a task well beyond the scope of any single book chapter. Fortunately, there are several scholars who have carefully and critically attended to this work.[1] The job of distinguishing fact from fiction is all the more difficult in this case because in many ways it was Crockett the man who created Davy the legend. If we accept that one definition of the modern individual is the ability to project oneself as "image," as an already formalized self, then Crockett serves as an early, partial example of this process. In fact, Andrew Paul Hutton (1987:xxi) states that Crockett was one of the first Americans "to make a living off his celebrity status."

David Crockett was born on August 17, 1786, in Greene County, Tennessee, to John and Rebecca Hawkins Crockett. John Crockett was a poor man, having lost his homestead to various debtors, who cared for his family by taking a series of odd jobs. Young David began working, like many of his frontier compatriots, at an early age. At twelve, for example, he was hired out by his father to help drive cattle to Rockbridge County, Virginia. After completing his contractual obligations, he was detained against his will and forced to work until he managed to escape and make his way back home.

On August 14, 1806, David married Mary (Polly) Finley in Jefferson County, Tennessee. After moving several times, Crockett and his wife and sons, John Wesley and William, settled in Franklin County, Tennessee, and there he joined the local militia. During this time, Crockett served under Andrew Jackson, who was to become his political adversary in later years (Shackford 1994:27). Crockett took part in several skirmishes of the Creek Indian Wars, including the battle of Tallussahatchee, on November 3, 1813, and continued to serve in various capacities in the militia.

Before Crockett was elected to the U.S. Congress and came to national prominence, he held several local offices. In 1817 he was justice of the peace in Lawrence County, Tennessee; in 1818 he was town commissioner of Lawrenceburg and continued to serve in the militia. In August 1821 he won a seat in the Tennessee state legislature. Crockett was reelected to this position in 1823 and completed his last term in October 1824.

After an unsuccessful bid for Congress in 1825, Crockett was elected to the House of Representatives in 1827 and reelected in 1829. He was an outspoken legislator, especially on issues related to public land policy in the West. It was on this issue that he broke ranks with his Tennessee delegation—as well as with Andrew Jackson, who was elected president in 1828—which resulted in his failed bid for reelection in 1831.

By this time, however, Crockett's celebrity status was already garnering national attention. In 1831 the play "The Lion of the West," by James Kirk Paulding, opened at the Park Theatre in New York City. The main character, Nimrod Wildfire, played by James Hackett, was a "thinly veiled imitation of Crockett" who spoke the lines later taken up by Crockett himself: "I can jump higher—squat lower—dive deeper—stay longer under and come out drier!" (Montgomery 1989:60).

In 1833 Matthew St. Clair Clark, a clerk in the House of Representatives, published an "unauthorized" biography of Crockett, *The Life and Adventures of Colonel David Crockett of West Tennessee.*[2] This book, along with Paulding's play, advanced Crockett's reputation and aided his reelection to Congress later that year. In response to this hyperbolic yet "authentic" work, Crockett published his autobiography, *A Narrative of the Life of Davy Crockett of the State of Tennessee,* in February 1834, ghostwritten by his congressional colleague, Thomas Chilton. Although Crockett dismissed the earlier biography, James A. Shackford and Stanley J. Folmsbee (1973) claim that it contains information that only Crockett could have provided. Crockett's autobiography is a more serious telling, not the "boisterous yarning" (Shackford and Folmsbee 1973:xii) of Clark's work. But Crockett lost his seat in Congress for the last time in 1835 to Adam Huntsman, a follower of Jackson, and along with several others left for Texas on November 1 of that year.

Crockett's career in Congress was not distinguished. He was, according to Hutton (1987:xxi), "too independent and too honest." The independent and honest Crockett is best witnessed in his unwavering support for his impoverished West Tennessee constituents, exemplified in his politicking for the Tennessee Vacant Land Bill. This bill called for the release of all federal lands in Tennessee by the U.S. government and allowing the state to then sell the land, placing the earnings in its educational fund (Shackford 1994:90). Crockett initially supported the bill, siding with James C. Polk, his Tennessee colleague, as he believed the land would be sold at an affordable price to the poor. As Shackford clearly shows, Crockett's primary concern was for his constituents in West Tennessee, not the use of money for education. It soon became obvious to Crockett, however, that Polk and the Tennessee delegation were interested only in selling the land for the highest price, a move that would leave the pioneers of West

Tennessee in "utter deprivation" (Shackford 1994:91). Crockett, it seems, and here we see where his political allegiance lay, regarded "these 'squatters' as the pioneering advance guard of the American nation" who were "entitled to the plot of land which they had improved, and on which they made their homes" (Shackford 1994:91).[3]

Advancing the concerns of his constituents, Crockett broke with Polk and his other Tennessee colleagues and introduced an amendment that would give the former federal lands directly to those already living on them. What is clear from Crockett's speeches on this issue is his incipient class awareness of the deep disparity between rich and poor.

> The grant for the support of colleges drained us of fifty-two thousand five hundred dollars in cash. Ay, sir, in hard cash, wrung from the hands of the poor men, who live the sweat of their brow. I repeat, that I was utterly opposed to this: not because I am the enemy of education, but because the benefits of education are not to be dispersed with an equal hand. The college system went into practice to draw a line of demarcation between two classes of society—it separated the children of the rich from the children of the poor. (Quoted in Shackford 1994:96)

If Crockett's position on the land issue was not responsible for his loss of support by the Tennessee delegation, his failure to vote for the Indian Removal Bill was. The bill, advanced by supporters of President Jackson, proposed relocating a number of peaceful tribes from Tennessee, Alabama, Mississippi, and Georgia to west of the Mississippi River. Crockett, following his conscience and ignoring pressure from the majority of the Tennessee delegation as well as Jackson himself, voted against the bill. His sympathies were for "the poor remnants of a once powerful people" (Davis 1998:176). But his vote in this case is not the only one in which his populist sentiments were made known. For example, he held a similar stance concerning an appropriations bill for West Point Military Academy, one that seems ironic when contrasted with the patriotic fervor that surrounds the legendary Davy. On January 22, 1830, Crockett, speaking on a resolution concerning patronage to the academy, stated he was against "the whole idea of West Point" (Shackford 1994:113). A few weeks later, on February 25, he introduced a resolution:

> That no one class of citizens . . . has an exclusive right to demand or receive . . . more than an equal and ratable proportion of the funds of the national treasury, which is replenished by a common contribution,

and, in some instances more at the cost of the poor man, who has but little to defend, than that of the rich man, who seldom fights to defend himself or his property.

That each and every institution, calculated at public expense, and under the patronage and sanction of the Government, to grant exclusive privileges except in consideration of public services, is not only aristocratic, but a downright invasion of the rights of citizens, and a violation of . . . "the Constitution."

*Further,* that the Military Academy at West Point is subject to the foregoing objections, inasmuch as those who are educated there receive their instruction at the public expense, and are generally the sons of the rich and influential, who are able to educate their own children. While the sons of the poor . . . are often neglected, or if educated . . . are superseded in the service by cadets educated at West Point Academy.

*Resolved, therefore,* . . . [t]hat said institution should be abolished, and the appropriations annually made for its support discontinued. (Quoted in Shackford 1994:114; emphasis in original)

In the end, it was Crockett's open and "monomaniacal antipathy toward all matters Jacksonian" (Shackford 1994:132) that ended his congressional career. Crockett's dislike for Jackson, however, was not present at the beginning of his public career. In fact, early on Crockett supported, quite openly, Jackson's political agendas. But, according to Shackford and Folmsbee (1973), it was Crockett's opposition to the Jackson-backed Indian Removal Bill and Tennessee Vacant Land Bill that led to his passionate dislike for the president. Turning against the Jackson supporters was turning against the president himself. As Crockett states, "I know'd well enough, though, that if I didn't 'hurra' for his name, the hue and cry was to be raised against me, and I was to be sacrificed, if possible" (quoted in Shackford and Folmsbee 1973:205). Crockett was correct, and the Jacksonians were responsible for running candidates against him, including Adam Huntsman, who defeated him by 252 votes in 1835. With his political career in shambles, believing he was abandoned by his West Tennessee voters, and in dire need of financial stability, Crockett left for Texas a defeated politician and with little money. According to Shackford (1994: 216–217), Crockett planned to relocate his family, become a land agent, and gain the affluence and respect he believed eluded him in Tennessee.

In January 1836 Crockett signed an oath of allegiance to the Provisional Government of Texas and arrived in San Antonio de Béxar a few weeks later, just a month before the Battle of the Alamo. Sam Houston had been appointed commander in chief of the Texas forces by the provisional governor, Henry Smith. But Houston's appointment was opposed by anti-Jacksonians who made up the General Council and who had selected Lt. Gov. James Robinson as the Texas leader. Both men, therefore, claimed authority to lead Texas until their differences were settled in March 1836. In the interim, Houston sent Jim Bowie to San Antonio with orders to Col. Jim Neill to abandon the Alamo. But on arrival, Bowie, like Neill, believed that San Antonio de Béxar was instrumental to the protection of Texas. William Travis, who replaced Neill when he was called away on a family emergency, also believed that a stand at the Alamo was important. How and why Crockett decided to go to San Antonio de Béxar is not clear, but his arrival in early February 1836 was met with great excitement and improved the morale of those already present. What is clear is that Crockett did not go to Texas to "join the revolution." He went there to begin a new life, to find economic security, and possibly to make his way back into politics as a Texan. Instead, arriving in the midst of a military confrontation he did not seek, Crockett joined the struggle for Texas independence.

### THE DEATH OF DAVY: HISTORY, LEGENDRY, AND THE BATTLE OVER MEANING

The debate over how exactly Crockett died began in the nineteenth century and became particularly strident in the last three decades. One narrative tells of Davy falling victim to the Mexican forces, fiercely battling until his last breath; the other speaks of Crockett and a handful of others surviving the bloodiest part of the battle and surrendering, only to be executed moments later on Santa Anna's orders. Contemporary historians generally agree that evidence for the capture and execution of Crockett is quite strong. Hutton (1989:29) even claims that there "really is very little room for doubt that Crockett was captured and executed at the Alamo."

Kilgore, in his small but important book, *How Did Davy Die?* (1978), provides a clear summation of the various documents and sources of conflict on this debate. He states that immediate reports of the fall of the Alamo already contained the news that Crockett, along with others, was executed after the battle. In fact, Houston's first news of the Alamo battle contained information that "seven men surrendered and called for Santa Anna and quarter" (Kilgore 1978:17). Relatedly, three weeks after the battle the *New Orleans Post-Union* printed a story it claimed to have received from traveler leaving Texas that said, "Crockett and others had tried to surrender but were told there was not mercy for them" (Kilgore 1978:18). The *Post-Union* story was reprinted in other cities as well as reproduced, almost verbatim, by Mary Austin Holly in her book, *Texas,* published in July 1836. The *New York Courier and Enquirer* also published an account of Crockett's execution that was taken from an interview with an unnamed Mexican prisoner captured at the Battle of San Jacinto (Kilgore 1978:20–21).

Like the *Courier and Enquirer* article, much of the evidence comes from Mexican sources. No survivors lived to tell the story of the Alamo from the inside except for Mrs. Dickenson and Travis's slave, Joe. Their accounts, however, do not deny or affirm either story as they did not depart the room in which they took shelter until some time after the siege had ended. And while Mrs. Dickenson reports seeing Crockett's body "lying between the church and the long barracks," Hutton shows how the chronology of her departure from the Alamo supports the execution of Crockett scenario (Hutton 1989:40 n. 30).

At this time I want only to address several of the Mexican sources that support Crockett's execution. The most influential, as well as controversial, is the diary of Lt. José Enrique de la Peña, one of Santa Anna's officers who also wrote critically of his superior's decisions. De la Peña's diary was first published in Mexico in 1955 and translated by Carmen Perry, then librarian of the Alamo Library for the DRT, and published in the United States in 1975. De la Peña participated in the final siege of March 6, 1836, and recalled the following events.

> Shortly before Santa Anna's speech, an unpleasant episode had taken place, which, since it occurred after the end of the skirmish, was looked upon as base murder and which contributed greatly to the coolness that was noted. Some seven men had survived the general carnage and, under the protection of General Castrillón, they were brought before Santa Anna. Among them was one of great stature, well proportioned, with regular features, in whose face there was the imprint of adversity, but in whom one also noticed a degree of resignation and nobility that did him honor. He was the naturalist David Crockett, well known in North America for his unusual adventures, who had undertaken to explore the country and who, finding himself in Béjar at the very moment of surprise, had taken refuge in the Alamo, fearing that his status as a foreigner might not be respected. Santa Anna answered Castrillón's intervention on Crockett's behalf with a gesture of indignation and, addressing himself to the sappers, the troops closest to him, ordered his execution. The commanders and officers were outraged at this action and did not support the order, hoping that once the fury of the moment

had blown over these men would be spared; but several officers who were around the president and who, perhaps, had not been present during the moment of danger, became noteworthy by an infamous deed, surpassing the soldiers in cruelty. They thrust themselves forward, in order to flatter their commander, and with swords in hand, fell upon these unfortunate, defenseless men just as a tiger leaps upon his prey. Though tortured and killed, these unfortunate died without complaining and without humiliating themselves before their torturers. (De la Peña 1975:53)

While William Groneman has attempted to invalidate the diary, James Crisp has authenticated, quite convincingly, de la Peña's authorship. The Groneman-Crisp debate is beyond the scope of this chapter but serves as a critical example of how debates over the past, specifically, myth taken as history, continue to serve an interest beyond that of understanding the past.[4]

Another crucial corroborating eyewitness account is that of Santa Anna's personal secretary, Ramón Caro, who reported the following:

Among the 183 killed there were five who were discovered by General Castrillón hiding after the assault. He took them immediately to the presence of His Excellency who had come up by this time. When he presented the prisoners, he was severely reprimanded for not having killed them on the spot, after which he turned his back upon Castrillón while the soldiers stepped out of their ranks and set upon the prisoners until they were killed. (Quoted in Castañeda 1970:105–106)

The last source I want to briefly address is Sgt. Francisco Becerra, whose story Kilgore (1978:24) refers to as the most "bizarre account of Crockett's death." Becerra's recollection is important because he later serves as the source for two key historical narratives of the battle, those of John S. Ford and Reuben M. Potter. Becerra was captured at the Battle of San Jacinto and stayed in Texas, first working for Mirabeau B. Lamar and later for Potter. He fought for the Texas forces in the Mexican War, under Lamar, and supported the South during the Civil War. As Kilgore (1980:10) notes, "[H]e fought many more battles and many more years for Texas than he did for Mexico." Ford first collected Becerra's account of the Alamo battle in Brownsville, Texas, in 1875 and used it extensively in his *Origin and Fall of the Alamo*, published in 1895. Ford's first telling of Becerra's account, however, is from 1875, and here Becerra tells of the following events.

While this was occurring another Texian made his appearance. He had been lying on the floor, as if resting. When he arose I asked:—"How many is there of you?" He replied:—"Only Two."

"The gentleman, who spoke Spanish, asked for Gen. Cos, and said he would like to see him. Just then Gen. Amador came in. He asked why the orders of the President had not been executed, and the two Texians killed. . . . In a few moments Gen. Cos, Gen. Almonte, and Gen. Tolza, entered the room. As soon as Gen. Cos saw the gentleman who spoke Spanish he rushed to him, and embraced him. He told the other generals it was Travis, that on a former occasion he had treated him like a brother, and loaned him money, etc. He also said the other man was Col. Crockett. He entreated the other generals to go with him to Gen. Santa Anna, and join with him in a request to save the lives of the two Texians. The generals and the Texians left together to find Santa Anna. The bugler and myself followed them. They encountered the commander-in-chief in the court yard, with Gen. Castrillon. Gen. Cos said to him:—"Mr. President, you have here two prisoners—in the name of the Republic of Mexico I supplicate you to guarantee the lives of both." Santa Anna was very much enraged. He said:—"Gentlemen generals, my order was to kill every man in the Alamo." He turned, and said:—"Soldiers, kill them." A soldier was standing near Travis, and presented his gun at him. Travis seized the bayonet, and depressed the muzzle of the piece to the floor, and it was not fired. While this was taking place the soldiers standing around opened fire. A shot struck Travis in the back. He then stood erect, folding his arms, and looked calmly, unflinchingly, upon his assailants. He was finally killed by a ball passing through his neck. Crockett stood in similar position. They died undaunted like heroes. (Becerra and Ford 1980:22–23)

Becerra also served as the source of Potter's well-known history of the Alamo. However, because Potter's representation of the battle fails to recount the execution of Crockett after the battle, I address it in a later section.

These narratives of Crockett's death, although contradictory on some points, display enough congruence so as to agree with Hutton's earlier claim that there is little doubt about how Crockett died. Kilgore's final reconstruction of Crockett's death concludes this section.

As the assault waned about six o'clock that morning of March 6, 1836, General Castrillón found Crockett and several others and marched them into the open Alamo yard. (It deserves repeating here that the most creditable of the eyewitnesses did not say the Texans surrendered.) Santa Anna had entered the blood-soaked grounds to address his assembling troops, and his reply to Castrillón's plea for mercy for the surviving Texans was immediate and terribly final. Soldiers still in the grip of battle fever sprang to execute his order of death. The evidence suggests that the entire episode—from the discovery of the Texans until their deaths—took place within only a few minutes. (Kilgore 1978:47)

### DAVY LIVES: LEGENDRY AND THE HEROIC

It is clear that David Crockett, through his ghostwritten autobiography, his political speeches, and the popularity of his views, was well known at the time of his death at the Alamo. Soon after Crockett published his autobiography the Whig party decided to capitalize on his name and released two more books claiming Crockett as the author. One was a satirical biography of Martin Van Buren, Jackson's successor in waiting; the other, *An Account of Colonel Crockett's Tour to the North and Down East,* fictitiously depicted Crockett on the campaign trail. As Michael Lofaro (1994:x) claims, "[Crockett was] no fool. He knew his image and continued to manipulate it." The summer after his death Carey and Hart, Crockett's publishers, released *Colonel Crockett's Exploits and Adventures in Texas.* The book was sold as Crockett's Texas journal found by General Castrillón and then recovered at San Jacinto. For years the author of this text was taken to be Crockett, until it was shown to be written by Richard Penn Smith with full acknowledgment by Carey and Hart. While the story of Crockett's death in Smith's book follows the Castrillón capture and subsequent execution, the fictionalized aspects of the journal only added to Davy's reputation: "Pop, pop, pop! Bom, bom, bom! throughout the day. No time for memorandum now. . . . Go ahead! Liberty and independence forever!" (quoted in Hutton 1989:30). Smith's work along with Crockett's 1834 biography and the ghostwritten *Account of Colonel Crockett's Tour to the North and Down East* were bound together and distributed, and thousands of copies were sold. As Hutton (1989:30) comments on Smith's book, "The hoax of authorship was not uncovered for years, and many believed it was truly Crockett's diary."

Just before Crockett's death, another major venue of Davy's legendry was published, the *Crockett Almanac.* Between its release in 1835 and 1856, nearly twenty volumes in all were published. Through Smith's bogus book and the continued publication of the almanacs, the stories of Crockett captured the imagination of Americans. Even Crockett's autobiography, Robert Hauck (1989:185) claims, is "an imaginative book, and his imagination is one of the subjects" as he "deliberately crafted a style of prose" that was idiomatic, recognizable, and in the language of legend. Hauck (1989:186) continues: "[The] stereotype of the frontiersman was already established by the time Crockett took it up, but he tailored it to his purposes, playing the role beautifully, enhancing it, refabricating it, making it very much his own." After his death the legends continued, including stories of his last moments in the Alamo.

The 1837 almanac was one of the first writings to build on Davy's legendary death.

> Fear was a word he [Crockett] knew not the definition of. It was calculated that during the siege he killed not less than 85 men, and wounded 120 besides, as he was one of the best rifle shooters of the west, and he had four rifles, with two men to load constantly, and he fired as fast as they could load, nearly always hitting his man; but the distance was so great that he could not put the ball through a mortal place every time. (Quoted in Kilgore 1989:9)

Such heroics were based on early, exaggerated reports of Crockett's death. On March 28, 1836, the town of Nacogdoches adopted the following resolution: "David Crockett (now rendered immortal in Glory) had fortified himself with sixteen guns well charged, and a monument of slain foes encompasses his lifeless body" (Kilgore 1989:10).

By the latter part of the nineteenth century Davy had become a national legend. In Tennessee Crockett County was created in 1871 from pieces of four other jurisdictions, and the county seat was renamed Alamo. In 1889 Benjamin Strong Rush purchased forty-seven acres near Crockett's birthplace and built a public historical site to celebrate Davy's 103d birthday (Cummings 1989:71). The following year Frank Murdock and Frank Mayo's play, "Davy Crockett: Or, Be Sure You're Right, Then Go Ahead," began a twenty-four-year run, ending only with the death of Mayo (who played the part of Crockett) in 1896.

Crockett was an important subject in the early days of cinema as well. The first film on him was *Davy Crockett—In Hearts United,* released by the New York Motion Picture Company in 1909. This was followed by *Davy Crockett* in 1910, made by Selig Polyscope Company. I have already discussed the Méliès film of 1911 as well as the 1915 *Martyrs of the Alamo* (which I address again shortly). Several other films that took Crockett as their subject were the 1916 Oliver Morosco Photoplay production, *Davy Crockett;* the 1926 Sunset silent movie, *Davy Crockett at the Fall of the*

*Alamo;* the 1950 *Davy Crockett, Indian Scout,* released by Reliance; and, of course, the Disney and Wayne productions (see chap. 5).

Hutton (1989:31) claims that little attention was given to Crockett after the Civil War: the exploits of Buffalo Bill Cody, Wild Bill Hickok, and George Armstrong Custer during this period overshadowed his. But Crockett was not forgotten. Between Murdock and Mayo's play, the Tennessee celebrations, and the six films that featured him, Crockett remained a central figure in the American imagination. And in 1939 Richard Dorson published *Davy Crockett: American Comic Legend,* which rekindled interest in the legendary Davy before the Disney craze of the mid-1950s. I want to discuss, however, a different, yet related, set of influences on the popularity of Crockett. I suggest that his popularity during this period emerges with a post–Civil War effort to reunite the nation by redefining the contours of patriotism and heroism. While I understand Hutton's claim that other frontier heroes eclipsed Crockett, I want also to suggest that the figure of Davy is one that is not bound by popular legends and culture but one that seeps into the American imagination through the conflation (or, better yet, collapsing) of history, myth, and legendry at the Alamo.

## CROCKETT, THE ALAMO, AND THE ABSENT CAUSE OF HEROISM

There should be little doubt by this point in my argument that the Alamo, not as battle, but as place and story, was created in the latter half of the nineteenth century due, in large measure, to the influences of the Texas Modern. By way of underscoring my thesis as well as extending it to the production of a wider social formation within American national consciousness, I want to rethink the place of Crockett and the Alamo through one of its primary motifs: the patriotic hero. That is, if the social transformations associated with the Texas Modern serve as the material base for the making of the Alamo, the patriotic hero, made visible here through the figure of Crockett, serves as a primary and idealized form through which the cultural work of the Texas Modern is achieved. By way of introducing this proposition concerning patriotism and its political conditions of production, let me briefly return to Crockett's death and demonstrate how patriotism and the heroic serve to rewrite the putative facts of Crockett himself.

I can cite several instances in which the historical Crockett was overlooked in favor of the legendary Davy, but perhaps none is more important to the Alamo story than that undertaken by Reuben Potter. Potter is credited with writing the first important historical account of the Battle of the Alamo, including a version of Crockett's heroic death. As Kilgore (1989:10) comments, Potter "vigorously denounced anyone who questioned that

he . . . did not die fighting to his last breath" and was absolutely committed "to the idea of the Alamo as a great heroic epic."[5] Recall that Potter
learned much of what he knew about the Alamo and Crockett from his
former employee, Francisco Becerra. And while the portion of Becerra's
story that concerns Bowie's and Travis's deaths seems unreliable to Potter,
Becerra's discussion of Crockett's demise is structurally congruent with
other Mexican eyewitness accounts, such as that of de la Peña.

Potter first proposed his account of the Alamo battle in an 1860 pamphlet
that was later reprinted in the *Texas Almanac* in 1868. He then expanded
this early work and published it in 1878 in the *Magazine of American History*. What I want to highlight here is what Potter fails to say. In Potter's
(1878:15) text, the only mention of Crockett's death is one he states was
relayed to him by Mr. Ruiz, mayor of San Antonio, who says "the body of
Crocket [*sic*] was found in the west battery." Potter is silent on how Crockett died. This silence is important, because he does report the discovery
and execution of several other men after the battle. He writes:

> Half an hour or more after the action was over a few men were found
> concealed in one of the rooms under some mattresses. General Hous-
> ton, in a letter of the 11th, says as many as seven; but I have generally
> heard them spoken of as only four or five. The officer to whom the dis-
> covery was first reported entreated Santa Ana [*sic*] to spare their lives;
> but he was sternly rebuked, and the men ordered to be shot, which was
> done. (Potter 1878:14)

This omission is more remarkable because it is quite clear that Potter
knew of reports of Crockett being executed with these "four or five" men
from his employee and historical informant, Francisco Becerra. Becerra
had fought with Santa Anna at the Alamo and remained in Texas after the
Battle of San Jacinto. He became a primary historical source on the Alamo
for Potter and Ford. In fact, Potter cites Becerra in his first endnote of the
article:

> I had for several years in Texas as a servant, one of the Mexican soldiers
> captured at San Jacinto, Sergeant Becero [*sic*], of the Battalion of Mata-
> moros. He was in the assault, and witnessed Dickenson's leap. He also
> saw the body of Bowie on his bed, where he had been killed, and wit-
> nessed the execution of the few men who were found in concealment af-
> ter the action was over. He did not know the names of Bowie or Dicken-

son, and related the circumstances, not in reply to inquiries, but in a natural way as recollections in narrating an experience. (1878:20)

Why does Potter not mention Crockett as one of those executed after the battle? Is it that he does not believe he has enough corroborating evidence for such a statement and therefore refrains from infusing hearsay or legend into his "historical" narrative? Or is it that he suppresses this information on the death of Crockett so as to keep "enshrined" the mythic image of Davy and the Alamo heroes? For reasons based on Potter's own writing, I believe the second of these positions is more accurate.

In the paragraph following the description of the four or five survivors who were shot, Potter relays the following story:

Lieutenant Dickenson commanded the gun at the east embrasure of the chapel. His family was probably in one of the small vaulted rooms of the north projections, which will account for his being able to take his child to the rear of the building when it was being stormed. An irrigating canal ran below the embrasure, and his aim may have been to break the shock of his leap by landing in the mud of that waterless ditch, and then try to escape, or he may have thought that so striking an act would plead for his life; but the shower of bullets which greeted him told how vain was the hope. The authenticity of this highly dramatic incident has been questioned, but it was asserted from the first, and was related to me by an eye-witness engaged in the assault. (1878:14–15)

The concluding sentence is important for two reasons. First, Potter admits that Dickenson's leap is a questionable event but reports it because it was "asserted from the first" by an "eye-witness account." Second, and more important, the eyewitness for Potter's narrative about Dickenson is, according to the note quoted above, Francisco Becerra. Becerra serves as the source on the execution of the "four or five" men after the battle as well as on Dickenson's leap. Why, then, does Potter not mention Crockett as one of the men executed after the battle? The most logical answer is that he had no information linking Crockett to those who were executed. But we know differently. John Ford's earlier, 1875 account of the Alamo battle, also based on Becerra's testimony, states that Crockett was one of those executed on Santa Anna's orders (Becerra and Ford 1980:23). Why does Potter not make the same claim about Crockett? If it is because he thought there was only hearsay evidence, why does he include the story of Dickenson? Potter, it seems, is quite willing to report information that is "questionable" when it enhances or supports his heroic image of the Alamo defenders, as in the case of Dickenson's leap. But when the information detracts from his heroic tale, Potter neglects to include it in his narrative.

Two years after this account was published, Potter seems even more emphatic about preserving the memory of the heroic Davy. Responding to an article in the *Independent Hours,* he claimed that "David Crockett never surrendered to bear or tiger, Indian or Mexican" (Kilgore 1978:27). Three years later Potter again responded to a story of Crockett's execution in the *Magazine of American History.* Then, in 1886, Becerra's story appeared in this same venue, to which Potter angrily replied in praise of Crockett's heroic death in battle (Kilgore 1978:28). These denouncements are somewhat surprising given that Potter depended so heavily on Becerra's account of the events and circumstances related to the Battle of the Alamo. Potter himself, however, suggests the motive for his statements: "[I]n a fight [when the hopelessly outnumbered] know they have all got to die, the bravest fall first; the last reached is certain to be a sneak. Thus it was at the Alamo. Travis and Crockett fell early on the outworks" (quoted in Kilgore 1989:11). Believing Crockett to be among the bravest, Potter could not have him executed after the battle.

The importance of Potter's history cannot be underestimated. In 1914 Eugene C. Barker reported that it was the most "'thorough' history to date," and it remained, besides Adina De Zavala's account, the only major study of the battle until Amelia Williams's 1931 doctoral dissertation at the University of Texas.[6] And in 1889 the eminent historian Hubert Howe Bancroft claimed that stories stating that Crockett, among others, "was one of the captives put to death, are utterly unworthy of credence" (quoted in Kilgore 1978:27).

We are left with the following question: Why were stories of Crockett's surrender and execution omitted from important historical and popular accounts of the Battle of the Alamo in the late nineteenth and early twentieth century? Could it be that all the evidence for Crockett's execution came from "Mexican" sources? Perhaps. But as Hutton (1987:liv) remarks, we have not one "single reliable eyewitness account of Crockett's death *in battle*" (my emphasis). When contrasted with the overwhelming number of eyewitnesses to Crockett's surrender and execution, stories of his heroic death, rifle and knife in hand, tell us more about the need to "see" the heroic Davy than to "know" Crockett the man.

It is here that we must rethink the enshrinement of the heroic Davy through the currents of its day. Re-visioning Crockett the hero in such a way allows for connections between the making and acceptance of legendry as fact and the historical conditions from which it emerges to become visible. In doing this I want to expand my earlier discussion of the Texas Modern to a position that now includes its relationship to an emerging nationalist, patriotic formation. In effect, I want to rethink the making of the heroic Davy so as to incorporate the politics of nationalism, patriotism, and the heroic as they evolved in the post–Civil War era. My suggestion is that the erasure of the historical Crockett in the works of Potter and others and the emergence of a legendary Davy result from, and serve to broaden, social and political ideologies that require an emphasis on nationalism and patriotism.

Notions of patriotism at the turn of the twentieth century were in flux, the result of shifting understandings of allegiance, honor, and national service in the Reconstruction period. I turn to this period and its debates first because it is also during this time that the legendary Davy is being "worked out." Second, we must remember that while Crockett died at the Alamo, his legend and reputation, both before and after his death, was as a southern politician, adventurer, and hero.[7] Third, the image of the heroic Crockett, and his valor, as well as that of his Alamo compatriots, is one that is almost always used in the service of the nation, or at least the dominant whose interest the nation serves.

Cecelia Elizabeth O'Leary (1996) nicely demonstrates how patriotism during the days of Radical Reconstruction served two purposes. It signified traditional ideas of "willingness to die for one's country" and "more radical notions of social, political, and racial equality" (O'Leary 1996:55). One of these radical notions was the sense among former slaves that they were "fully American" (O'Leary 1996:55). By 1883, however, any notion of black racial equality began to fade, undermined on various fronts, including the 1883 Supreme Court decision that the Civil Rights Act of 1875 was unconstitutional. This resulted, as O'Leary (1996:57) suggests, in the remittance "to the Southern people, temporarily at least, [of] control of the race question."

In this same period there is a growing national interest in the past, manifested in the formation of organizations such as the Daughters of the American Revolution and the Daughters of the Republic of Texas and various veterans' groups. In addition, there is the construction of two national enemies, both connected to the expansion of the United States: the Plains Indians and Spain. After Custer's defeat in 1876 at Little Big Horn, the Plains Indians emerged as a common enemy for U.S. military forces that a decade before were divided North and South. As a result, Confederate soldiers now volunteered for duty and served alongside forces from the North. In effect, the Indian Wars served as a foundation for national unity (O'Leary 1996:58).

Still, for a country divided by war only a few years before, reconciliation between the North and the South was a slow, tedious, and conflictual process, especially for those who fought and for those whose job it was to interpret the war for future generations. It was the Spanish-American War of the late 1890s that served to solidify relations between northern and southern soldiers, including the "full exoneration" of Confederate officers (O'Leary 1996:60). As Michael Kammen (1991) has argued, this was also a period of increased immigration and concomitant efforts of "Americanization." The rewriting of history, including the redefinition of the Civil War, like that of the Alamo, was instrumental in this process. Equally important was the recognition of the military efforts of Confederate soldiers as acts of valor, not treason. Many of these issues were played out on the national scene through ideological readjustments between the members of the Grand Army of the Republic (GAR) and the United Confederate Veterans (UCV).

By the early 1900s the rewriting of the Civil War had nearly been accomplished. At the fiftieth anniversary of the Battle of Gettysburg in 1913, neither slavery as a cause nor the unification of race relations between whites and blacks as a goal of the victor was mentioned as part of the memory of the Civil War; instead the war was recast as "a heroic struggle between brothers whose blood had strengthened and purified the nation. It was neither southern nor northern but American valor that Civil War soldiers had vindicated when they each fought for what they considered to be right" (O'Leary 1996:77-78). In this refiguring, valor no longer reflected the ideological or moral cause of one's fight but self-sacrifice in battle.

The recasting of valor as a central tenet of patriotism is critical for the construction of the heroic Davy as it underscores why he could be recognized as an "American" hero. It mattered little that his purpose in traveling to Texas was personal, not political or patriotic. What did matter was his death in "battle." Thus Potter and others could not have Davy surrender only to be executed. This is what Potter (1878:17) suggests when he says of the heroics of the Alamo defenders, "The main element of defense was the individual valor and skill of men who had few advantages of fortification, ordinance, discipline or command."

The Civil War serves as only one key example of how cultural, civic, and political organizations in the late nineteenth and early twentieth century attended to the invention of the nation. The rewriting of the Civil War that facilitated the emergence of a new patriotism and a rise in "Americanism" resulted in the abandonment of racial equality as a goal of Reconstruction, silencing "black Americans and white supporters of social justice" (O'Leary 1996:80). This new patriotic fever transferred to other areas as a united North and South now stood together against the rise of immigrants and for the reinforcement of racism. In the South, the common enemy was black social life; or more precisely, the North and South found an area of convergence around a renewed racism manifest in Jim Crow segregation. Coupled with a rise in xenophobia at this moment, it took little for this sentiment to develop in Texas and other areas of the Southwest where Mexicans had long served as the racial Other. This redefinition of the past had severe implications for immigrants and racial minorities. As Kammen states:

> Those who remained content to romanticize the past and perpetuate faith in that fantasy world were able to maintain a reasonable coherent vision of how the present had evolved and why certain values, such as racial supremacy and separation, should be maintained. (1991:196)

In the fervor of historical revisionism the heroic Davy was reproduced and the Alamo was "made" into a site of national (not only Texan) liberty at the cost of racial strife. Two key examples demonstrate Andrew Neather's (1996:89) point that "the nation's racial integrity could mean almost the same thing as 'patriotism.'" Here I point to the 1915 films *Birth of a Nation* and *Martyrs of the Alamo*. Both serve to infuse their intended white audiences with a sense of historical understandings: *Birth of a Nation* on the perils of Reconstruction, *Martyrs of the Alamo* on the taking of Texas. In doing so, both films posit a radical alterity to blacks and Mexicans so as to justify their continued subjugation through social and political segregation and economic dominance. By collapsing a discourse of fear for blacks in the South with Mexicans in Texas, these films rewrite the past and render all efforts of social control through a patriotic idiom: to stand for the nation is to uphold a social order of dominance. Erased from the Civil War and Reconstruction are goals of racial equality; written into the Battle of the Alamo is a racial perspective that ignores the historical and political conditions of 1836. O'Leary (1996:59) claims that in the South, valor, not treason, provided southerners with an interpretation of the Civil War; the same could be said about the Alamo defenders.

My concern here is not with the historical Crockett but with the legendary Davy. The erasure of the historical Crockett by Potter and others in favor of the legendary Davy coincides with efforts nationwide to rewrite the past in the spirit of nationalism, patriotism, and valor. But here patriotism works to enforce a racial hierarchy and class formation that privileges a few. This is clear for the Texas Modern; it is also clear in the South. Like remembering Confederate soldiers for their valor, not their cause, Davy must die fighting heroically, not executed for his beliefs. In effect, the heroic Davy is made in the image of the new American patriot whose valor reproduces the nation and whose death purifies the polis from those whose racial formation or cultural heritage darkens the American landscape.

### DAVY ON THE TWILIGHT OF MODERNITY

The reproduction of the legendary Davy continues to this day. Popular culture has continued to forge a heroic image even as evidence of Crockett's execution has been validated. In fact, Hutton (1989:37) has claimed that when it comes to Davy Crockett, we find "the absolute triumph of popular culture over historical fact."

The triumph of popular culture surely began with films such as *Martyrs of the Alamo*, but it reached its apex in 1954 and 1955 with the Disney television series (see chap. 5). For seven months the craze was coonskin caps and other Crockett paraphernalia, including the selling of several million copies of "The Ballad of Davy Crockett." If one was too young to remember Fess Parker as Davy, one could not avoid the ballad. At the same time, *The Last Command* was released, showing the legendary Davy die heroically as he blows up the powder magazine at the end of the Alamo battle. The same scene is repeated in 1960 in Wayne's *The Alamo*. Granted, popular culture is under little or no obligation to represent the past accurately, but these depictions have become the standard image of Crockett's death for generations. Even the DRT suggested that Wayne's film was accurate on this point. As late as 1985, Pat Dibrell claimed, "There were plans made before the battle to blow up the gunpowder stored in the main shrine if it was overrun and Davy Crockett was attempting to do that when he was killed" (quoted in Hutton 1989:36). And Walter Lord's book, *A Time to Stand*, "the best book to date on the Alamo" according to Hutton (1989:34), does not include the Crockett execution in the body of the book but reproduces the following narrative:

> Crockett's Tennesseans, at bay near the palisade, battled with a wild fury that awed even the attackers. Individual names and deeds were lost forever in the seething mass of knives, pistols, fists, and broken gunstocks;

but Sergeant Felix Nuñez remembered one man who could stand for any of them, including Crockett himself:

> He was a tall American of rather dark complexion and had on a long buckskin coat and a round cap without any bill, made out of fox skin with the long tail hanging down his back. This man apparently had a charmed life. Of the many soldiers who took deliberate aim at him and fired, not one ever hit him. On the contrary, he never missed a shot. He killed at least eight of our men, besides wounding several others. This being observed by a lieutenant who had come in over the wall, he sprang at him and dealt him a deadly blow with his sword, just above the right eye, which felled him to the ground, and in an instant he was pierced by not less than 20 bayonets. (Lord 1961:161–162)

At the end of the book, however, in an unnumbered chapter titled "Riddles of the Alamo," Lord outlines the main evidence for Crockett's surrender. Still, he finishes by stating, "There's a good chance Crockett lived up to his legend, and in some circles it remains dangerous even to question the matter" (Lord 1961:207).

This brings me to my final point: Why was it dangerous to question the death of Crockett in the mid-twentieth century?[8] At the time Lord is writing it is clear, at least in popular formulations, that both Davy Crockett and nationalistic patriotism have collapsed into each other. If *Martyrs of the Alamo* served to "repress" and "manage" fears, not only of Mexicans, but also of the contradictory conditions of the Texas Modern, the Crockett craze of the 1950s works toward a similar end. Only now the conditions that warrant management have shifted and include at least two distinct fronts. There is no doubt that the major fear in post–World War II America was communism and its perceived threat to "liberty" and "freedom." Witness Wayne's intense political beliefs and constant conflation of the Alamo heroes with his notion of (anticommunist) liberty and freedom. But like the Texas Modern and *Martyrs of the Alamo,* the Crockett and Alamo craze of the fifties warrants a social understanding, which is to say, who are the "Mexicans" of this period? They are, as I have noted, Mexican Americans. It is not coincidence that George J. Sánchez concludes his award-winning history of Mexican Americans in Los Angeles, *Becoming Mexican American,* with a story from 1945 that "marks the transition from a Mexico-centered leadership to one focused on political and social advancement *in* American society" (1993:274; my emphasis). The period after World War II was one of social and economic advances and increased political activity on the part of Mexican Americans as they laid claim to their American rights.

Juan Gómez-Quiñones (1990), in a work that presents much of what can be said of this period, discusses the multiple fronts and locations of Mexican-American activism and political practice from the 1940s on. He demonstrates how Mexican Americans with various social agendas and in different political voices began to speak and demand the rights due them as citizens and residents of the United States. Although this is not the place to recount the numerous efforts by Mexican Americans to redress their sociopolitical position, let me discuss at least two organizations, highlighted by Gómez-Quiñones, that serve as key models of social action: the Community Service Organization (cso) and the American G.I. Forum.

The cso emerged in Los Angeles in 1947 out of the failed city council election of Edward Roybal. Partially funded and advised by the Industrial Areas Foundation (iaf)—perhaps the most successful training institute for community organizers to date—the cso successfully registered and educated more than forty thousand voters in the Los Angeles area (Gómez-Quiñones 1990:53). Roybal was the "single most important Mexican elected official in California during the post–World War II period" before losing the 1947 election (Gómez-Quiñones 1990:54). With cso, Roybal and numerous others changed the face of Mexican-American politics in Los Angeles and elsewhere in southern California. Their goals were "to challenge effectively the social problems plaguing the city's Spanish-speaking people and to provide the community with a level of political representation which it had lacked for three-quarters of a century" (Gómez-Quiñones 1990:54). Besides voter registration, cso and its membership sought redress for police harassment and housing discrimination, and by the 1960s it had expanded to twenty-two chapters in California and Arizona. While the impact of the cso was experienced locally through the development of site-specific social agendas, its successes served as an example for other initiatives, especially those associated with the iaf throughout the Southwest.

The American G.I. Forum, and its predecessor, the League of United Latin American Citizens (lulac), was neither radical nor militant in its approach to change. Both, however, served as key national organizations that promoted the interest of Mexican Americans as they worked toward full inclusion in the American social arena. The American G.I. Forum was established to serve the needs of Mexican-American military veterans, but it was the death of Felix Longoria that thrust the organization into national prominence. Longoria, a Purple Heart recipient, was refused burial in his hometown, Three Rivers, Texas, because he was a Mexican American. This led to the intervention of Dr. Hector García, from Houston, Texas, who arranged for Longoria to be buried in Arlington National Cemetery. After this incident, the G.I. Forum established itself as a major contributor to the advancement of the social needs of Mexican Americans with initiatives in voter registration, job training, bilingual education, and educational parity (Gómez-Quiñones 1990:61).

The 1950s were important politically for Mexican Americans. There were myriad efforts by national groups such as LULAC to integrate Mexican Americans into the American social fabric. Local organizations arose throughout the Southwest: trade unions, local church groups, community organizations, and student groups. From Fresno, California, where the Mexican American Political Association (MAPA) was organized in 1959, to Texas, where the Political Association of Spanish-Speaking Organizations (PASSO) was started in 1961, Mexican Americans were actively challenging the status quo in an effort to attain the rights and privileges of educational and housing equity and to end the discrimination their community had long experienced. Gómez-Quiñones (1990:98) claims that Mexican Americans had tired of living with "the most debilitating effect of prejudice," which emerged from "the continued maintenance of the dominant Anglo American attitude of superiority toward Mexicans, a combination of ethnocentrism and supremacism." As the Mexican-origin population increased their efforts to effect social change, their sense of self coalesced into what Mario T. García (1989) has called the "Mexican American generation."

The Crockett craze of Disney and Wayne cannot be separated from this political moment. As was the case with the denial of racial reconstruction in the South after the Civil War, this new wave of Crockett patriotism was an effort to divert attention from issues of inequality and racial injustice. In the face of growing civil strife, in the midst of institutionalized segregation and racism that resulted in Jim Crow laws against Mexican Americans, and in the continued denial of civil rights in the post–World War II era, the renewed interest in the heroic Davy renders valor supreme and ideological critique of the nation a communist plot. Especially for those involved in ethnic politics, the Cold War ideology—epitomized by the McCarren Act of 1950 and the McCarren-Walter Act of 1952, both aimed at protecting the nation from "subversives"—had a severe impact (M. García 1989:213). Any criticism of the status quo, especially by ethnic and racial minorities, was taken as unpatriotic and a threat to the sovereignty of the United States. Models of valor, as in Crockett and the Alamo defenders, were reproduced as public reminders of the "authentic" American character. Anything less was unacceptable.

My concern, primarily, is with a form of patriotism that elides the real conditions of history for constructed notions of the nation. The Crockett of history spoke and battled bravely for the dispossessed of his state; he believed, perhaps naively for our day but no less heroically, that individuals could make a difference within the institutions of power so as to share that power with the underprivileged. But this is not the Crockett we have come to know over the past generations, nor is it the Crockett that has been reproduced in popular culture or at sites like the Alamo. This Crockett died in 1836 giving birth to a heroic Davy and the invented notions of liberty and freedom that have long been used against the likes of those whom the historical Crockett unabashedly defended.

# Conclusion

꘏꘎

## THE ALAMO AS TEX(MEX)
## MASTER SYMBOL OF MODERNITY

By 1960 and Wayne's production of *The Alamo,* modernity was in a
state of flux. I even suggest that the intense interest in Crockett coupled
with the Alamo films of the 1950s—almost as intense as the years from
1909 to 1926—was an attempt to hold firm the eroding conditions of
American modern social life by embracing one of its key symbols. Without fully accepting periodizing dates for the modern, it is not coincidental
that the birth of the postmodern is, according to David Harvey (1990), associated with the mid-1960s. Wayne's *Alamo,* I offer, is a facile effort at preserving a modernist, post–World War II sensibility before the social rumblings of that era erupted into the tumultuous years of the Vietnam war
and the Civil Rights and feminist movements.

Wayne's aseptic portrayal of Mexicans, we now see, emerges not only
from his personal views but also from the changing, historically condi-
tioned racial politics of this era. And yet, as noted in chapter 5, the symbolic logic of the modern could not but portray Mexicans as Other, witnessed in Wayne's portrayal of the Mexican women and Juan Seguín.
Wayne's film, then, marks the twilight of the Alamo as master symbol before the coming years would see critiques, demonstrations, and parodies
not only of the Alamo itself but also of the modern project more generally.[1]

### MODERNITY AND SYMBOL MAKING

By way of conclusion, I want to elaborate more fully the relationship between modernity and the making of symbols. This is necessary, I offer, because the general orientation of the Alamo, as master symbol, is one of a
token to a type. I suggest that while the historical and social particularities
of the Alamo, and its place in cultural memory, may be unique, it follows
a general pattern that I believe is endemic to modernity. To fully come to

terms with the Alamo as master symbol, therefore, we need to underscore the process of meaning making more generally.

In my discussion of the Texas Modern I underscored the historical specificity, an always necessary aspect, of the modern in relation to its Texas manifestation. I have showed how the forces of modernity wreaked havoc on Mexicans and Mexican Americans as they were displaced through the forces of technology, industrialization, and capitalism, or social production more generally. At this point I want to undertake a more general discussion of modernity in relation to the consequences of its selective forces on symbolic practice. By way of definition, I use the similar yet distinctive understandings of modernity proffered by Anthony Giddens and Fredric Jameson.

For Giddens (1990:21), a critical marker of modernity is "disembedding": "the 'lifting out' of social relations from local contexts of interaction and their restructuring across indefinite spans of time-space." One of the means by which local contexts are lifted out and replaced is what Giddens (1990:22) refers to, not coincidentally, as "symbolic tokens": "the media of interchange that can be 'passed around' without regard to the specific characteristics of individuals or groups that handle them at any particular junction." While Giddens takes money as his example, informed more perceptively for him by Simmel, not Marx, the process through which specific, historical features or "tokens" are disembedded from the events of their making and reconstructed in radically distinct spatial-temporal locations is emblematic of modernity and its associated practices. Let me be clear on what I believe Giddens means. First, he is not suggesting that "disembedding" is unique to modernity; in fact, numerous anthropologists and folklorists, informed by models of diffusion, have examined in detail the movement of cultural forms from one site to another. But diffusion entails cultural contact. Giddens, by contrast, suggests that modernity is marked by a disjuncture between space and time so that, for example, a local place like the Alamo or the person of Davy Crockett no longer signifies the conditions of their making but represents values and meanings that were nonexistent in 1836.

Jameson's formulation of modernity, informed by his nuanced and finely honed Marxian hermeneutic, is one inseparable from a capitalist cultural logic. Critical to his understanding is the process of differentiation—distinct but not unlike Giddens's notion of disembedding—that is fueled by the effects of reification. For Jameson (1981:63), reification is a modern force through which the "'traditional' or 'natural' (*naturwüchsige*) unities, social forms, human relations, cultural events, even religious systems, are systematically *broken up* in order to be reconstructed more efficiently, in the form of new post-natural processes or mechanisms" that obtain a sense of autonomy and "serve[s] to compensate for the dehumanization of experience reification brings with it" (my emphasis). Between Jameson and Giddens, then, I take modernity to be a transformational process through which earlier social and cultural complexes are broken up, disembedded, or removed from the social relations of their making and reconstituted and relocated, under the weight of routinized re-presentations, into distinct, spatial-temporal domains. As noted earlier, one of the effects of modernity is the redefinition of Self and Other as social rubrics from the past are no longer capable of organizing or mapping new forms of social and cultural relationships. I will return to this definition of modernity below. However, before proceeding I want to recognize that both Giddens and Jameson understand the production of an autonomous subject—a self disembedded from its social relations of formation—as one of the key features of modern thought and practice.

If modernity constitutes a process of transformation by which previous social and cultural formations are reorganized through a distinctively new organizational rubric, what is the effect of this rubric on the symbolic? It is this question that leads me to formulate the master symbol of modernity, a heuristically cobbled notion that suggests sign-images do not arbitrarily lose their links with the subjects they were first predicated on but are in fact uncoupled from their "natural" unities by the historical contingencies of rationality, technology, the capitalist market, routinization, and myriad other forces emerging from modern practice at the local level.

The literature on symbols, signs, and metaphors is extensive, emerging from various key theorists in the humanities and social sciences who have defined the field of semiology. For reasons that will become clear below, I want to begin my discussion of the master symbol with the work of James Fernandez (1986). As an anthropologist, Fernandez is keenly aware of the persuasive and performative utility of symbols as constituent features of cultural production. Fernandez (1986:29) in fact argues for a deep understanding of tropes as they emerge in "behavior" or practice.

Fernandez's articulation of the "mission of metaphor," one of the key tropes itself constituted from symbolic formulations, is one that I find most useful. He begins by discussing the fitful position of symbolic analysis as a result, in part, of the complex and not always clearly stated relationship among symbol, sign, and signal and their often-ambiguous referents.[2]

Fernandez (1986:31) defines symbols as "abstracted sign-images which have lost their direct link with the subjects on which they were first predicated in specific contexts, developing their plausible links with multi-tudinous subjects in multitudinous contexts." Let me accentuate Fernandez's definition with elements of Max Black's (1962:44) interactional theory of metaphor, which, like Fernandez's, emphasizes the active process of metaphorical production as one that selects, emphasizes, suppresses, and organizes meaning. What is instructive about Black's understanding, as reread through Fernandez, is that symbolic thought is not merely reflective or passive but assertive. Symbols, through practice and their association with metaphor, produce, not merely represent, meaning (see Turner 1991). As such, symbols and symbolic forms serve not only as a way of reflecting the world but also as a way of shaping social reality and social identities; they are, as Geertz (1973) says, "models of" and "models for" a social order.

Identity serves as a key area of symbolic production. According to Fernandez, symbols construct identity by differentiating a subject from the "natural" world and "other" subjects. Totemism is a key example for Fernandez (1986:36), one that "represents a mastery by the subject over the plurality of its natural predicates." This is a process that moves from inchoateness to subjectivity as metaphors are invoked to imagine and produce a differentiated self through multiple predications (1986:37). The result of such predications, Fernandez (1986:37) states, is, first, the making of an "identity" for a self; and second, a sense of "mastery" where the self achieves "social movement or social order." Fernandez's notion that symbols lead to a sense of mastery through which the self achieves social order is precisely the most salient feature of his discussion and the point at which I want to extend his views not through the case of totemism and primordialism, as he does, but through the process of modernity.

From this perspective, Fernandez's understanding of the unlinking and relinking of the symbolic process that leads to a "masterful self" (1986:37) warrants further reflection. In the primordial and totemic examples of Fernandez, mastery is achieved as a "Self" is differentiated from an "Other," a process that keeps in place distinct sociospatial domains. As Fernandez (1986:36) states, "[T]he power in totemism is that it at once preserves a sense of these primordial identification processes and achieves a sense of separation both from nature and from other social subjects." But the logic of modernity offers a distinctive turn on mastery, where the forces of differentiation and reification lead not to separate sociospatial domains with their concomitant Self-Other identities but to a hierarchical engagement whereby Self and Other are reconfigured through multiple discursive mechanisms and practices that slot social actors through relations of dominance. As such, the "Self" and "Other" of modernity are constructed not on the same social plane but on the structured and hierarchical field of reified, disembedded, and socially constituted difference.[3]

## THE TEX(MEX) MASTER SYMBOL OF MODERNITY

With this brief foray into symbolic theory I want to now rethink the relationship between the Alamo and modernity. The Alamo, with its various symbolic inflections and articulations, serves as a key example of a master symbol of modernity. Its reproduction through various discursive forms, spatial terrains, and cinematic and historical texts reveals its depth, complexity, and complicity with the emergence of the Texas Modern. Thus, with this newly articulated formulation of symbolic production in modernity, I want to return to the specific features of the Alamo as it is symbolically reconfigured through various genres of cultural memory.

As noted in chapter 3, capitalist spatial reorganization and consumer culture were mainly responsible for the reorganization of San Antonio from its Spanish and Mexican spatial arrangement to its American urban form. But why is it that this newly configured American city was recentered on the Alamo before its emergence as a place of public history? The answer, I argue, is that here the spatial form of the built environment serves an anticipatory, ideological, and nondiscursive role. Recall that the spatial reorganization of the late nineteenth century is concomitant with the social readjustments of Texas society, including its racial and ethnic elements. It is perhaps clearer to see how discursive ideologies of racial and ethnic superiority and inferiority serve the changes of the Texas Modern. The spatial reorganization of San Antonio works in the same way. Besides reproducing discursive images of treacherous, unclean, radically other Mexicans, one merely has to affirm this understanding by walking through the city streets of San Antonio. The new, the modern, the American are marked by the respatialization of property, while the old, the traditional, the Mexican is dissolved into the folkloric, the quaint, the foreign. Is it a surprise that this respatialization takes as its focal point the plaza of the Alamo? In this case, the forces of respatialization anticipate, in reconstructing the built environment, the symbolic role of the Alamo. The ruins of the Alamo, even before 1905, serve as a material reminder of Mexican tyranny and corruptness. "The awakening of the dead in those revolutions," Marx writes, served the purpose of glorifying the *new struggles,* not of parodying the old; of magnifying the given tasks in *imagination,* not of taking flight from their solution in reality; of finding once more the spirit of revolution, not of making its ghost walk again. (1978:596; my emphasis)

The development of the Alamo at the end of the nineteenth century has little to do with knowing the past but re-visioning it for a new social order. As Marx suggests, the awakening of these old ruins works both for the advancement of "new struggles" (or social orders) and of escalating such struggles through "imaginary," which is to say, symbolic, forms. The Alamo as symbol, however, is pressed into service not for the proletariat but for the ruling classes as they attempt to solidify, through spatial dominance, their hold on the local terrain.[4]

Here, one of the modernizing apparatuses used is the built environment as it fixes in the urban topography of San Antonio an imaginary past of Mexican tyranny through the material presence of the Alamo. The eruption of commercial enterprises facilitated by technological innovations and increased industrialization is not unique to San Antonio, but the coalescing of these forces and practices in conjunction with the shifting of the historically Mexican heart of the city to the area around the Alamo reveals a spatial unconscious of power and class formation intrinsic to modernity.

But modernity is actualized through a number of material, symbolic, and social transformations imparted discursively as well. As such, the literary and historical narratives of De Zavala and Driscoll reveal the exclusions, displacements, and disavowals of modernity, as do their own biographies. The lives of these two women were deeply implicated in their shared passion for the Alamo. In their struggles to stamp the Alamo with their sense of the past, their particular, historically shaped subjectivities informed their differential understanding of Texas's racial and ethnic past and kept them from collaborating fully in their work. It was no accident that De Zavala's vision of the past as a differentiated but ongoing flow of people, places, and events was reconfigured by the sentimentally informed regionalism of Driscoll. Nor was it coincidence that the socially induced divisions of the Texas Modern were rewritten as personal and racial flaws on the part of Mexicans by Driscoll. Both women experienced, full force, although from different social positions, the stigmatizing effects of the racial politics of this period and imbued their historical visions with these same inflections.

In making the Alamo a place of public history and culture in the early

1900s, the work of De Zavala and Driscoll allows us to witness the looming task of redefining American culture and society at a time of increased
immigration and expanding capitalist economies instrumental to modernization. During this time, the search for collective icons that could fix
particular images and identities yielded places of public culture.[5] Such
fixings detach places and persons from their collective past and reattach
them as ideological sources of meaning, a process that converts the private
visions of cultural elites into public markers of a new social order.

Nowhere are these historical detachments and their social reattachments experienced more profoundly during the early twentieth century
than in the visually selective images of cinema. The product of modernist
technology, motion pictures introduced a stimulating, powerful, and
never before experienced medium of representation. The sheer weight of
this new visual apparatus allowed for the reproduction of culture in new
and powerfully realist images, including its visualization of the past. I am
not suggesting that the past was not used ideologically before the arrival
of motion pictures, but the novelty and sensorial experience of this new
medium brought such efforts to a new height. Cinema, therefore, emerges
as a primary apparatus for the dissemination of this new social order's
Othering discourses that underscore the modern project itself. Here the
movies of Méliès, Griffith, and Carbanne are not simply the works of individual filmmakers exploring the medium of film. They are, I offer, engaged
in the very reproduction of the medium by participating in the differentiating logic of modern social life. While the historical and cultural content
of their works may be distinct, their works emerge from the same understanding of power and desire that slots Others into hierarchical patterns.[6]

By 1915 the Alamo had emerged as a master symbol, uncoupled from its
Texas parochial setting and rewritten to incorporate a new social imaginary through a dynamic process of meaning making, memory marking,
and contemporary identity creation. The effect of these reproductions
was the making of a "Self"—or more precisely, the fashioning of a masterful Anglo Self—over a Mexican "Other" within a structured relationship of dominance. Trouillot, in discussing the emergence of the Haitian
revolution, says that a "negro" uprising was, to the French officials and
slave owners, unthinkable. This view, he states, was epistemological, not
ideological: for the French, such an event was not within the realm of practical possibility. This point is instructive in terms of the Alamo. The structured relation of dominance between Anglos and Mexicans emerges from
the logic of modernity that slots masterful selves and subjugated others.
My suggestion is that such a position emerges between and within episte-

mology and ideology. On the one hand, the logic of a masterful self and subjugated Other is one that stems from reified notions of social life that construct difference by essentializing Others; on the other hand, essentialized Others serve the social, economic, and political imagination of the dominant. While symbols are models for understanding and actualizing our most deeply held convictions of social life, they are not blindfolds that prevent us from seeing Others in a perceptively distinct light. We must take into account that images, projections, and meanings of class, racial, and ethnic relations produced during this period, while dominant, are not totalizing. Mexicans and Anglos resisted the prescriptive sensibilities of this period. The point to be made, however, is, first, that master symbols like the Alamo shape and inform a wide spectrum of social experiences and cultural meanings in ways that often go unnoticed and uncritiqued; and, second, that these forms work in tandem with other generative processes like those construed around patriotism, heroism, and the nation so as to further mark as delinquent any critique of or variation from the norm.

Master symbols, therefore, not only order relations between Self and Other but also underscore the modern project and its apparatuses. They serve as double-helixed signs through which a semiotics of project and place inform power relations between social actors. Let me explain. Trouillot (1991:32), quoting Edouard Glissant, states that "[t]he West is not in the West. It is a project, not a place." I would like to suggest that the Western project of modernity emplotted in the Alamo as symbol is both project and place and that master symbols are precisely those constructions that coalesce around these articulations. As inflections of power, master symbols serve as a semiotics of place in shaping, regulating, and informing relations between social actors in history; as a semiotics of project, master symbols mimetically connect local struggles with the movement to world culture. A semiotics of place serves to anchor meaning in a foundational and thereby mythical past; a semiotics of project binds social actors in the present with a sense of historical subjectivity and attempts to silence the stories of those whose presence may unravel the tightly wound strands of meaning in the master symbol.

The Alamo as master symbol serves as a critical map for the exploitation and displacement of Mexicans, legitimized by the Texas Modern. Uncoupling the events of 1836 from their historical past and reconfiguring them to the social and political needs of the Texas Modern serves to sanction one way of life over another. The case of the Alamo demonstrates how events from the past serve to advance various plots in the present by endowing them with a sense of historicality and genuineness. But we cannot dismiss how the story of the Alamo is emplotted by the project of modernity and its construal of a new, hierarchically constituted society. It is through this larger tale that the story of the Alamo, as a master symbol of modernity, must be read. The events of 1836, then, serve as an episodic element that advance a plot of social and racial difference with a myth of origin. While historians, both professional and popular, may debate the "factual" details of how Davy died, or the location of various persons during the engagement, or the names and racial/ethnic identities of those involved in the battle, the "meaning" of such discussion is warranted only as a result of the formative weight we give to 1836 as an explanatory factor for the present social order. The Alamo exists as an event in the past but emerges in culture through its semantic ability to unite place and project. Is it coincidence that the heroic, mythic tale of the Alamo is itself a story about the birth, not merely of Texas, but of the United States and the western frontier? While the West, as a place — not a project — was surely present before 1836, it is the West — as a project of modernity — that emerges full force with the cultural birth of the Alamo.

# NOTES

## INTRODUCTION

1. This experience is not mine alone. Linenthal (1988:526) describes how several Chicano educators whom he interviewed in San Antonio concerning the Alamo reported, "[W]e learned in third or fourth grade that we killed the Alamo heroes."

2. My use of the terms "Texans," "Anglos," "Mexicans," and "Mexican Americans" follows the well-known meanings associated with these names in the Southwest. Historically, the Battle of the Alamo was fought between "Texans" and "Mexicans," but this refers to national identities, not cultural or ethnic ones. The often-overlooked feature of this is that there were a number of Mexicans fighting alongside the Texans, who themselves were a varied lot, including Europeans (for more on this point, see chap. 2). The term "Anglo," especially when contrasted with "Mexican" or "Mexican American," is used to refer to a non-Mexican, as is customary in this part of the world. "Mexican" and "Mexican American" are often interchanged, since in many cases, especially historical ones, identity and citizenship were not overlapping features. Thus one could be an American citizen but consider oneself Mexican. See Montejano 1987 for the historical development of these terms.

## CHAPTER ONE

1. My discussion of modernity is influenced by a number of theorists on the subject, including but not limited to Berman (1982), Habermas (1979), Jameson (1992a), and Harvey (1990).

2. The notion of a "complex structure" emanates from Althusser as he attempts to rethink his way through the all too often deterministic notions of the relationship between a material base and a cultural or ideological superstructure. This Althusserian totality posits a multiply inflected structure constituted from relatively autonomous and at times contradictory unities (Althusser and Balibar 1970). Crucial for Althusserianism is the complex but quite necessary relationship between ideology, or a system of signs, and the "Real" as a thing-in-itself. It is this

conjuncture of the historical production of signs and its at times contradictory relationship to the Real that I want to develop through the notion of a material semiology. Refusing historicism but not the role of history, economism but not modes of production, symbolism but not a system of signs, a material semiology underscores that the work of meaning making is both expressive and constitutive of social life. As a conjuncture, the relationship between material life and signification admits a complex, historically specific structure of relationship. See also Hall 1980.

3. See Limón 1998 for an important discussion of this relationship that extends beyond economic formations and into literary production itself.

4. I am aided in this analysis by Jameson's discussion of modes of production. In his attempt to untangle various historicisms from Marxism, Jameson (1979:68) discusses how "advanced" modes of production must include previous modes, "which it has had to suppress"; and, at the same time, in which future modes can be detected through the "various local forms of class struggle." By incorporating this notion, both during the moment of the peace structure and in 1900, the various contradictions and tensions of this aptly described cultural revolution come into focus.

5. One of the strategies of state violence is to reproduce its competition as "primitive" and "other" so as to feign a kind of frontier imagery of savagery that rationalizes violence.

6. Althusser's (1971:162) more detailed formulation of ideology as both representation and an imaginary relationship to one's social condition is instructive here once again. As representation, Althusser's notion of ideology is accessible only through signifying practice: the production of narrative, art, icons, fetishes, and other expressive forms. Through these forms, signs "underwrite" our stories about the real (Saldívar 1990:211). The signifying forms of ideology emerge as the products of particular conditions of history. As Althusser further reminds us, these forms provide imaginary relationships to the Real because the Real, as a thing-in-itself, is unrepresentable. These imaginary signs serve as "a way of grappling with a Real that must always transcend it" (Saldívar 1990:212) but by necessity must always signify one's lived relationship to it.

7. Analytically, the rethinking and regrounding of both symbol making and symbolic thought in history is what I refer to as a historical materialist semiology. These pages, then, suggest two important foci of symbolic analysis: first, the need to rethink symbolic production through its historical content; and second, the need to reground analysis of symbolic productions through the conditions of their own making.

CHAPTER TWO

1. This summary of the film produced and projected at the Alamo is based on multiple viewings. All quotes are taken directly from my notes as I recorded them at each viewing.

2. Like other factors of the official narrative, the historical evidence of Bowie's fascination with the Alamo is slim, if that. See Glazer 1985 for more on this point.

3. In summer 2000, after showing this film every twenty minutes every day for nearly fifteen years, the Daughters of the Republic of Texas finally acted on criticisms of its portrayal and hired a professional filmmaker from California to create a new one. The new film will be discussed in a follow-up to this work.

4. For an overview of literature concerning memory, see Wachtel 1986; Le Goff 1992; Nora 1989; and Ruffins 1992. See Stewart 1996 for a stimulating discussion of how narratives circulate through a variety of public markers and spaces.

5. There is a growing literature that explores various understandings of the past, including notions of history, tradition, and memory. See Benson, Brier, and Rosenzweig 1986; Chartier 1988; Friedman 1992; Gathercole and Lowenthal 1990; Handler and Linnekin 1984; Hobsbawm and Ranger 1983; Lowenthal 1985; Ricoeur 1980; Shils 1981; Sturken 1997; White 1987.

6. Meaning in this case is constructed primarily through its ability to unite a series of events into a conjunctural whole, or plot. Here, the distinction between plot and chronicle serves as an important distinction. Historical, literary, mythic, and memorial narratives conjoin a series of events or happenings — the chronicle — into a unified whole with a beginning and an end — the narrative. In brief, these narratives tell stories and in this process share common structures and devices of meaning production. This is not to say that historical narratives cannot be evaluated for their truth value, but such an evaluation is made on the conjunction of events and happenings referred to as the historical discourse's chronicle. As Louis O. Minks states:

> One can regard any text in direct discourse as a logical conjunction of assertions. The truth-value of the text is then simply a logical function of the truth or falsity of the individual assertions taken separately: the conjunction is true if and only if each of the propositions is true. Narrative has in fact been analyzed, especially by philosophers intent on comparing the form of the narrative with the form of theories, as if it were nothing but a logical conjunction of past-referring statements; and on such an analysis there is no problem of *narrative truth*. The difficulty with the model of logical conjunction, however, is that it is not a model of narrative at all. It is rather a model of a chronicle. Logical conjunction serves well enough as a representation of the only ordering relation of chronicles, which is ". . . and then . . . and then . . . and then . . ." Narratives, however, contain indefinitely many ordering relations, and indefinitely many ways of *combining* these relations. It is such a combination that we mean when we speak of the coherence of narrative, or the lack of it. (Mink 1978 : 143 –144; emphasis in original)

7. These issues are not unique to sites of public history and culture but are present in various other sites where issues of representation are important. See Appadurai and Breckenridge 1992; Karp, Kreamer, and Lavine 1992; Karp and

Lavine 1991; Leon and Rosenzweig 1989; Potter and Leone 1992; Strong 1996; Wallace 1986.

8. For discussions on the place of plot in historical discourse, see White 1987; Ricoeur 1980.

9. See Bakhtin 1981:343 on authoritative discourse in the novel.

10. The structure of the oppositional discourse between Texans and Mexicans goes undisputed, while the details of where Travis really died or where Bowie's bedroom was located are pored over in minute detail. The deep structure of this place does not change, while the multiplicity of historical minutiae are viewed as the "real" elements of the Alamo's historical identity.

11. See Trouillot 1995 on this point. Also on this point, Gadamer (1990:303) believes that memory needs no validation since it thinks itself complete: ambiguity is dispelled, motives understood, winners and losers clearly marked. Historical narratives, on the other hand, are noisy: they are open, shifting, changing with the emergence of new evidence, other perspectives, and possible interpretations; they are contested, dialogical, and open to revision, debate, and "can never be complete."

12. For further reading on this subject, see Meyer and Sherman 1995.

13. The ambivalence that hindered the making of the Alamo until the late nineteenth century is the same ambivalence Homi Bhabha (1990c:1) claims "emerges from a growing awareness that . . . the cultural temporality of the nation inscribes a much more transitional social reality." This ambivalence, one we have been "obliged to forget" (Bhabha 1990a:311) is what remains silent at the Alamo today.

### CHAPTER 3

1. In the last decade the study of space has become an important area of cultural theory. For key texts that have informed this analysis, see Castells 1983; Harvey 1973, 1985; Katznelson 1988, 1992; Lefebvre 1991; Simmel 1950; Soja 1989.

2. Yet we cannot minimize the role of indigenous plazas in the urban topography of Spanish towns in the New World.

3. For a discussion of mercantile exchange as distinct from capitalist production, see Habermas 1993:17.

4. The reference to Alamo Plaza as "high ground" is not clear. Is it the case that the area surrounding Alamo Plaza is higher in elevation, a point I still need to explore; or is it that Alamo Plaza is higher in terms of social space and not marked as low ground as apparently Main Plaza is?

5. See Montejano 1987 on this point.

6. This point is made in the opposite direction by Mary Ann Noonan Guerra in her historically detailed tourist book on San Antonio: "That Parade ground—the Plaza de Armas, Military Plaza—was the city. With the Plaza de las Islas [Main Plaza] alongside just east, it held its place as the center of San Antonio until 1900" (1988:65).

7. There is a link between the respatialization of Alamo Plaza after 1875 and the building of the cathedrals and national palace over indigenous sites in Tenochtitlán. In both sites, earlier, culturally distinct forms are reproduced in ways that maintain a spatial link to the past but under radically different social practices. The result is a spatial reproduction that in appearance or form builds on past practices so as to maintain a certain level of continuity while concurrently breaking the social forces that shaped previous spatial usages.

8. For a rigorous discussion of forms and their social and historical content, see Jameson 1971.

9. The effort of city officials to "landscape" Alamo Plaza cannot be dismissed too easily, since as Zukin (1992:224) argues, "landscape refers to . . . the special imprint of dominant institutions on the natural topography."

## CHAPTER 4

1. There was, according to Gould (1882), a growing trade in Mexican curiosities and souvenirs of the Alamo, although these items were only loosely tied, if at all, to the physical place of the Alamo.

2. Documents of the Twenty-ninth Legislature—Regular Session for January 23, 1905, contain a resolution thanking the DRT with amendments that specifically recognize De Zavala, Driscoll, and others.

3. Adina De Zavala Collection, University of the Incarnate Word, San Antonio, Texas.

4. De Zavala (Adina) Papers, Box 2m163, Center for American History, University of Texas at Austin. DRT Proceedings, April 21, 1906.

5. Adina De Zavala File, Daughters of the Republic of Texas Library, The Alamo, San Antonio, Texas.

6. De Zavala (Adina) Papers, Box 2m127, Center for American History, University of Texas at Austin.

7. Supplemental petition, "DRT v. ADZ, Docket no. 43344." Quoted in Ables 1967:406.

8. De Zavala (Adina) Papers, Box 2m163, Center for American History, University of Texas at Austin.

9. Adina De Zavala File, Daughters of the Republic of Texas Library, The Alamo, San Antonio, Texas.

10. De Zavala (Adina) Papers, Box 2m163, Center for American History, University of Texas at Austin.

11. It is these same maps and plats that are part of De Zavala's historical chronology in *History and Legends of the Alamo.*

12. Adina De Zavala Collection, University of the Incarnate Word, San Antonio, Texas.

13. *Holland's Magazine,* December 1935. Adina De Zavala File, Daughters of the Republic of Texas Library, The Alamo, San Antonio, Texas.

14. Adina De Zavala File, Daughters of the Republic of Texas Library, The Alamo, San Antonio, Texas.

15. De Zavala (Adina) Papers, Box 2m128, Center for American History, University of Texas at Austin.

16. One of the other vice presidents in the Texas Folk-lore Society was Col. M. L. Crimmins of Fort Sam Houston in San Antonio, who also served with De Zavala as an officer of the THLA.

17. From an advertisement of the book found among her papers in the Adina De Zavala Collection, University of the Incarnate Word, San Antonio, Texas.

18. Adina De Zavala Collection, Letter file 1925–1926, University of the Incarnate Word, San Antonio, Texas.

19. Adina De Zavala Collection, Letter file, University of the Incarnate Word, San Antonio, Texas.

20. Adina De Zavala Collection, University of the Incarnate Word, San Antonio, Texas.

21. For example, the letter quoted earlier from her uncle Lorenzo de Zavala, Jr., was written entirely in Spanish.

22. It is no coincidence that a majority of the caricatures of South Texas *mexicanos* depict them as lazy and unproductive, a stereotype based not on practice but on views informed by the social cleavages that erupted in the wake of social and structural reformation. Texans and Mexicans, at the turn of the century, inhabited and were products of distinct social places. After some time, these attitudes themselves became the reified and naturalized images of the Other that informed practice. For works that discuss this critical period in Texas-Mexican historiography, see De León 1983; De León and Stewart 1985; Flores 1993; Limón 1983; Montejano 1987.

23. Jameson (1981:53) refers to this as a "strategy of containment" whereby narrative forms provide discursive authority to social practices that, in this case, inscribe Mexicans as members of an inferior and lower class.

24. De Zavala (Adina) Papers, Box 2m129, Center for American History, University of Texas at Austin.

25. This is a rather interesting example, especially soon after World War II and the anti-German sentiment it produced.

26. De Zavala (Adina) Papers, Box 2m163, Center for American History, University of Texas at Austin.

27. Adina De Zavala Collection, University of the Incarnate Word, San Antonio, Texas.

28. While it is not clear how close De Zavala and González were, De Zavala refers to her several times in her notes from meetings they attended, specifically referring to a talk she gave on "the social conditions in Southern Texas." De Zavala (Adina) Papers, Box 2m138, Center for American History, University of Texas at Austin.

29. The legend of the Woman in Blue seems to have been particularly important for De Zavala. Not only does it play a key role in her embedded political critique,

but she collected numerous variants of the legend and disseminated them to people she knew. For example, in a letter to James Walsh of New York, she writes, "I am writing other legends and stories. I think you will be interested in the Woman in Blue. You will find a reference to her in the chronicles of the early Tejas Indians—in my little book—also she appears in the histories of the kindred or associate tribes. I am fascinated by her." Adina De Zavala Collection, University of the Incarnate Word, San Antonio, Texas.

30. Adina De Zavala Collection, University of the Incarnate Word, San Antonio, Texas.

31. See Rodríguez 1994 for an overview of the meaning and importance of Our Lady of Guadalupe in the lives of Mexican and Mexican-American women.

32. The distinction between social actors, subjects, and agents (developed in the next paragraph) is drawn from Trouillot 1995:23.

33. For a fuller discussion and examples of this point, see Flores 1992 and 1994; Limón 1983, 1994; Paredes 1958.

34. See Brear 1995.

### CHAPTER FIVE

1. For an overview of Alamo films, see Thompson 1991; Graham 1985; Huberman and Hugetz 1985; Hutton 1986.

2. Film File, Daughters of the Republic of Texas Library, the Alamo, San Antonio, Texas.

3. The spelling of Almeron and Suzanna Dickenson's names varies from author to author and from one historical period to another. To be consistent, I have regularized the spellings as presented here.

4. It is not coincidental that this same "flawed" aspect of Mexican subjectivity is found in the stories of Clara Driscoll discussed in chapter 3.

5. On this point in relation to the role of diasporic communities in Britain, see Brah 1992:130–131.

6. They do not mention *Davy Crockett at the Fall of the Alamo* presumably because no complete copy of this film is available.

7. Zuber's story, as well as J. Frank Dobie's romantic acceptance of it, appears in Dobie, Boatright, and Ransom 1939.

8. The story of the line was so popular that it was reproduced, quite uncritically, in Anna Pennybacker's *History of Texas for Schools,* which was published in 1888 and went through six editions in its twenty-five-year press life (Dobie, Boatright, and Ransom 1939:11).

9. *San Antonio Light,* March 19, 1961.

10. According to Crisp (2001), this portrait of the Mexican army was also reported by Reuben Potter, author of the first major historical account of the Alamo battle, in a letter to Henry A. McArdle, the artist whose painting, *Dawn at the Alamo,* adorns the Texas state capitol. For reasons that are not clear, by the time McArdle's

painting was completed in 1905, his representation of Mexicans had completely changed. Instead of upright and chivalrous, they were portrayed as more grotesque and suspicious, even cowardly. This, of course, fits well with the interpretation in the film, *Martyrs of the Alamo.*

11. It is interesting that Wayne pays little attention to the men of San Antonio de Béxar, except for Juan Seguín, whom I discuss below, and a minor scene in which several men are hoarding gunpowder in the church. Even in the latter case, however, it is not clear if these men are Mexicans as the leader is named Emil Sand.

12. It is correct that Seguín served as an early mayor of San Antonio, but this was not until the 1840s, some years after the Battle of the Alamo.

### CHAPTER SIX

1. The literature on Crockett is extensive, ranging from scholarly to popular and less rigorous. Those that have proven to be most useful to me are Hutton 1987, 1989; Kilgore 1978, 1980; Lofaro 1994; Shackford 1994; Shackford and Folmsbee 1973.

2. The authorship of this work was unknown until it was established by Shackford in his 1994 biography of Crockett.

3. Tennessee, according to Cummings (1989:68–69), is divided socially and geographically between the East, Middle, and West. To West Tennesseans, Jackson and his supporters "represented a greedy aristocracy" compared to their "poor homesteading" families. East Tennessee also acted more like the North, later supporting the Union during the Civil War.

4. For key points and counterpoints in this debate, see Crisp 1994, 1995, 1996; Groneman 1994, 1995a, 1995b, 1996.

5. Kilgore includes the work of W. P. Zuber along with that of Potter. I believe, however, that Potter's work has long been taken as a historically important and faithful reporting of the story. Zuber's work, on the other hand, has been questioned for some time. See Dobie, Boatright, and Ransom 1939.

6. See Williams 1931, published in abridged form in the *Southwestern Historical Quarterly.*

7. At the same time a cautionary note must be appended, as John Seelye (1985) has carefully demonstrated that the Crockett Almanacs, main contributors to Crockett's post-Alamo reputation, are the work of eastern writers.

8. This question really has two moments: the first in 1961 at the time Lord is writing; the second, in the current political moment when writers such as Kilgore, Hutton, and Crisp have been criticized for their academically informed views.

### CONCLUSION

1. It is important to note that just a few short years after Wayne's film, in typical postmodern parody, the film *Viva Max,* starring Peter Ustinov, takes none other

than the Alamo as its subject for an iconoclastic critique of modernity. This is not a singular example but signals, at least in terms of the Alamo, the eruption of a wave of protests, critiques, and parodies that continue into the present. Along these lines, Pee Wee Herman's bike is not in the basement of the Alamo.

2. For this reason Fernandez regrounds his discussion of symbol in that of metaphor through which the associated processes of sign-images were first predicated. While I fully recognize and agree to some extent with Fernandez's move to the discussion of metaphor, I will continue to invoke the term "symbol," albeit from a position, like Fernandez's, that understands symbols as instrumental to metaphorical practice. As I show below, it is not with the "how" of symbol, metaphor, or tropic formulation that I am concerned here but with the "logic" through which symbols are actualized in practice.

3. Foucault (1970:227) discusses how the transition from described structure to classifying character emerged in the eighteenth century through the rubric "organic structure." An example of this, for Foucault, is seen in the various taxonomic distinctions that are denoted hierarchically according to various complexities of structure. If scientific (modern) thought—through the principle of organic structure—classifies according to hierarchical difference, so do other forms of ordering, such as symbolic predication.

4. As Marx's theorizing of the imaginary suggests (a position that is developed later by Althusser), symbolic, ideological discourses impel the material transformations of modernity by legitimating a change in the social relations of production. As such, strategies that legitimate the social and economic displacement of others, as Other, are necessary elements in the social transition to modernity. Jürgen Habermas (1993) claims that civil society comes into existence when under state and bureaucratic authority household economies emerge as essential elements of the public sphere. Likewise, the logic of labor that fosters the formation of Others, as in the case of San Antonio's Mexicans, must also produce its public analogue through which a notion of dominance enters the public sphere and serves the general interest of the polity.

5. Arjun Appadurai and Carol A. Breckenridge (1992) discuss how museums and their holdings both fix and destabilize group identities through the display of material artifacts. While the Alamo is a museum, shrine, and reconstructed physical structure, the private vision made public contributes to the same kind of meaning making discussed by Appadurai and Breckenridge.

6. The cinematic images of these early filmmakers not only cast Mexicans, blacks, and natives in an Othering light but likewise illuminate the contours of the dominant. These early portrayals of the Alamo defenders, specifically Davy Crockett, serve as master symbols of the master as well, providing important normative roles for members of the dominant group.

# REFERENCES

Ables, L. Robert. 1967. "The Second Battle for the Alamo." *Southwestern Historical Quarterly* 70(3):372–413.

Almaguer, Tomás. 1987. "Ideological Distortions in Recent Chicano Historiography." *Aztlán* 18(1):7–28.

Althusser, Louis. 1971. *Lenin and Philosophy and Other Essays.* Trans. Ben Brewster. New York: Monthly Review Press.

Althusser, Louis, and Etienne Balibar. 1970. *Reading Capital.* Trans. Ben Brewster. London: Verso.

Appadurai, Arjun, and Carol A. Breckenridge. 1992. "Museums Are Good to Think: Heritage on View in India." In *Museums and Communities: The Politics of Public Culture,* ed. Ivan Karp, Christine Mullen Kreamer, and Steven D. Lavine, 34–55. Washington, D.C.: Smithsonian Institution Press

Arreola, Daniel D. 1992. "Plaza Towns in South Texas." *Geographical Review* 82(1):56–73.

Bakhtin, M. M. 1981. *The Dialogic Imagination.* Austin: University of Texas Press.

Barr, Alwyn. 1971. *Reconstruction to Reform: Texas Politics, 1876–1906.* Austin: University of Texas Press.

———. 1990. *Texans in Revolt: The Battle for San Antonio, 1835.* Austin: University of Texas Press.

Barrera, Mario. 1979. *Race and Class in the Southwest: A Theory of Racial Inequality.* Notre Dame: University of Notre Dame Press.

Becerra, Francisco, as told to John S. Ford. 1980. *A Mexican Sergeant's Recollection of the Alamo and San Jacinto.* Austin: Jenkins Publishing Company.

Benson, Susan Porter, Stephen Brier, and Roy Rosenzweig, eds. 1986. *Presenting the Past: Essays on History and the Public.* Philadelphia: Temple University Press.

Berman, Marshall. 1982. *All That Is Solid Melts into Air: The Experience of Modernity.* New York: Simon and Schuster.

Bernardi, Daniel. 1996. "The Voice of Whiteness: D. W. Griffith's Biograph Films." In *The Birth of Whiteness: Race and the Emergence of U.S. Cinema,* ed. Daniel Bernardi, 103–128. New Brunswick: Rutgers University Press.

Bhabha, Homi. 1990a. "DissemiNation: Time, Narrative, and the Margins of the Modern Nation." In *Nation and Narration,* ed. Homi Bhabha, 291–322. London: Routledge.

———. 1990b. "Introduction: Narrating the Nation." In *Nation and Narration,* ed. Homi Bhabha, 1–7. London: Routledge Press.

———, ed. 1990c. *Nation and Narration.* London: Routledge.

———. 1994. *The Location of Culture.* London: Routledge.

Black, Max. 1962. *Models and Metaphors: Studies in Language and Philosophy.* Ithaca: Cornell University Press.

Bonet Correa, Antonio. 1982. "La Puerta del Sol de Madrid, Centro de Sociabilidad." In *"Plazas" et sociabilité en Europe et Amerique Latine,* Fasc. 6. Madrid: Boccard, 1982.

Brah, Avtar. 1992. "Difference, Diversity and Differentiation." In *"Race," Culture and Difference,* ed. James Donald and Ali Rattansi, 130–131. London: Sage.

Brear, Holly. 1995. *Inherit the Alamo.* Austin: University of Texas Press.

Cardenas, Gilberto, Jorge Chapa, and Susan Burek. 1993. "The Changing Economic Position of Mexican Americans in San Antonio." In *Latinos in a Changing U.S. Economy,* ed. Rebecca Morales and Frank Bonilla, 160–183. Newbury Park, Calif.: Sage.

Castañeda, Carlos E. 1970. *The Mexican Side of the Texan Revolution.* Dallas: Graphic Ideas.

Castells, Manuel. 1983. *The City and the Grassroots.* Berkeley: University of California Press.

Charney, Leo, and Vanessa R. Schwartz. 1995. *Cinema and the Invention of Modern Life.* Berkeley: University of California Press.

Chartier, Roger. 1988. *Cultural History: Between Practices and Representations.* Ithaca: Cornell University Press.

Clark, Donald, and Christopher Andersen. 1995. *John Wayne's "The Alamo": The Making of the Epic Film.* New York: Citadel Press.

Clifford, James. 1988. *The Predicament of Culture: Twentieth-Century Ethnography, Literature, and Art.* Cambridge, Mass.: Harvard University Press.

Colquitt, Oscar B. 1913. *Message of Governor O. B. Colquitt to the Thirty-third Legislature Relating to the Alamo Property.* Austin: Von Boeckmann-Jones Co., Printers.

Cook, Gertrude, and Esther MacMillan. 1976. "San Antonio in 1776." In *San Antonio in the Eighteenth Century,* ed. Frances K. Hendricks, 129–135. San Antonio: San Antonio Bicentennial Heritage Committee.

Crisp, James E. 1994. "The Little Book That Wasn't There: The Myth and Mystery of the de la Peña Diary." *Southwestern Historical Quarterly* 97 (October): 260–296.

———. 1995. "A Reply: When Revision Becomes Obsession, Bill Groneman and the de la Peña Diary." *Military History of the West* 25(2):143–155.

———. 1996. "Letters to the Editor: Truth, Confusion, and the de la Peña Controversy—A Final Reply." *Military History of the West* 26(1):99–104.

———. 2001. "An Incident in San Antonio: The Contested Iconology of Davy Crockett's Death at the Alamo." *Journal of the West* 40(2):67–77.

Crouch, Dora P., Daniel J. Garr, and Axel I. Mundigo. 1982. *Spanish City Planning in North America.* Cambridge, Mass.: MIT Press.

Cruz, Gilbert R. 1988. *Let There Be Towns: Spanish Municipal Origins in the American Southwest, 1610–1810.* College Station: Texas A&M University Press.

Cumberland, Charles C. 1954. "Border Raids in the Lower Rio Grande Valley— 1915." *Southwestern Historical Quarterly* 57:285–311.

Cummings, Joe. 1989. "Celebrating Crockett in Tennessee." In *Crockett at Two Hundred: New Perspectives on the Man and the Myth,* ed. M. A. Lofaro and J. Cummings, 67–82. Knoxville: University of Tennessee Press.

Davis, William C. 1998. *Three Roads to the Alamo: The Lives and Fortunes of David Crockett, James Bowie, and William Barret Travis.* New York: HarperCollins.

de la Peña, José Enrique. 1975. *With Santa Anna in Texas: A Personal Narrative of the Revolution.* Trans. and ed. Carmen Perry. College Station: Texas A&M University Press.

de la Teja, Jesús. 1991. *A Revolution Remembered: The Memoirs and Selected Correspondence of Juan N. Seguín.* Austin: State House Press.

de la Teja, Jesús F., and John Wheat. 1985. "Béxar: Profile of a Tejano Community, 1820–1832." *Southwestern Historical Quarterly* 89(1):7–34.

De León, Arnoldo. 1982. *The Tejano Community, 1836–1900.* Albuquerque: University of New Mexico Press.

———. 1983. *They Called Them Greasers: Anglo Attitudes toward Mexicans in Texas, 1821–1900.* Austin: University of Texas Press.

De León, Arnoldo, and Kenneth L. Stewart. 1985. "A Tale of Three Cities: A Comparative Analysis of the Socio-Economics of Mexican-Americans in Los Angeles, Tucson, and San Antonio." *Journal of the West* 24(2):64–74.

De Zavala, Adina. 1917. *History and Legends of the Alamo and Other Missions In and Around San Antonio.* San Antonio: Privately published by the author. Reprint, edited and with an introduction by Richard R. Flores. Houston: Arte Público Press, 1996.

Dobie, J. Frank, Mody C. Boatright, and Harry H. Ransom. 1939. *In the Shadow of History.* Texas Folk-Lore Society Publications, vol. 15. Austin: Texas Folk-Lore Society.

Douglas, Ann. 1977. *The Feminization of American Culture.* New York: Doubleday.

Driscoll, Clara. 1905. *The Girl of La Gloria.* New York: G. P. Putnam's Sons.

———. 1906. *In the Shadow of the Alamo.* New York: G. P. Putnam's Sons.

Driscoll, Clara, and Robert B. Smith. 1905. *Mexicana: A Comic Opera in Three Acts.* New York.

Fernandez, James. 1986. *Persuasions and Performances: The Play of Tropes in Culture.* Bloomington: Indiana University Press.

Flores, Richard R. 1992. "The Corrido and the Emergence of Texas-Mexican Social Identity." *Journal of American Folklore* 105:166–182.

———. 1993. "History, 'Los Pastores,' and the Shifting Poetics of Dislocation." *Journal of Historical Sociology* 6(2):164–185.

———. 1994. "'Los Pastores' and the Gifting of Performance." *American Ethnologist* 21(2):270–285.

Foucault, Michel. 1970. *The Order of Things: An Archaeology of the Human Sciences.* New York: Vintage Books.

———. 1980. *The History of Sexuality. Volume I: An Introduction.* New York: Vintage Books.

Fox, Anne A., Feris A. Bass, Jr., and Thomas Hester. 1976. *The Archaeology and History of Alamo Plaza.* Archaeological Survey Report, no. 16. San Antonio: Center for Archaeological Research, University of Texas at San Antonio.

Friedman, Jonathan. 1992. "Myth, History, and Political Identity." *Cultural Anthropology* 7(2):194–210.

Frisch, Michael. 1989. "American History and the Structures of Collective Memory." *Journal of American History* 75(4):1130–1155.

Gadamer, Hans-Georg. 1990. *Truth and Method.* New York: Crossroad.

García, Mario T. 1989. *Mexican Americans: Leadership, Ideology, and Identity, 1930–1960.* New Haven: Yale University Press.

García, Richard. 1991. *Rise of the Mexican American Middle Class.* College Station: Texas A&M University Press.

Garrison, George P. 1906. *Texas: A Contest of Civilizations.* Boston: Houghton Mifflin.

Gathercole, Peter, and David Lowenthal, eds. 1990. *The Politics of the Past.* London: Unwin Hyman.

Geertz, Clifford. 1973. *The Interpretation of Culture.* New York: Basic Books.

Giddens, Anthony. 1990. *The Consequences of Modernity.* Stanford: Stanford University Press.

Glazer, Tom W. 1985. "Victory or Death." In *Alamo Images: Changing Perceptions of a Texas Experience,* ed. Susan Prendergast Schoelwer, 61–103. Dallas: DeGolyer Library and Southern Methodist University Press.

Gómez-Quiñones, Juan. 1970. *"Plan de San Diego* Reviewed." *Aztlán* 1:124–132.

———. 1990. *Chicano Politics: Reality and Promise, 1940–1990.* Albuquerque: University of New Mexico Press.

Gould, Stephen. 1882. *The Alamo City Guide.* New York: MacGowan & Slipper Printers.

Graham, Don. 1985. "Remembering the Alamo: The Story of the Texas Revolution in Popular Culture." *Southwestern Historical Quarterly* 89(1):35–66.

Gramsci, Antonio. 1971. *Selection from the Prison Notebooks.* Trans. Quinton Hoare and Geoffrey Nowell Smith. New York: International Publishers.

Green, Rena Maverick. 1989. *Memoirs of Mary A. Maverick*. Introduction by S. L. Myres. Lincoln: University of Nebraska Press.

Groneman, William. 1994. *Defense of a Legend: Crockett and the de la Peña Diary*. Plano: Republic of Texas Press, Wordware Publishing.

———. 1995a. "The Controversial Alleged Account of José Enrique de la Peña." *Military History of the West* 25(2):129–142.

———. 1995b. "A Rejoinder: Publish Rather than Perish—Regardless Jim Crisp and the de la Peña Diary." *Military History of the West* 25(2):157–165.

———. 1996. "Letters to the Editor: A Last Final Reply, Or, How I Learned to Stop Worrying and Love Jim Crisp." *Military History of the West* 26(1):105–106.

Gunning, Tom. 1991. *D. W. Griffith and the Origins of American Narrative Film: The Early Years*. Urbana: University of Illinois Press.

Guerra, Mary Ann Noonan. 1988. *The History of San Antonio's Market Square*. San Antonio: Alamo Press.

Gupta, Akhil, and James Ferguson. 1992. "Beyond Culture: Space, Identity and the Politics of Difference." *Cultural Anthropology* 7(1):6–23.

Habermas, Jürgen. 1979. *Communication and the Evolution of Society*. Trans. Thomas McCarthy. Boston: Beacon Press.

———. 1993. *The Structural Transformation of the Public Sphere*. Trans. Thomas Burger with Frederick Lawrence. Cambridge, Mass.: MIT Press.

Hager, William M. 1963. "The Plan of San Diego: Unrest on the Texas Border in 1915." *Arizona and the West* 5(4):327–336.

Hale, Grace Elizabeth. 1998. *Making Whiteness: The Culture of Segregation in the South, 1890–1940*. New York: Vintage Books.

Hale, Will. 1959. *Twenty-four Years a Cowboy and Ranchman in Southern Texas and Old Mexico*. Norman: University of Oklahoma Press.

Hall, Stuart. 1980. "Race, Articulation and Societies Structured in Dominance." In *Sociological Theories: Race and Colonialism*, ed. UNESCO, 305–345. Paris: UNESCO.

Handler, Richard, and Joyce Linnekin. 1984. "Tradition, Genuine or Spurious." *Journal of American Folklore* 97:273–290.

Hardin, Stephen L. 1994. *Texian Iliad: A Military History of the Texas Revolution*. Austin: University of Texas Press.

Harvey, David. 1973. *Social Justice and the City*. London: Edward Arnold.

———. 1985. *Consciousness and the Urban Experience*. Baltimore, Md.: Johns Hopkins University Press.

———. 1990. *The Condition of Postmodernity*. Cambridge, Mass.: Blackwell.

Hauck, Richard Boyd. 1989. "The Real Davy Crockett: Creative Autobiography and the Invention of His Legend." In *Crockett at Two Hundred: New Perspectives on the Man and the Myth*, ed. M. A. Lafaro and J. Cummings, 179–191. Knoxville: University of Tennessee Press.

Hobsbawm, Eric J. 1987. *The Age of Empire, 1875–1914*. Cambridge: Cambridge University Press.

Hobsbawm, Eric, and Terence Ranger, eds. 1983. *The Invention of Tradition.* Cambridge: Cambridge University Press.

Huberman, Brian. 1992. *John Wayne's The Alamo: MGM-United Artists.* Video documentary.

Huberman, Brian, and Ed Hugetz. 1985. "Fabled Facade: Filmic Treatments of the Battle of the Alamo." *Southwest Media Review* (Spring):30–41.

Hutton, Andrew Paul. 1986. "The Celluloid Alamo." *Arizona and the West* 28(1):5–22.

——. 1987. Introduction to *A Narrative of the Life of David Crockett by Himself,* v–lvii. Lincoln: University of Nebraska Press.

——. 1989. "Davy Crockett: An Exposition on Hero Worship." In *Crockett at Two Hundred: New Perspectives on the Man and the Myth,* ed. M. A. Lofaro and J. Cummings, 20–41. Knoxville: University of Tennessee Press.

Jameson, Fredric. 1971. *Marxism and Form.* Princeton: Princeton University Press.

——. 1979. "Marxism and Historicism." *New Literary History* 11(1):41–73.

——. 1981. *The Political Unconscious.* Ithaca: Cornell University Press.

——. 1988. "Cognitive Mapping." In *Marxism and the Interpretation of Culture,* ed. Cary Nelson and Lawrence Grossberg, 347–357. Urbana: University of Illinois Press.

——. 1992a. *Postmodernism, or, The Cultural Logic of Late Capitalism.* Durham: Duke University Press.

——. 1992b. *Signatures of the Visible.* New York: Routledge.

Jennings, Frank. 1995. "Adina De Zavala: Alamo Crusader." *Texas Highways* 42(March):15–21.

Johnson, David R. 1990. "Frugal and Sparing: Interest Groups, Politics, and City Building in San Antonio, 1870–1885." In *Urban Texas: Politics and Development,* ed. C. Miller and H. T. Sanders, 33–57. College Station: Texas A&M University Press.

Kammen, Michael. 1991. *Mystic Chords of Memory: The Transformation of Tradition in American Culture.* New York: Vintage Books/Random House.

Karp, Ivan, Christine Mullen Kreamer, and Steven D. Lavine, eds. 1992. *Museums and Communities: The Politics of Public Culture.* Washington, D.C.: Smithsonian Institution Press.

Karp, Ivan, and Steven D. Lavine, eds. 1991. *Exhibiting Cultures.* Washington, D.C.: Smithsonian Institution Press.

Katznelson, Ira. 1988. "Reflections on Space and the City." In *Power, Culture and Place: Essays on New York City,* ed. J. H. Mollenkopf, 285–300. New York: Russell Sage.

——. 1992. *Marxism and the City.* London: Clarendon Press.

Kearney, Michael. 1991. "Borders and Boundaries of State and Self at the End of Empire." *Journal of Historical Sociology* 4(1):52–74.

Kilgore, Dan. 1978. *How Did Davy Die?* College Station: Texas A&M University Press.

———. 1980. Introduction to *A Mexican Sergeant's Recollections of the Alamo and San Jacinto,* by Francisco Becerra as told to John S. Ford in 1875, 5–11. Austin: Jenkins Publishing Company.

———. 1989. "Why Davy Didn't Die." In *Crockett at Two Hundred: New Perspectives on the Man and the Myth,* ed. M. A. Lofaro and J. Cummings, 7–19. Knoxville: University of Tennessee Press.

King, Edward. 1875. *The Great South.* Hartford: American Publishing Company.

Knox, William John. 1927. *The Economic Status of the Mexican Immigrant in San Antonio, Texas.* Ph.D. dissertation, University of Texas at Austin. Reprint, San Francisco: R and E Research Associates, 1971.

Lass, Andrew. 1988. "Romantic Documents and Political Monuments: the Meaning-Fulfillment of History in 19th-Century Czech Nationalism." *American Ethnologist* 15(3):456–471.

Lefebvre, Henri. 1991. *The Production of Space.* Oxford: Blackwell.

Le Goff, Jacques. 1992. *History and Memory.* New York: Columbia University Press.

Leon, Warren, and Roy Rosenzweig, eds. 1989. *History Museums in the United States: A Critical Assessment.* Urbana and Chicago: University of Illinois Press.

Limón, José E. 1974. "El Primer Congreso Mexicanista de 1911: A Precursor to Contemporary Chicanismo." *Aztlán* 5:85–117.

———. 1983. "Folklore, Social Conflict and the United States–Mexico Border." In *Handbook of American Folklore,* ed. R. Dorson, 216–226. Bloomington: Indiana University Press.

———. 1994. *Dancing with the Devil: Society and Cultural Poetics in Mexican-American South Texas.* Madison: University of Wisconsin Press.

———. 1998. *American Encounters: Greater Mexico, the United States, and the Erotics of Culture.* Boston: Beacon Press.

Linenthal, Edward Tabor. 1988. "'A Reservoir of Spiritual Power': Patriotic Faith at the Alamo in the Twentieth Century." *Southwestern Historical Quarterly* 91(4):509–531.

Lipsitz, George. 1998. *The Possessive Investment in Whiteness.* Philadelphia: Temple University Press.

Lofaro, Michael A. 1994. Introduction to *David Crockett: The Man and the Legend by James Atkins Shackford,* ed. J. B. Shackford, ix–xx. Lincoln: University of Nebraska Press.

Longoria, Mario D. 1982. "Revolution, Visionary Plan, and the Marketplace: A San Antonio Incident." *Aztlán* 12(2):211–226.

Lord, Walter. 1961. *A Time to Stand.* New York: Harper & Brothers.

Low, Setha M. 1993. "The Cultural Meaning of the Plaza: The History of the Spanish-American Gridplan-Plaza Urban Design." In *The Cultural Meaning of*

*Space,* ed. R. Rotenberg and G. McDonogh, 75–93. Westport, Conn.: Bergin & Garvey.

———. 1995. "Indigenous Architecture and the Spanish American Plaza in Mesoamerica and the Caribbean." *American Anthropologist* 97(4):748–762.

Lowenthal, David. 1985. *The Past Is a Foreign Country.* Cambridge: Cambridge University Press.

MacCannell, Dean. 1992. *Empty Meeting Grounds: The Tourist Papers.* London: Routledge.

Marx, Karl. 1978. "The Eighteenth Brumaire of Louis Bonaparte." In *The Marx-Engels Reader,* 2d ed., ed. R. Tucker, 594–617. New York: W. W. Norton.

Matovina, Timothy M. 1995a. *The Alamo Remembered: Tejano Accounts and Perspectives.* Austin: University of Texas Press.

———. 1995b. *Tejano Religion and Ethnicity, San Antonio, 1821–1860.* Austin: University of Texas Press.

Meyer, Michael C., and William L. Sherman. 1995. *The Course of Mexican History.* New York: Oxford University Press.

Mink, Louis O. 1978. "Narrative Form as a Cognitive Instrument." In *The Writing of History: Literary Form and Historical Understanding,* ed. Robert H. Canary and Henry Kozicki, 143–144. Madison: University of Wisconsin Press.

Montejano, David. 1987. *Anglos and Mexicans in the Making of Texas, 1836–1986.* Austin: University of Texas Press.

Montgomery, Michael. 1989. "David Crockett and the Rhetoric of Tennessee Politics." In *Crockett at Two Hundred: New Perspectives on the Man and the Myth,* ed. M. A. Lofaro and J. Cummings, 42–66. Knoxville: University of Tennessee Press.

Neather, Andrew. 1996. "Labor Republicanism, Race, and Popular Patriotism in the Era of Empire, 1890–1914." In *Bonds of Affection: Americans Define Their Patriotism,* ed. J. Bodnar, 82–101. Princeton: Princeton University Press.

Nora, Pierre. 1989. "Between Memory and History: Les Lieux de Mémoire." *Representations* 26(Spring):7–25.

O'Leary, Cecilia Elizabeth. 1996. "'Blood Brotherhood': The Racialization of Patriotism, 1865–1918." In *Bonds of Affection: Americans Define Their Patriotism,* ed. J. Bodnar, 53–81. Princeton: Princeton University Press.

Olmsted, Frederick Law. 1857. *Journey through Texas; or a Saddle-Trip on the Southwestern Frontier.* New York: Dix, Edwards & Co.

Paredes, Américo. 1958. *With His Pistol in His Hand: A Border Ballad and Its Hero.* Austin: University of Texas Press.

Patterson, John S. 1989. "From Battle Ground to Pleasure Ground: Gettysburg as a Historic Site." In *History Museums in the United States,* ed. Warren Leon and Roy Rosenzweig, 128–157. Urbana and Chicago: University of Illinois Press.

Potter, Parker B., and Mark P. Leone. 1992. "Establishing the Roots of Historical Consciousness in Modern Annapolis, Maryland." In *Museums and Communities: The Politics of Public Culture,* ed. Ivan Karp, Christine Mullen Kreamer, and Steven D. Lavine, 476–505. Washington, D.C.: Smithsonian Institution Press.

Potter, Reuben M. 1878. "The Fall of the Alamo." *Magazine of American History* 2(1):1–21.

Poyo, Gerald E., and Gilberto M. Hinojosa. 1991. *Tejano Origins in Eighteenth-Century San Antonio.* Austin: University of Texas Press.

Prassel, Frank Richard. 1961. "Leisure Time Activities in San Antonio, 1877–1917." M.A. thesis, Trinity University.

Remy, Caroline M. 1960. "A Study of the Transition of San Antonio from a Frontier to an Urban Community from 1875–1900." M.A. thesis, Trinity University.

Richmond, Douglas W. 1980. "La Guerra de Texas se renova: Mexican Insurrection and Carrancista Ambitions, 1900–1920." *Aztlán* 11(1):1–32.

Ricoeur, Paul. 1970. *Freud and Philosophy: An Essay on Interpretation.* New Haven: Yale University Press.

———. 1980. "Narrative Time." *Critical Inquiry* 7(1):169–190.

Rimmer, Tony. 1978. "The Martyrs of the Alamo." *Cinema Texas* 14(4):27–32.

Rodríguez, Jeanette. 1994. *Our Lady of Guadalupe: Faith and Empowerment among Mexican-American Women.* Austin: University of Texas Press.

Rogers, Will Chapel, III. 1968. "A History of the Military Plaza to 1937." M.A. thesis, Trinity University.

Rojas-Mix, Miguel A. 1978. *La Plaza Mayor: El urbanismo, instrumento de dominio colonial.* Barcelona: Muchnik Editores de Idiomas Vivientes.

Rony, Fatimah Tobing. 1996. *The Third Eye: Race, Cinema, and Ethnographic Spectacle.* Durham: Duke University Press.

Rosenbaum, Robert J. 1981. *Mexicano Resistance in the Southwest: The Sacred Rights of Self-Preservation.* Austin: University of Texas Press.

Ruffins, Fath Davis. 1992. "Mythos, Memory, and History: African American Preservation Efforts, 1820–1990." In *Museums and Communities: The Politics of Public Culture,* ed. Ivan Karp, Christine Mullen Kreamer, and Steven D. Lavine, 506–611. Washington, D.C.: Smithsonian Institution Press.

Saldívar, Ramón. 1990. *Chicano Narrative: The Dialectics of Difference.* Madison: University of Wisconsin Press.

San Antonio, City of. April 15, 1844–December 3, 1848. Journal of the Council of the City of San Antonio.

———. January 1824–April 1827. Spanish Minute Book: City of San Antonio.

———. March 1, 1839–April 5, 1844. Journal of the Council of the City of San Antonio.

Sánchez, George J. 1993. *Becoming Mexican American: Ethnicity, Culture and Identity in Chicano Los Angeles, 1900–1945.* New York: Oxford University Press.

Schoelwer, Susan Prendergast, ed. 1985. *Alamo Images: Changing Perceptions of a Texas Experience.* Dallas: DeGolyer Library and Southern Methodist University Press.

Seelye, John. 1985. "A Well-Wrought Crockett." In *Davy Crockett: The Man, the*

*Legend, the Legacy, 1786–1986,* ed. M. A. Lofaro, 21–45. Knoxville: University of Tennessee Press.

Sennett, Richard. 1974. *The Fall of Public Man.* New York: W. W. Norton.

Shackford, James Atkins. 1994. *David Crockett: The Man and the Legend.* Lincoln: University of Nebraska Press.

Shackford, James A., and Stanley J. Folmsbee. 1973. "Annotations and Introduction." In *A Narrative of the the Life of David Crockett of the State of Tennessee by David Crockett,* ix–xx. Knoxville: University of Tennessee Press.

Shils, Edward. 1981. *Tradition.* London: Faber and Faber.

Simmel, Georg. 1950. "The Metropolis and Mental Life." In *The Sociology of Georg Simmel,* ed. K. Wolff, 409–424. New York: Free Press.

Smith, Horace R. 1966. "History of Alamo Plaza from Its Beginning to the Present." M.A. thesis, Trinity University.

Soja, Edward. 1989. *Postmodern Geographies: The Reassertion of Space in Critical Social Theory.* London: Verso.

Spell, Lota M., trans. and ed. 1962. "The Grant and First Survey of the City of San Antonio." *Southwestern Historical Quarterly* 1(July):73–89.

Spofford, Harriet Prescott. 1877. "San Antonio de Bexar." *Harper's New Monthly Magazine* 55:836–847.

Stallybrass, Peter, and Allon White. 1986. *The Politics and Poetics of Transgression.* Ithaca: Cornell University Press.

Steinfeldt, Cecilia. 1978. *San Antonio Was: Seen through a Magic Lantern, View from the Slide Collection of Albert Steves, Sr.* San Antonio: San Antonio Museum Association.

Stewart, Kathleen. 1996. *A Space on the Side of the Road: Cultural Poetics in an "Other" America.* Princeton: Princeton University Press.

Stewart, Kenneth L., and Arnoldo De León. 1993. *Not Room Enough: Mexicans, Anglos, and Socio-economic Change in Texas, 1850–1900.* Albuquerque: University of New Mexico Press.

Strong, Bernice Rhoades. 1987. "Alamo Plaza: Crossroads of a City, 1724–1900." M.A. thesis, University of Texas at San Antonio.

Strong, Pauline. 1996. "Animated Indians: Critique and Contradiction in Commodified Children's Culture." *Cultural Anthropology* 11(3):405–424.

Sturken, Marita. 1997. *Entangled Memories: The Vietnam War, the AIDS Epidemic, and the Politics of Remembering.* Berkeley: University of California Press.

Taussig, Michael. 1993. *Mimesis and Alterity: A Particular History of the Senses.* New York: Routledge.

Thompson, Frank. 1991. *Alamo Movies.* Plano: Republic of Texas Press, Wordware Publishing.

———. 1996. *The Star Film Ranch: Texas' First Picture Show.* Plano: Republic of Texas Press, Wordware Publishing.

Trouillot, Michel-Rolph. 1991. "Anthropology and the Savage Slot: The Poetics and Politics of Otherness." In *Recapturing Anthropology: Working in the Pres-*

*ent,* ed. Richard G. Fox, 17–44. Santa Fe, New Mex.: School of American Research.

———. 1995. *Silencing the Past: Power and the Production of History.* Boston: Beacon Press.

Turner, Terence. 1991. "'We Are Parrots,' 'Twins Are Birds': The Play of Tropes as Operational Structure." In *Beyond Metaphor: The Theory of Tropes in Anthropology,* ed. James Fernandez, 121–158. Stanford: Stanford University Press.

Vélez-Ibáñez, Carlos. 1996. *Border Visions: Mexican Cultures of the Southwest United States.* Tucson: University of Arizona Press.

Wachtel, Nathan. 1986. "Memory and History: Introduction." *History and Anthropology* 2(October):207–221.

Wallace, Michael. 1986. "Visiting the Past: History Museums in the United States." In *Presenting the Past: Essays on History and the Public,* ed. Susan Porter Benson, Stephen Brier, and Roy Rosenzweig, 137–161. Philadelphia: Temple University Press.

Weber, David J. 1988. *Myth and the History of the Hispanic Southwest.* Albuquerque: University of New Mexico Press.

———. 1992. *The Spanish Frontier in North America.* New Haven: Yale University Press.

Weber, Max. 1946. *From Max Weber: Essays in Sociology.* New York: Oxford University Press.

White, Hayden. 1987. *The Content of the Form: Narrative Discourse and Historical Representation.* Baltimore: Johns Hopkins University Press.

Williams, Amelia W. 1931. "A Critical Study of the Siege of the Alamo and of the Personnel of Its Defenders." Ph.D. dissertation, University of Texas. Published in abridged form in *Southwestern Historical Quarterly* 36(April 1933):251–287; 37(July 1933):1–44; 37(October 1933):79–115; 37(January 1934):157–184; 37(April 1934):237–312.

Wills, Gary. 1997. *John Wayne's America: The Politics of Celebrity.* New York: Simon and Schuster.

Wolf, Eric. 1982. *Europe and the People without History.* Berkeley: University of California Press.

Yoakum, H. 1855. *History of Texas from Its First Settlement in 1685 to Its Annexation to the United States in 1846.* 2 vols. New York: Redfield; facsimile, Austin: Steck-Vaughn Co., 1939.

Zamora, Emilio. 1993. *The World of the Mexican Worker in Texas.* College Station: Texas A&M University Press.

Zukin, Sharon. 1992. "Postmodern Urban Landscapes: Mapping Culture and Power." In *Modernity and Identity,* ed. Scott Lash and Jonathan Friedman, 221–247. Oxford: Blackwell.

# INDEX